HARDPRESS.NET
HOME OF HARD-TO-FIND BOOKS

Elsie Seymour, Or, the Contrast
by A. Wygorn

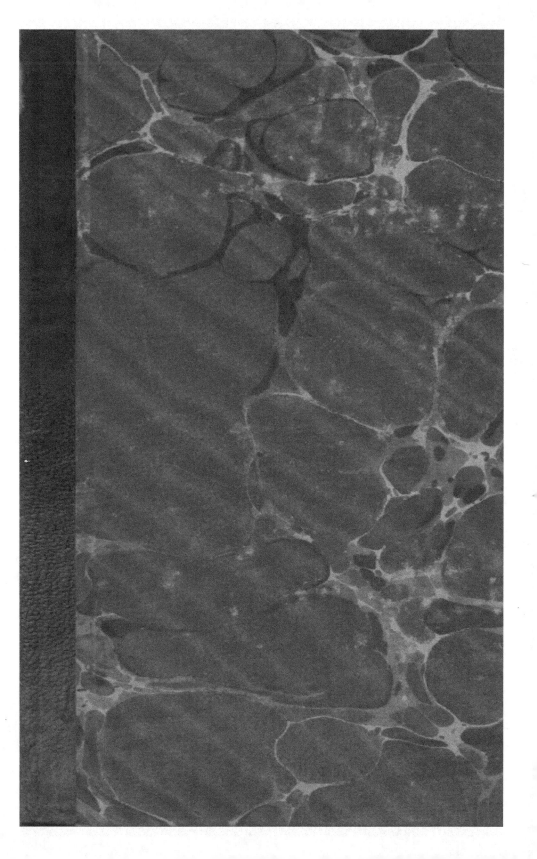

600073021J

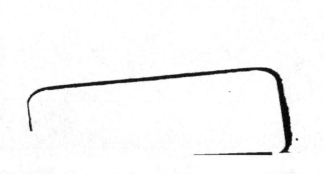

POPULAR NEW WORKS.

ELSIE SEYMOUR;

OR,

The Contrast.

By A. Wygorn.

IN THREE VOLUMES.

VOL. III.

LONDON:

THOMAS CAUTLEY NEWBY, PUBLISHER,

30, WELBECK STREET, CAVENDISH SQUARE.

1856.

ELSIE SEYMOUR.

CHAPTER IX.

LOVE'S LABOUR LOST.

IT was some ten days after the events related in the last chapter, that Elliott and Morden were seated in a white-washed room at the Latin convent, at Jerusalem, where Herbert had persuaded them to stay after their return from Eyn Sultaun.

Frank was recovering slowly from the severe attack which had threatened his life. He was seated in a chair, the most comfortable which the convent could furnish, while Frederick was lolling on the table blowing through the jessamine tube of a chibouque, to discover whether it was properly cleaned.

" You see I am as anxious as you can be,

my dear fellow, to get away from this awfully slow place, but the what you may call him won't hear of it ; the hakim, that's it."

" He will keep me as long as he can get a fee out of me," returned Frank.

" I don't doubt it—the rascal—but what am I to do ? I promised that fellow, Lisle, and the cerulean, not to let you stir without the hakim's permission. So you are a fixture here until he has bled your purse to death."

" Confound the fellow ! I wish I was out of his clutches ; I am sure I should get well sooner."

" It is a sell for you, I must confess," rejoined Morden, who felt it some relief to his own ennui to torment his unfortunate companion : " your amiable divinity is probably amusing herself with Lisle some-where near Damascus, I should think, by this time."

" Hang it, I say, Morden, I am quite up to travelling," returned Frank with considerable warmth, " I'll tell the fellow, Braschi, plainly,

that I will not go on any longer with his mede-
cines."

"I'll take a bet that Lisle marries that girl,"
continued his tormentor.

Frank was silent.

"A good match, too, don't you think?"

Frank was seized with a slight coughing
fit.

"You see it is not everybody," pursued
Morden, "that would suit the blue divinity.
She wants a sort of fellow like Lisle. For one
thing, she'd never be happy without a good
large fortune. She is an ambitious girl, I am
sure, and would like to act the patroness, and
be a grand lady."

"She has a good fortune of her own," ven-
tured Elliott, at length.

"Not till her father dies; at least, not
enough to be a very grand lady upon."

"I don't think she cares a bit about that
sort of thing," said Frank.

B 3

Morden laughed, and Frank made an effort to change the conversation.

Many days elapsed before the invalid could persuade his companion, who was himself tired to death of Jerusalem, to commence the journey.   There were two reasons which may have weighed in inducing Fred to persist in his opposition to their departure, one of which was his promise to Herbert and Elsie, and the other, his dread of again joining their party. At length Frank was well enough to order the horses and insist upon starting.   He was burning with anxiety to catch Elsie, before she left Beyrout, and, if possible, to overtake her at Damascus.   He knew that the Seymours would travel slowly, and would make frequent delays upon their journey, as Elsie never willingly left anything unseen, and he used every imaginable argument to hurry forward his friend, who was as obstinate as a baggage mule in the matter.

At length, Elliott and Morden made their

exit through the Damascus Gate, and pro-
ceeded over the hill country of Judæa, in the
direction of Nablous.

Sychar, Jezreel, Erdraelon, Nazareth and
Tabor, were almost lost upon poor Elliott,
whose one desire was to overtake Elsie. Their
destiny was Beyrout, since the hope of finding
letters there seemed to be the best bait to hurry
Morden forward upon the journey.

They had started from Jeneen at day-break,
and were riding in a hot sun across the wide
plain of Esdraelon, bounded in front, by the
mountains of Galilee, among which they could
distinguish the lesser Hermon (called by the
inspired poet-king, the little hill of Hermon),
and Tabor, and to the west, by Mount Carmel
and the sea. Morden appeared to take an
especial interest in seeing everything, and, in-
stead of pressing forward, as formerly, he was
for delaying at every point of historical interest,
whereas Frank, (who had always made a point
of investigating the lions), was now for pushing

on at the risk of losing the main object of their
tour.   Frederick's sudden taste for the sacred
localities was, if not solely, at all events in a
great measure, the result of his fear of over-
taking the other travellers, but he also ex-
perienced more pleasure from the actual travel-
ing than he had done hitherto, being mounted
upon a very tolerable steed, in place of the
rough dromedary which he had ridden through
the desert.   Frank desired to proceed at a
brisker pace, but his animal, chosen for the
invalid on account of its steadiness, was not
eager for any such excitement, and Fred was
equally unwilling to allow him to heat himself
under such a burning sun.

"I say, Deira!" said Morden, turning to
the dragoman, "how long are we to remain at
Nazareth?"

"Oh, my dear fellow!" exclaimed Frank,
"you don't intend to stay there, do you, more
than a night—I don't see the object."

"Oh, ma, you must stay, two, dree days,

and go to Tabaria, and Mount Tabor, and Cana Ghalil, and all de blaces," put in the draga-man, "to see dose blaces, he take you dree four days, and den you come back and go to Mount Carmel and Acre. Unless you like go straight to Damascus, by Saafed and Banias?"

"Of course we must see everything," said Morden, "you wouldn't miss Tiberias?"

Frank groaned in anguish.

"I am afraid we shall be so long getting to Beyrout, and, you know, we may find impor-tant letters there."

"Oh, ma, you be sorry after, to miss Ta-baria, where your religion was first make known, you know, and den so beautiful you can't tink."

"And, after all," continued Morden, "what difference does it make? A few days' delay can be of no great consequence. I should not mind going round by what's the name of the place?"

"Ah! By Saafed and Banias to Sham, to Damascus. That berry good way."

"No—that will never do," rejoined Frank, "I want to go the shortest way to Beyrout. I am expecting letters."

"Ma, we get letters sent to Damascus to meet you—you must see Damascus; so berry, berry beautiful, you know."

"Of course, I am going there afterwards!" exclaimed Frank somewhat pettishly.

"My dear fellow!" rejoined Morden, "one would think your fortune depended upon a letter. I never heard you make such a point of getting letters before, and if you want to overtake the young lady with the blue stockings, you will be quite as likely to find her at Damascus as Beyrout."

Deira drew back and fell into conversation with the cook, while Elliott, endeavoured to resign himself to his fate.

When they reached the convent at Nazareth, they learnt that the Seymours' party, after remaining there for more than a week and making expeditions to Carmel and Djerash, had started for Damascus by Tabaria and Saafed. Their long delay made it evident to Frank that, by going straight to Damascus, he should still find them there, and he began to repent of having so strongly urged their proceeding immediately to Beyrout. After strolling to the church of the Annunciation, and seeing other sacred sites in the city of the Saviour's early years, they returned to dine in their rooms at the convent.

"Well, Elliott!" said Frederick Morden, as he lolled back in his chair, awaiting the arrival of their dinner : "I think you are right after all, about going straight to Beyrout. I don't fancy you are up to the other journey."

"Not up to it? How do you mean? I am all right again now."

"That's all very fine, my dear fellow," returned Morden, whose tactics were now

B 3

changed through fear of overtaking the Seymours at Damascus : " but I am sure you would be running a risk. Besides you told me you were expecting important letters at Beyrout ?"

" Deira said he could get them forwarded to Damascus," retorted Frank.

" Only you seemed quite put out this morning when this road was even suggested. I suppose you want to overtake a certain fair lady in blue—eh ?"

" Pooh ! No, nonsense, Morden. I think we had better go the short way to Damascus."

" You must see all the places about here first," replied the other.

" Very well."

" Deira says that if we go by Banias, we ought to make an expedition from this to Acre and Mount Carmel, and I, for one, don't feel inclined to miss anything, even for the sake of Miss Elsie Seymour."

Elliott concealed his disgust and made up

his mind to accompany his friend to mount Carmel.

It is scarcely within the province of this tale to describe the mountain of Elijah or the forest of His Carmel where the wood of oak was, at that spring-tide season, interspersed with anemones and ranunculuses, more brilliant than Solomon in all his glory. Frank could not see without some slight emotion the mount of the Transfiguration, or the blue lake where the greatest marvels of divine love were enacted. There is no spot on earth more consecrated than that little sea, which produced the fishers of mankind. It is encinctured by the same mountains, and subject to the same storms as when the myriads were fed with the loaves or when the Lord walked upon its waters.

Three easy days from Tiberias brought them to the most lovely site in all Palestine, Banias, the ancient Cesarea Philippi, where Christ founded His Church and pronounced the words

which encircle the dome of the most splendid
cathedral in Christendom.

At the foot of mount Hermon, with its crest
of snow, lies, interspersed amid the Roman
ruins of Cesaræa Philippi, the modern village
of Banias. This fountain-head of the Christian
priesthood stands at the very source of the
river Jordan, the fertilizer of the promised land
of the Old Testament, as if to show the analogy
between the river of plenty and those waters
of life, which flow freely through the channels
of grace. The cascades and streams which
pour in all directions around the ruins
of Banias give it a resemblance to Tivoli, while
the rich verdure of its groves and the snow
peaks of the anti-Lebanon in its rear, render it
yet more lovely than that gem of the campagna
where Hadrian built his villa.

Their tents were erected beneath an ash-
tree of vast dimensions, growing on an open space
within the ancient walls of the town. While

Deira and Morden were superintending the operation of pitching the tents and preparing the repast, Elliott took his sketch-book and quietly made his escape. Poor Frank was not up to much fatigue, but his love of solitude induced him to wander to some distance among the groves and rivulets of this romantic spot. As the sun was setting behind the southernmost hills of Lebanon, he found himself at the foot of a ruined tower surrounded by oaks interspersed with fern and bright flowers of Galilee. The whole scene became tinted with a roseate hue well suited to the flights of his imagination. A thousand day dreams crowded upon his fancy and, among them all, he pictured Elsie as the absorbing object of his life. He was seated on a stone and had opened his book to draw. He turned over the pages and his eyes rested upon the Pylon and Hall of Philœ where he had first been inspired with love for his divinity. A variety of other scenes then floated before his mind and a thousand visions

of Elsie were rapidly conjured up, but many
were as rapidly discarded, and no memory of
the past seemed so cheering to his heart
as the hours of sickness at Eyn Sultaun,
when she had deigned to watch beside his
couch.

The doubts which followed these pleasant
recollections reacted so painfully upon him, in
his yet feeble state of health, as to prompt him
to seek relief by endeavouring to fix his mind
upon his sketch.   He was thus employed when
a tall personage in a black tunic and wearing
the green turban of a Hadji (or pilgrim from
Mecca) came, unperceived by Frank, and seated
himself at the distance of a few paces from
where he was.   When the latter raised his
head and became aware of the stranger's pre-
sence, he merely greeted him with the usual
salutation of "Barhaba," and concluding his
motive in sitting there to be the mere curiosity
of a native, was resuming his drawing, when
the man, finding he had gained his attention,

commenced addressing him in Arabic, accompanying his phrases with gesticulations, which, to the English hawagee, were, perhaps, more intelligible than the words. Nevertheless, with both these expletives combined, the whole argument was yet so entirely beyond poor Elliott's comprehension, that he imagined, from what little he could interpret that the man desired to conduct him to some curiosity in the neighbourhood, perhaps the ruined castle which, standing upon one of the acclivities of mount Hermon, overhangs the village of Banias and forms a glorious object in the panorama. However, as he had been told by Deira that it was situated at the distance of more than one hour's march from the village, he did not feel tempted, at that moment, to avail himself of the escort. After a vain endeavour at explanations, he arose from his seat and, closing his book, bade adieu to his talkative companion and returned towards the village.

The man follo¯ed at a respectful distance, and might have been more successful in making known his sentiments, had not Deira been away purchasing fowls and eggs. Frank was tired with his ramble, and, not finding Morden in the tent, threw himself on his bed, and, in spite of fleas, in which Banias abounds to such an extent as to oblige the inhabitants to dwell in houses perched upon poles during the three hottest summer months, fell into a profound sleep.

"Ma, Hawagee Elliott, your dinner get quite cold!" was the greeting which met Frank's ears as he aroused himself from his pleasant slumbers: " Mr. Morden he dine and go off."

" How so, Deira ? What time is it ?"

" Near nine o'clock.   Dime to go bed."

" Why the d——l did not you wake me before ?"

" Mr Morden he call you, ma you no wake,

so he go off to see Hawagees. There come a Hadji who say he see you drawing, and ask you to go, ma you no want to go. Suppose you are berry tired."

"What do you mean?" enquired Frank, with some degree of asperity, for he felt put out upon finding that he had overslept himself: "who are these Hawagees?"

"Your friend, you know—Hawagee Inglees —the Inglees gentleman, you know, wid de lady that take care of you."

"Confound it!" exclaimed Frank, springing up from his bed in a paroxysm of passion, ill-befitting a gentle lover: "do you mean to say that that fellow Morden is gone off to Mr. Seymour's tent without me? Why the d——l didn't you wake me? How far is it off? Tell me."

"It be long way—berry long way—more than two, dree hour."

Frank felt his heart sink within him, as he enquired :

" And when did Morden start off ?"

" 'Bout four hours ago, we come back and find one Hadji, who say he meet you, and tell you 'bout de Hawagee, but you go into de dent, and we find you fast asleep."

This was a terrible blow to Frank. He, who had been dreaming of nothing else but Elsie, to miss this opportunity of seeing her, and to feel, at the same time, that it was partly his own fault, as he might have taken more pains to interpret the words of the messenger. It was with great difficulty that the kind-hearted dragoman was able to soothe him. The quick-sighted Egyptian readily interpreted the real motives which were at work in his mind, and endeavoured to console him thus :

" Neber mind—you see de lady to-morrow. We get to Hasbeyah togeder, and encamp at de same blace, I bromise you. After all, de Hawagee, Mister Morden, he get berry late, after dey all gone to bed. I dink he no see dem to-night."

By degrees, Elliott became more consoled, and was, after much coaxing, induced to eat some dinner. He was still doubtful in his own mind as to whether he should set off in quest of his adored one or not, but Deira's entreaties prevailed upon him to await his friend's return.

Hour after hour passed, and yet Fred Morden did not return. Frank looked at his watch, and perceiving that it was midnight, called Deira, who had fallen asleep, and declared that he would set off at whatever hazard.

"I don't know de way——you cannot find de way. You better go to sleep, and I take you in de morning."

At that moment a face peered into the tent, and a voice called——

"Hawagee!"

It was an Arab boy, who brought a letter for Elliott, which he hurriedly opened.

" My dear Elliott,

    " The road is so terribly bad in
the dark that I have accepted Lisle's offer to
share his tent for the night, but I hope to be
back with you early in the morning.

         " F. Morden."

" Confound the fellow !" muttered Frank,
in his jealousy, and then threw himself on the
bed, and endeavoured to escape from his wrath
and vexation in slumbers, broken by agonizing
dreams.

He slept more profoundly towards morning,
and, when at length fairly aroused, he found
Fred Morden in the tent, re-adjusting his
neglected toilet, and preparing for breakfast.

" Well, old fellow, I saw your lady-love
last night, looking as blooming as you could
wish, and asking tenderly after you."

There was something soothing in this commencement which tended to soften Frank's feelings.

"Well, I wish you had only awoke me, and told me you were going!" replied Elliott.

"My dear fellow, you'd have been tired to death—you could not have stood it. Why, even your fair nurse, who, of course, is all impatience to see you, said she was glad you did not attempt it."

"Shall I be able to overtake them this morning? In which direction are they gone?"

"Overtake them? You will overtake them at Hasbeyah to-night, no doubt—if the length of journey is not too great for you."

"My good fellow, it is absurd to talk as if, after having had a fever, I was to go on nursing myself all my life."

Fred Morden was too well satisfied at having succeeded in blunting the edge of Frank's wrath, to feel much annoyed by his peevish temper, and under the circumstances, considered it more prudent to leave him to his grumblings and adjourn to the breakfast-table, which was placed out of doors beneath the shade of the wide spreading ash.

For some hours after leaving Banias their route lay through a wild forest-district, where the stunted oaks were interspersed with turf and flowers. Herds of goats and occasional villages afforded a pleasing variety to the scene. No country can be more abundantly supplied with water than the whole of the anti-Lebanon, and, as they ascended that range, they continued to cross a vast number of transparent rivulets. After a long and tedious march, they, at length, reached the vale of Hasbeyah. This capital of the Druses occupies the most picturesque site of any town in Syria. It stands upon the eastern slope of a deep and narrow ravine, at the bottom of which flows an impetuous mountain torrent, while its western bank is thickly wooded with olive groves. In the centre of the town, which is of considerable extent, rises the Saracenic Castle, a vast build-

ing dating from the days of the Crusaders.
The streets and bazaars of Hasbeyah are en-
livened by the presence of a Druse population,
which has a marked advantage over a Moham-
medan crowd through the circumstance of many
of their women being unveiled. The female
Druses, who appear, more than any others, to
have inherited the old Jewish customs, wear,
as is well known, the horn so frequently alluded
to in holy Scripture.

Pretty as many of their merry faces ap-
peared, they were unheeded by Frank, who
was intent only upon overtaking Elsie. As he
descended the steep road from the town, his
eyes caught the cheering sight of travellers'
tents among the olive groves upon the opposite
slope. His heart beat high as he forded the
torrent and approached the encampment. He
spurred forward his jaded steed and was the
first to reach the spot where, alas, fresh cause
for jealousy was destined to greet his arrival, since

the first person whom he met, was Herbert
Lisle.

"I am delighted to see you, Elliott!" ex-
claimed Herbert, heartily shaking his hand:
"upon my word how well you look! It is quite a
pleasure to see you again."

Frank could not feel much jealousy towards
Lisle, and returned his cordial welcome.

"Come," continued Herbert, "let me look
after your horse. Miss Seymour will be de-
lighted to see you. She is with her father up
yonder, sketching. But wait, you must want
some refreshment after your ride."

"No thank you! I am ashamed to give you
the trouble of holding my horse."

"My dear Elliott, don't say that," returned
Lisle good-naturedly, for he readily perceived
Frank's anxiety to join the Seymours, "never
mind the horse. I'll see to it. You will find
them up there, just beyond that clump of olive
trees."

The ardent lover did not fail to profit by the generosity of his supposed rival, and hastened towards the spot indicated by Herbert, with so much impetuosity as to fail to recognize Mr. Winslow, whom he passed upon the way.

In an another minute he found himself in the presence of Elsie. She was alone, for her father had strayed to some distance.

"Oh, Mr. Elliott! I am delighted to see you!" exclaimed Miss Seymour, with far more than her wonted cordiality.

"You see, that, thanks to your care and kindness, I am now quite well."

"You do not look quite strong yet!" returned Elsie, interrupting Frank's intended outpouring of thanks.

"How ungrateful you must have thought me in not coming yesterday—last night, I mean, when Frederick Morden paid you a visit."

"Oh no, do not say so, Mr. Elliott!" pursued Elsie in her kindest manner, "I would

not, for the world, have had you expose your-
self at night after your fever. To tell you the
truth I felt a good deal alarmed at hearing of
your having started so soon upon this long
journey."

Frank could no longer contain himself. For
weeks this passion had been fermenting in his
heart, and now, the interest which she ex-
pressed in his welfare, seemed to him, like an
echo of his dreams.

"Miss Seymour! How can I ever make a
return for all your kindness?"

"Oh, pray do not say so!" exclaimed Elsie.

"My whole life would be insufficient. I
feel that I am unworthy of you; but if you
would only allow me to prove my gratitude."

"I beg you will not speak so!" rejoined
Elsie, with an intonation of command in her
voice, not unmingled with dread.

"You must hear me!" persisted Frank, who
fancied that he had gone too far to recede: "my
happiness depends upon it; but what is that,

Miss Seymour, compared with yours? I feel that, in short, that I am unworthy of the place in Elsie Seymour's heart which she will, for ever and for ever, hold in mine. Can you, oh! Miss Seymour, can you so far pity me as to afford me one word, not of promise, but of hope—only hope?"

"How can you talk so foolishly? Mr. Elliott, pray do not!" said Elsie, in a state of mingled terror and annoyance: "you will make yourself ill by this excitement. It is not right. Forget it."

"Forget it I cannot. Pray, let me hope."

"I should be deceiving you if I did. You cannot really think that we are suited to each other. Reflect upon this. Remember Miss Morden, and endeavour so to direct your course that, if possible, we may not meet again, unless you can bear to meet, as alone we may—that is, as ordinary friends and acquaintances."

This was spoken with such firmness that

c 3

there was no replying to it, and, at its conclu-
sion, Elsie turned and called her father.

When Mr. Seymour approached she ran to
meet him and, having whispered a word, left
him to join Frank, while she retreated towards
the tents.

It was a terrible blow to Elliott, who had
not sufficiently recovered himself to greet Mr.
Seymour with ordinary courtesy. The latter,
however, seemed to attribute his absent fit to
illness or fatigue, and recommended him to rest
after his journey.

*　　*　　*　　*　　*

"I have just been with poor Elliott," said
Lisle, "as he came into the Seymours' tent
that same evening, "he looks very ill. I am
sure he has been travelling too fast, and is not
sufficiently careful."

Mr. Seymour was present, and Elsie slightly
coloured and made an evasive reply, for she
felt that Frank's proposal had given a foun-

dation to her father's scruples with regard to her acting nurse at Eyn Sultaun. Herbert did not fail to notice these circumstances, but the conversation took another turn until Mr. Seymour left them for his accustomed conference with Achmet.

"Tell me, Miss Seymour," enquired Lisle, laughing, "what have you done to Elliott? When I happened to name you to him, he coloured deeply and scarcely spoke another word. He talks of avoiding Damascus, and going straight to Baalbec and Beyrout.

Elsie was wretched at the unexpected result of her devotion, and longed to make known her error and contrition to him whom she had already consulted upon her duty. She sighed, and looking him full in the face, was encouraged by his candid countenance to pour forth the truth itself without disguise.

"Have I done wrong?" she said: "he proposed to me, and I refused him."

"Impossible! And yet—"

"Do you blame me?"

_ "Miss Seymour!"

She almost wished he would call her Elsie. Mr. Seymour once more returned at an unlucky moment, and Lisle walked for four hours upon the banks of the torrent of Hasbeyah, musing in the moonlight. It was long past midnight when he regained his tent, but he awoke the dragoman at that late hour to inform him that he should probably go straight to Baalbec with Morden and Frank Elliott.

"Alas!" thought Herbert: "if she had but understood the symbolism of the agate trinket!"

BOOK V.

THE TWO LOVES.

CHAPTER I.

HEARTACHE.

It was towards the beginning of May ; Lady
Elliott and her daughters had been residing for
the last few months in a house overlooking the
sea at Brighton. Although Kate had been
benefitted by the change of air, her cheeks had
lost much of their former bloom and, notwith-
standing her efforts to banish it, a trace of
sadness overcast her features. There was,
perhaps, cause enough for it ; nor was Lady
Elliott free from the same infection, and Ka-
tharine felt it a duty, in some degree, to subdue
her own feelings, in order to support her mother
in her afflictions. They were both seated near
the window in the front drawing-room, while

c 5

Mary was reclining upon a sofa at the farther side of the apartment. The day was pouring wet, and without that internal consolation of a good fire which cheers an English winter. The dismal roaring of the sea, the pattering of rain-drops upon the window, and the splashing of vehicles and pedestrians on the pavement beneath, gave a gloomy aspect to the external world, which may possibly have harmonised with the feelings of the mourners within that chamber. Lady Elliott was occupied with some work, and Kate was directing and sealing some black-edged letters at a little table near the window. All three were dressed in deep mourning and, from their faces, a stranger might have told that they were sorrowing for a loss which they all felt.

"Mamma," said Kate, "do you think it will do if I tell John to prepay this letter to Frank, or must it be stamped?"

"It will do if he pays it, I should think," returned Lady Elliott, with a deep sigh.

"I have a foreign postage stamp up-stairs," said Mary, "I am going up and will send it down to you."

After the invalid had left the room, Lady Elliott seemed to place less restraint upon her grief and to feel less loth to indulge in conversation.

"Poor Frank!" half sighed the mother, "how have you broken the terrible news to him?"

"Oh, mamma!" exclaimed Kate, afraid lest her mother should relapse into hysterics, "he will have heard from me before he gets this. You know I wrote to Malta, and this is to meet him at Marseilles."

"Dear boy—my own dear, dear, boy!" said the mother, as the hot tears came trickling down her cheek.

"Don't, dearest mamma—it is not right, indeed it is not—he is far, far happier, in heaven."

Lady Elliott was sobbing convulsively.

"Dearest mother!" continued Kate, taking her hand and kissing it, "you should not give way. If Mary comes in and sees you it may do her great harm—she is so excitable!"

"If they had brought his poor body home! But to think of my dear child in the cold sea, and his last words about his mother! If God had but granted me to be by his side to nurse him!"

"Mamma!" put in Kate, supplicatingly.

"When I last saw dear Godfrey, I remember his saying :—'Oh, mother, I hope I may be spared to see you all again.' He was the image of your poor father. So good, and gentle, and thoughtful. Oh, my darling, darling boy!"

Kate had, in early life, been deeply attached to Godfrey, but, in late years, had been more thrown with Frank, and had, perhaps, learnt to lavish upon him, some of that sisterly affection which, under other circumstances, might have been bestowed upon his elder brother. All that her mother said was deeply felt by the affectionate sister, and it required more than an ordinary effort to retain the composure which, for her mother's sake, she forced herself to assume.

"Mamma! have you written to Aunt Fortescue?"

"No—not to-day! It would have been better if—if he could have been buried on shore."

"Mamma! Providence orders these things for the best. We ought not to repine, you know."

"Repine! No child. Poor boy, if it had only been God's will to spare him."

And she wept bitterly.

A few days only had elapsed since Lady Elliott had received intelligence of her son's death on ship-board, as he was returning round the Cape, from India. Abcess had formed upon the liver, and, having broken into the lungs, already exhausted by disease, had suffocated him. His body had been buried in the sea, somewhere between the Cape and the Tropics.

This news, which had been so terrible a blow to the widowed mother, was not less deeply felt by her daughters, although, to Kate, it proved, in some sort, a relief, inasmuch as, by drawing her thoughts from her own secret sorrows, it fixed them upon griefs which she could share with others, and enable them to bear with greater fortitude.

It appeared to Kate as if the sunshine of her life were passed away for ever. The bright recollections of six months ago had been eclipsed by sorrows which seemed destined to darken the whole course of her future existence. There was a root of bitterness in her cup, which, with a less excellent disposition, might have soured her temper, and led to open repining, discontent, or anger. She could not but feel that her mother had acted incautiously towards her betrothed, and that it

might have been more prudent to have allowed
her some farther voice in rejecting him for
ever. It is true that the evidence against
Cecil Montagu appeared overwhelming, but to
her adoring heart it had seemed hard to be
asked to cast him off without affording him a
chance of clearing himself, and, notwithstand-
ing the proofs which had sufficed to convince
her relations, she either could not or would not
believe him guilty. It was an additional
source of affliction to Kate, to feel that she had
herself acted in a manner which, however pure
the motive, was such a manifestation of distrust
towards Montagu as he could not easily over-
look. At a moment when her mind was
weakened by bodily sickness, her mother had
extorted a consent to her proceedings, and a
promise that she would not see her lover again.
It is true that Kate had qualified this latter
condition, by adding, " until he should have
cleared himself." In the meantime the mar-
riage was entirely broken off, and all communi-

cations necessarily ceased between them. The
daughter's silence sufficiently ratified the
mother's rejection, and poor Kate felt that she
had sacrificed the happiness of her life upon
grounds which did not fully satisfy her own
judgment.

Although these blighted hopes could not but
weigh down Katharine's once buoyant spirits,
yet she never gave way to any bitter thoughts
towards her mother, and endeavoured to con-
vince herself, by every argument in her power,
that her parent had acted for the best. When
the bright image of the hero of her fancy in-
truded itself among her day-dreams, she strove
hard to banish the thought, but it came again
and again, at morn and even, winding
itself with her daily toil, and brooding like
a familiar spirit over her nightly meditation;
and, when Lady Elliott spoke with momen-
tary harshness to her daughter, for her
temper was hasty at times, it required
a double measure of patience to endure the

angry word, and an increased diligence in prayer to obtain strength for the conflict. Lady Elliott was not without a certain degree of hypochondria which increased and magnified those symptoms of feeble health to which she was undoubtedly a victim. She often grumbled over small misfortunes, and was seldom sufficiently overwhelmed by greater ones to bear them patiently. Upon the occasion of her present affliction, her daughters had been seriously alarmed by the violence of her grief, and the hysterical fits with which she was seized, had induced her to consult her medical attendant, who warned Kate that she should withdraw her thoughts, as much as possible, from the subject of her loss, and divert them into other channels. When she commenced sobbing, Kate felt alarmed, and bethought her of the doctor's advice.

"Dearest mamma," she said, coaxingly: "I suppose we shall have Frank home in a few days now. Do you know, I can't help think-

ing, from some of his later letters, that he is
an admirer of Miss Seymour's.   I almost think
that, if she would accept him, she might make
him an excellent wife."

Kate had done violence to her own feelings
by this speech, which she improvised solely as
a means of turning her mother's thoughts from
Godfrey.

"Poor Frank; how can you think about
such things at such a time, Kate?   My own
dear Godfrey, whom I always looked upon as
the honour of the family!"

"It is all for the best, if you could but see
it, dearest mamma; he is happy in heaven
now."

"Yes, that is what you all say, and I hope
and believe he is there, but it is a cruel,
cruel blow."

"Mamma, don't speak so," said Kate, im-
ploringly.

"I receive no sympathy!" exclaimed the
mother.

" Mamma ! mamma !" returned Kate, terrified, when she remembered the doctor's injunctions : " why will you keep your thoughts upon that terrible subject ?"

" Oh ! Kate !" rejoined the weeping mother ; " but I forgot. Your thoughts are elsewhere, no doubt ! It is very well to refer me to Providence, but who thinks their own trials for the best when they come ?"

This was meant as an allusion to her engagement with Montagu, and Kate did not fail to understand the taunt. She became silent, and was soon relieved from farther conversation by the entrance of Lady Elliott's maid, which gave her an opportunity of escaping to her own room.

In the solitude of her chamber she was able to indulge in a grief which, to say the least, was quite as deep as her mother's. It was many years since she had seen Godfrey, but she had taught herself to expect in him a brother to whom she might discreetly confide

her sorrows, and from whom she should obtain
sound advice and warm sympathy. His career
in India had earned him the reputation of very
superior abilities, and the sister had looked
forward with pride to his return, that is, as
much as she could muster under the humiliat-
ing circumstances in which she was placed.
The news of his illness and embarkation for
Europe may have served to give her something
to think of, besides her own grief, but his
death seemed, more than ever, to throw her
back upon the sorrows of her forlorn heart.

What a contrast between the present May
and the last November! When she looked
back at that bright period of her life it ap-
peared utterly unreal and dream-like.

"Was it wrong," thought she, "to indulge
in such a retrospect?"

How could she do otherwise? All her life
beforehand, even the bright days at Naples,
seemed so dull and blank compared with those
hours of felicity; but, how much more desolate

appeared the dark present, and the gloomier future! It was a relief to re-create the past. There was the first meeting at Alfreton, the same day upon which she had met Herbert Lisle. Then there was that early walk, and her first bright impressions. The fatal ride! How pleasant to recall the distant past, and to dwell, again and again, upon its incidents, leaving untouched those nearer scenes which formed the real subject of the episode.

Oh! if the worldly hero knew of the supplications and sighs which arose for him from the virgin heart of that poor desolate maiden, would he not have loved her even more than upon the day when he claimed her hand! His every look and word were treasured like holy relics in that bosom, and the beautiful girl was framing her whole existence into one long living prayer for Cecil Montagu.

"It is wrong," she thought, "to dwell upon it!"

Kate had a strong natural sense of right, and endeavoured to mould her thoughts, as well as her actions, to that standard. Religion did not, it is true, form the one subject, or object, of her existence, and therefore her will was not influenced by it to any extraordinary degree. On the other hand, she would not knowingly have offered violence to its precepts, and, whenever its claims were urged, either by others or by her own conscience, she recognized, and bowed before, them. Her coldness was partly owing to the system in which she had been brought up. She had been nurtured in the repulsive rather than in the attractive theory of faith, and scarcely believed herself to be a favoured child of Heaven. The world-wise proverb is literally true even in things not of this world; and if you give a person a bad name you repel him from what is good, and frustrate the object you desire to effect. Had she been early taught that she possessed the new life, she would more readily have embraced the new will, and have found consolation and joy amid her trials.

When she recalled her mother's taunt, she felt as if her only consolation were in the recollection of her hero. For her mother's sake, she had discarded him, and had even broken her pledge, for she could not forget that night at Thornwood, when her lover, as if in preparation for such a trial as this, had taken her hand, and had said : "you trust me, Katharine. Whatever failings may have sullied the past, I pledge you an unblemished future," and she had replied—" I trust you with all my heart, and without reserve."

This was upon the very eve of that illness, during which her engagement had been broken off. She had done this to please her mother— as a sacrifice to her tears and prayers—and now that mother had seemed to taunt her with it. She felt as if she had made a holocaust of

her life, and had been spurned. Poor girl!
weep on, but be not utterly dejected! It is
the way of the cross, if thou could'st but see
it! There is no other way but the way of
sorrows.

*   *   *   *   *

While she was thus immersed in grief, a
knock at the door recalled her from her mus-
ings. It was her maid who came to tell her
that her uncle had called, and that her mother
wished her to go down to receive him, as she
felt too ill to do so.

Kate endeavoured to wash away the tears
from her eyes, and hastened to the drawing-
room, where she found her uncle Reginald
awaiting her with some impatience.

Mr. Reginald Elliott was a tall, stout, good-
looking man of fifty, with greyish hair, and a
ruddy complexion, who spoke in a loud, off-
hand, decided tone of voice.

"Ha! Kate—I am glad to see you. Terrible affliction for you all. I suppose your poor mother feels it very deeply? Poor fellow—such a fine boy as I remember him!"

Kate's tears began to flow afresh.

"Mamma is not at all well—I am afraid she cannot see you."

"Oh, no, I wouldn't think of it. I ran down from town to know if I could be of any use to you, and am obliged to go back by this train," he continued, looking at his watch. "Your aunt would be glad to be of service in any way. We want you to come to Lockwood, where you will be quite quiet. Do promise me to persuade your mother, will you, my dear?"

"The doctors recommend her quiet," ventured Kate, timidly, as she sought vainly for some good reason to refuse the invitation, and recollected that their real advice had been diversion, as well as quiet.

" Quiet ! she will be perfectly quiet with us."

" She is so very nervous and hysterical."

" Change of scene is what she wants," rejoined her uncle : " come, Kate, you must promise to get her to pay us a visit. You are not looking well. Change of air will do you all the good in the world !"

" I am very well."

" Well ! not much amiss, I hope ! I know all about it. I hope that little affair is all blown over now. You are well out of it. Terrible scamp ! We will look out for you, and find something better. Your aunt is fond of a bit of match-making, you know, and has a very brilliant affair in her eye—but we won't talk of these things at such a time as this. Poor Godfrey, he was a great favourite of ours ! I suppose it was for the best, if we could only see it. Where is Frank now ?"

" On his way home, I hope. I have written to him to Malta and Marseilles."

"Well, I am afraid I must be off, to be in time for the train. Give our best love to your mother, and to Mary, and tell them how deeply we all feel with them; and remember you press them to come to Lockwood. Your aunt has written to your mother, but we depend upon your arguments. Good bye, my dear Kate. God bless you."

And the uncle hurried off, leaving his niece to ponder upon his words, and reflect with no very kindly feelings upon her worthy kinsman. "Well out of it," and, "terrible scamp!" "A million times better," she thought, "than the brilliant affair of the match-making aunt, would be a life of solitude spent in keeping her vow to Cecil Montagu, whom she had promised "to trust with all her heart and without reserve."

Katharine faithfully reported her uncle's message to her mother, who received pressing letters to the same effect, both from Mrs. Elliott and her sister, Mrs. Fortescue; the latter having been requested to urge her

D 3

visiting Lockwood, for the sake of that change
of scene which appeared important in her
present state of health. Lady Elliott was
pleased with the suggestion, and, in her
replies, stated that she only awaited Frank's
return to avail herself of the invitation.

CHAPTER II.

EMMELINE AND LAURA.

ALFRETON was lovely in the month of May, but its springtide beauty was no sufficient compensation to Emmeline, for the gaieties of the London season. The fact is, that Sir Edward was so much occupied with improvements upon his estate, that he preferred remaining in the country ; and Lady Morden did not care for being in London until Frederick returned to England, when she proposed that they should go up to meet him.

In the meanwhile, Emmeline was wasting her sweetness on the desert air, and sighing for some less sylyan scene. Arcadia is not to be found in the country, but it rather exists upon the borders of the Serpentine, or, in still greater perfection, on the stage of the opera. So felt Emmeline, as she sighed for London.

On a lovely afternoon she had strolled out with a straw hat upon her head, and a book in her hand, through the groves which bordered on the Trent. Seated in a secluded nook overlooking the river, she turned over the pages of her novel and reflected upon her melancholy fate.

No one in the whole world could ever have guessed that the destiny of the merry girl was overclouded, and, indeed, it required a good deal of imagination to conjure up those phantasies of grief of which she imagined herself the victim.

"I wonder how papa ever expects me to be married, if he leaves me in this dismal solitude while the London season is at its height!" thought Emmeline: "after all, I firmly believe I shall end by being an old maid; a horrid, hateful, old maid. Spiteful too, yes, that I would! I would be as spiteful as an old cat. I would ten thousand times rather die than be an old maid. It really is very, very, cruel of papa and mamma not to take me to London! I am determined I will marry the first person that proposes to me. I wonder if Mr. Elliott cares for me any longer? I almost think I should not even refuse him now, but, perhaps, he has forgotten me. I am afraid he will be very poor, and that would be dreadful, to be very poor, and not able to go to London, or travel abroad, or give parties and all that kind of thing! And then, Fred said something about his having fallen in love with Elsie, and of her having nursed him when he was ill. She would never accept him I am sure. I suppose he did not care the least for poor me all the time he pretended to be in love, and I do believe Elsie is a little bit of a flirt—I always thought so. It was not a very nice thing for a girl to nurse a man in that way, I must say! No, Miss Elsie, I am very angry with you about it!"

Her meditations rambled from one theme to another, until they were suddenly interrupted by the sound of voices approaching her retreat. She listened and recognized her mother's tones. At first, she felt half inclined to escape, but curiosity induced her to remain, and, in another minute, Lady Morden appeared in sight, accompanied by Laura Lisle. Concealing her disappointment, Emmeline went to meet them, and greeted her mother's visitor with her usual cheerful and easy manner.

"I shall leave you with Emmeline," said Lady Morden, " while I go back to Mrs. Lisle. Remember, Emmie," she continued, turning to her daughter, " you must come in presently to see Mr. and Mrs. Lisle, whom I have left with your father."

Emmeline thought it a bore, and wondered whether Miss Pinsant was there as well.

" I am afraid I must be returning to the house," said Laura, " for my father is obliged to go home rather early, having some business in his parish."

"In that case we can all go together," returned Lady Morden, " but I hoped you would have stayed and gone round the gardens with Emmeline."

Emmeline, who could not endure the Lisles, was delighted at the reprieve.

"Only think, Emmie," said Lady Morden, "I have just seen, in the paper, the death of Godfrey Elliott, Lady Elliott's eldest son, during his voyage from India. I do not know whether you remember a Miss Elliott, who was staying with us last year?" she continued, addressing Laura.

"Yes, perfectly—with her brother. You brought them to Carrowsby. Is he dead?"

"No, not that brother. He is with my son in the East. It will be a terrible blow to poor Lady Elliott, her son being away from her at the time."

D 5

" I remember that Herbert mentions him in some of his letters," said Laura.

" Godfrey was the eldest, and I suppose that Francis will be very well off now that his poor brother is dead. Katharine will feel it deeply."

This was addressed by Lady Morden to her daughter, who appreciated the facts as highly as her mother could have wished, but who felt more jealous than ever of Elsie Seymour.

" I suppose you often hear from Mr. Lisle ?" she enquired of Laura.

" Not very often, but his letters are full of interest when they do come."

" I suppose he mentions having met the Seymours and my brother ?"

" Yes," replied Laura, smiling archly, but speaking in a hasty tone : " though he does not say very much about Miss Seymour, we half suspect that there lies a story underneath. He seems certainly, I think, to admire her. She

is an acquaintance of yours I believe? Pray
what sort of person is she?"

"Oh! she is a great friend of ours," rejoined
Lady Morden: "she is a charming person
and extremely accomplished."

Emmeline was no longer jealous of her
friend Elsie and could afford to praise her as
she deserved. She had never before felt so well
pleased with Laura, and her own existence ap-
peared to have assumed a more rosëate tinge
than that which overshadowed it half an hour
before.

"I suppose you are going to London soon?"
asked Laura.

"I hope so," returned Emmeline.

"We intend to meet my son directly he
arrives," remarked Lady Morden. "You are
going from home I think you said?"

"Yes, I leave to-morrow. I am about to
pay a visit to my sister in Wiltshire."

"You are always visiting, I think," replied
Emmeline.

"I have been at home a long time now, ever since November."

"So have we.   We never leave home!" exclaimed Emmeline.

"But you are going to London?"

"Mamma always encourages one with that prospect, but it is like the bundle of hay which the poor donkey follows without ever reaching, and, at last, I suppose, gets to distrust, unless he is a terrible donkey indeed," said Emmeline, laughing.

"We are going directly my son Frederick returns," rejoined Lady Morden, in a voice which expressed a slight degree of pique. "Emmeline, you see, does not share our love for the country.   Sir Edward dislikes London."

"So do I," said Laura: "it is true I have been there very little, but I never wished to remain longer."

Emmeline tossed her head and inquired half satirically :

"Have you often been to the opera?"

"Once I went," replied Laura: "but I do not wish to go again."

"Oh! I idolize it; but, perhaps, you do not care for music?"

"Yes I do," she answered: "I am very fond of some music."

"Sacred, I suppose?" enquired the *espiègle* girl.

"Well there is no music so beautiful as Handel and Mendelsohn," put in Lady Morden, in an apologetical tone.

"But oratorios are so dreadfully long, I always think. So very English to suppose you can never have too much of a good thing," replied Emmeline.

"I agree with you there," remarked Laura: "I would rather have less at a time. I like beautiful music scattered through church services rather than long isolated compositions."

"It makes the service so long," said Emmeline : " I always find it long enough without music."

" For shame, Emmie !" rejoined her mother.

" Well, mamma, it is really dreadful now with all those hymns," replied Emmeline, who added, turning to Miss Lisle, " our clerk, who manages the singing, gives out no less than four hymns during the service. The one after the sermon makes me so angry that I should like to get up and walk out of church. But you must not think that I am referring to our church as an example of beautiful music, as the four cracked voices which form our choir are all at sixes and sevens. To do you justice, I do not think you would set up ours as a fair contrast to the opera," and her merry laugh resounded again.

" Emmie is incorrigible," said Lady Morden, whose affable dignity seemed strangely at variance with the unrestrained hilarity of her daughter, who was as much bent upon saying something to shock Miss Lisle as her mother was studious to please her.

It was not until the Lisles were gone that Emmeline had leisure to reflect upon what she had heard, and she soon discovered that a similar train of thought was running in her mother's mind.

"A sad thing this death of poor Godfrey Elliott," she said. "I should think Mr. Francis Elliott will feel it much. I had hoped we should have seen him on his return, but I suppose this will prevent our meeting for the present. Perhaps we may persuade him to come down here in the summer, after the London season."

Emmeline pretended indifference and replied:

"I should think he scarcely remembered his brother."

"So Mr. Lisle has taken a fancy to Elsie! It would be a charming *parti*."

"He is not half good enough for her,

mamma!" answered Emmeline, with more than
her usual warmth.

"He is of much better family and large
fortune, and most people think him very
agreeable."

"What is that, mamma? Elsie is worthy of
a Duke! There is but one Elsie."

"So you think, but I will venture to say
that her admirers are quite as rare as Mr.
Herbert Lisle's. You must remember that
she is peculiar; they are both peculiar. I am
sure that she is not a general favourite with
gentlemen."

"It shows their bad taste, but I half believe
you are right, mamma, for gentlemen naturally
like something more stupid, if possible, than
themselves. Still, mamma, you must allow
that she is a thousand times too good for Mr.
Herbert Lisle."

"She may improve him and, remember, he
is very clever they say, and who knows but

she may push him forward when he goes into Parliament ?"

"Oh ! mamma, if it had been Mr. Montagu, then I should have said nothing. He appreciates Elsie and is worthy of her; at least, I mean, in point of talent and accomplishments. I will never believe that Elsie would throw herself away upon Mr. Lisle until I hear it from herself, or see the marriage in the paper."

    *   *   *   *   *

In the meantime the Lisles had returned to Carrowsby Vicarage, and Laura sauntered through the garden with her mother while Mr. Lisle went about his parish business.

" You will remember to tell dear Mary about the boots for little Herby and the wine for Edith. I am sure, in her weak state, she ought to have a wine glass of port wine in an equal quantity of water at her dinner; and remember to tell me about baby's teething— dear Mary has never written again about the convulsions, but if you find they still go on, mind you persuade her to have my prescription made up, and see that they give him four or five drops every hour, not more, mind."

"I will remember, dear mamma, and see that grand-mamma's receipts are all attended to."

"Dearest Mary! I wish you could bring her back with you. Edward might surely let her come and see her old mother."

"There are the children in the way, as well as Edward, remember."

"It seems so long since they have been. You know you promised, Laura, to try and get Mary here sometime this year."

"I will do my best, certainly; but I can't promise more. I am sure, dearest Mary will be as anxious as any one to come."

"She went last autumn to Cawthorne; but that is not so far."

"Oh, mamma, I am sure she will come if she can."

" I wish Edward's living were nearer to us.
It seems to be such a long time without seeing
one's children."

" I wonder if cousin Herbert is come back
to England ?"

" Why, dear ? Do you think of going to
Cawthorne to see the Drislows ?"

" I should have liked to have seen some of
my pets there, very much. The poor old
people must have had a hard winter without
any of the family there. Poor old Sally
Dolby !"

" I thought you received a letter from some
one at Cawthorne last week ?"

" From Phœbe Elton, mamma, from Lon-
don ; but she enclosed one from Perdon, the
schoolmaster at Cawthorne. She is still at the
Training school, but expects to return soon.
Oh ! if I could be there for her wedding—poor
girl ! I should be afraid that old Dolby's cot-
tage will be less of a home for her since the

return of the daughter I told you about; Ann
Dolby that *was*."

"I wonder if Herbert is going to be mar-
ried!" said Mrs. Lisle.

"Who knows?" rejoined Laura, turning
away her face.

"I do not quite fancy I shall like this Miss
Seymour, from all I hear of her."

"I am sure cousin Herbert would not marry
any one you would dislike, dear mamma. The
Mordens seem very fond of her. But, after
all, we are jumping at conclusions upon very
insufficient grounds. We have no reason to be-
lieve that there is anything serious in it."

"Well, dear, I dare say you will hear more
about it before you return."

*   *   *   *

CHAPTER III.

WEST-LANGTON.

IT was a treat to Laura to visit her brother-in-law's parish, and to trace, from year to year, the progress which he made in setting forth, in their completeness, the doctrines of the cross and in winning souls to the crucified.

Edward Baring's orthodoxy was untinged by that dry and freezing formalism which centres its efforts in obtaining strict rubrical accuracy. It was not in his nature to love forms for their own sake, and no such lesson had been taught him by the Divine grace which kindled in his heart, and led him, above all other things, to labour for the conversion of sinners.

As Laura was seated by the tea-table in the homely little parlour, between her sister and Edward, she happened to enquire:

" And how does the church go on?"

" It remains in *statu-quo*. It has not moved from where it stood," replied Edward, laughing.

" How can you, Edward?" ventured his wife.

" No, but tell me about the singing," said Laura.

" We have no chaunting at all—nothing but the hymns. You have seen Edward's little book?" asked Mary.

" Yes—I was delighted with it. But don't they even chaunt the canticles?"

" No," returned Edward, " I have got them to sing hymns very well, and I prefer all the rest plain, unless it could be done very well indeed."

" You know Edward wishes to make it as short as possible," rejoined his wife.

"I am convinced," he said, "that the great length of the prayers is very prejudicial to the devotion of the poor. It is impossible for them to concentrate their thoughts the whole time, as they ought."

"You should divide the services," returned Laura.

"So we do. We have the litany in the afternoon, and evening-prayer at night."

"Have you many communicants?"

"A great many," rejoined Mary : "oh! I should almost think they had doubled since last year—have not they, Edward?"

"Scarcely that, darling—but, thank God, they are increasing."

"You celebrate it frequently?"

"Very frequently. It is the one evangelical worship, bequeathed to us by our Lord Himself, to shew forth His death continually."

"You don't think it is dangerous, lest persons should come unprepared."

"What ! dangerous to obey our Lord's command ?"

. "But after so many years of neglect people are ill prepared."

"Were they ever otherwise ? It is the pastor's duty to feed and tend the flock. We exercise the ministry of reconciliation in Christ's stead, but He alone can prepare His people by His Holy Spirit. You speak, dear Laura, as if you thought that the operations of the Spirit had ceased."

"But so many have sullied their baptismal robes."

And may they not wash them in the blood of the Lamb ? You complain of their being faint and languishing, and yet refuse them the food for the way, the bread of life."

"Then you don't admit them without preparation ?"

"I endeavour not to admit any without true change of heart and conversion to God. That

is my aim, but of course, I do not always suc-
ceed. We can only judge the tree by its fruits,
you know."

" And can we judge ourselves by any other
test ?" enquired Laura.

" It is, perhaps, the safest ; but the heart
alone knows when the love of God is kindled
within it, and feels when it can dwell in
that unspeakable and uncreated love. Although
such assurance is not universal, I am per-
suaded that it is not uncommon."

Laura became silent and pensive.

On the day following she accompanied her
brother-in-law to his cottages and to his pretty
little church, where, late in the evening, he
preached a short extempore sermon to a consi-
derable number of labouring people. There
was something very real and stirring in his
words, in which earnestness and burning love
supplied the place of eloquence. Many work-

ing people came from neighbouring parishes to
hear him proclaim the gospel to the poor and,
at late hours, when their daily toil was over,
obeying his invitation, rough peasants would
find him at his vicarage and ask him what they
should do to be saved.   He urged them to seek
the heavenly treasure in prayer, to ask where
they were sure to obtain and to knock, until
the door of acceptance was opened.   Many of
them found it hard to pray in their crowded
cottages, and, for their convenience, he left the
church doors open, that they might enter at all
hours, and pour forth their petitions without
distraction.

One morning, as the trio sat at their early
breakfast in the little vicarage, a letter arrived
by post for Edward Baring, which he opened
the more eagerly, as he recognised the hand-
writing of Herbert Lisle.

"Is he in England?" enquired Mary anxi-
ously, for she already knew from whom it
came.

" Yes, darling. Wait a minute, and you shall see it.."

" Is he coming to us, I wonder ?"

" One minute, dearest !"

" I didn't mean to interrupt. How I long to hear all about it."

" You shall, dearest. I will read it after you."

" No, darling husband, go on ; I didn't mean to interrupt you," and at last he succeeded in finishing his letter.

" Herbert is coming to pay us a visit in a few days."

" I am very glad to hear it," said Laura.

" I think he will bring his uncle with him."

" Mr. Winslow ?"

" Yes, do you know him ?"

" If I ever saw him, it was many years ago at Cawthorne, but I have no recollection of him."

" I suppose you scarcely wished to know him

B 2

formerly," rejoined Edward. "How wonderful an instance of God's dealings amongst us! I have always felt that those who speak of miracles having ceased in the church take a most short-sighted view of the gospel scheme; for to disbelieve in miracles is to deny direct answer to prayer. It is certain that our Blessed Lord never set bounds to His promise, that the prayer of faith should remove mountains. Here, at all events, is a miracle—as great, almost, as the conversion of St. Paul."

"From all one hears," replied Laura, "he seems quite sincere; but I confess, I always feel inclined and, it is, perhaps, very wrong of me to doubt very sudden conversions."

"To doubt miracles?"

"Well, I always feel that a more gradual change is likely to be more lasting."

"You mistake conversion for a human change. The gifts of the Holy Spirit are all sudden. The day of Pentecost, the waters of baptism, the laying on of hands. There may be a gradual preparation, but conversion *must* be sudden."

She did not agree with him, and yet felt unprepared or unwilling to discuss the question and, consequently, remained silent.

*   *   *   *   *

It was a lovely day, and Laura offered to take her little nephew and niece a walk. The garden of the vicarage was bright with spring flowers, and the aunt was obliged, at the outset of the excursion, to admire the borders appropriated to the children and to accept a somewhat unwieldy nosegay at their hands. From the garden they passed over a stile into a meadow gay with cowslips and butter-cups, and its hedges bright with May flowers. Allured onwards by the balmy atmosphere of the morning, they continued to follow the pathway through the meadows and beneath the shade of a copse, until they reached a hollow lane, of which the banks were strewed with violets and blue-bells.

"Aunty Laura, Herby says I must not have those pretty flowers!" said Edith, running up to Miss Lisle.

"No, aunty, must she? Mamma says it's poison!" rejoined the little boy.

"The blue-bells do you mean?" returned Laura: "they are not poison."

"No, aunty, not the blue bells," pursued the boy, "those purple flowers with yellow in the middle.

"Oh! That night-shade! You must not think of touching it, Edith."

"See here, aunty, there are some, oh! such pretty pink flowers, with spotted leaves. May I gather them?" and the little girl beckoned her aunt forward to look at a wild orcus.

Induced to prolong the walk, and forgetting how the time passed, Laura followed the lane until it brought her into a wider road with a broad margin of grass, upon which there lay some felled timber. Tempted by the sight of these trees, the children began to jump and stride across them, as if they were on horseback.

For a few moments she sat and watched their merry gambols.

While thus engaged, she seemed to hear voices in the distance, as of persons approaching along the lane, and she presently saw a lady and gentleman cantering up the greensward, towards the place where she sat.

On drawing near they slackened their pace, and she called to the children to notice the pretty horses, when it flashed across her that she had seen the lady's face before.

"Miss Lisle!" exclaimed the stranger, who had been the first to recognize her acquaintance.

"I thought I knew your face," said Laura, "how strange to meet you here!"

"Allow me to introduce my uncle to you."

The gentleman bowed, and she continued: "are you staying near here?"

"Yes. These are my sister's children. I am staying at the vicarage."

"At West-Langton?" enquired the uncle, "Is Mr. Baring your brother-in-law?"

"Yes."

"I hope Mrs. Lisle is well?" pursued the lady.

"I left her very well a few days since. Pray how is Lady Elliott? I was grieved to hear from the Mordens of the sad loss you have all had."

Katharine sighed as she replied.

Laura was struck with her faded expression and the absence of her former amination.

"I have long intended doing myself the pleasure of calling upon Mr. Baring," said Mr. Elliott, who felt, that, as he lived within the range of their visiting neighbourhood, he ought to make some apology for not being acquainted with him : " the fact is that we have been absent and have had some building going on and, with one thing or another, we have had less time than we could have wished to visit and become acquainted with our neighbours."

"I hope the Mordens are well?" said Kate who willingly lingered upon a reminiscence of those happy days when she had first seen Montagu.

"Yes. They are awaiting Mr. Frederick Morden's return with your brother, to go to London."

Katharine would have liked to ask other questions, but that she fancied her uncle might be impatient to proceed. She warmly pressed Laura's hand as she bade her farewell and proceeded on her way.

Miss Lisle returned homewards with the children, for whose long absence she apologized by an account of her morning's adventure.

On the following day, Mrs. Elliott of Lockwood drove over to West-Langton, and Mrs.

E 5

Baring being from home, she left cards, and a note containing excuses for not having previously called, coupled with a pressing invitation to dinner, in which Miss Lisle was especially included, for the day but one from that time.

The Barings were most unsociable neighbours. Edward Baring had, as far as a married man ever can, foresworn society. He felt that a parish priest ought to devote his whole time and a large portion of his income to his flock, and that, as his family duties already abstracted a considerable share of both, he was bound to give up all the rest to those over whom he was appointed a steward and overseer in Christ. This had been his determination when he first came to reside at the vicarage, and he had almost invarably informed his neighbours, at least such as had called upon him, that it was not his intention to visit. Mary had remonstrated feebly at first, and had afterwards, silently acquiesced in his whims. It was not his wish to tie her quite so rigorously, but in practice he found that she could not go to parties without him.

"Edward dear," said Mary, as she entered her husband's study with this note, "it is very annoying. I was out when Mrs. Elliott called, and 1 find that she has left a note asking Laura to accompany us there to dinner. There is an old friend of Laura's staying there! What are we to do?"

"When is it for?"

"The day after to-morrow."

"Saturday! well, Mary dearest, you know that I never dine out, but Herbert will be with us then, and if you like to take him and Laura, you can do it. I will be bound that Winslow will stay at home with me."

"What do you think, dearest Edward? You see it seems so hard to deprive Laura of meeting an old friend!"

"Oh yes! You had better accept it as I tell you, but be sure you inform Mrs. Elliott that I make it a rule never to dine out."

" Is that necessary ?"

" I am sure it is better, especially as I have refused so many others upon the same ground, You must ask to be allowed to bring Herbert in my place."

And thus Mary Baring succeeded, for the first time, in accepting an invitation in the neighbourhood.

The next day, Herbert and Arthur Winslow arrived, and Edward Baring met them at the station.　　They both returned with sun-burnt faces, Herbert looking all the better for his eastern tour.　　His companion was very silent and, to say the truth, Baring was a little dissatisfied at his apparent apathy and reserve. If he had expected from the new convert eloquence upon his spiritual experiences, he could not fail to be disappointed, for it was very rarely now that he ventured to speak of his own state, even to Herbert, who had been anxious to introduce his uncle to Edward Baring, as he felt convinced that the former would find great comfort from one so spiritually-minded from whom he himself had derived so much benefit.

It was a delightful meeting. Herbert had, all his life, been on terms of excessive intimacy with Mary and Laura, whom he had been accustomed to regard in the light of sisters rather than cousins. There were many things to relate and questions to ask, and the hours at West-Langton vicarage passed pleasantly during the few days of their visit.

Upon the first evening of his arrival, as they came out of church, Herbert stopped to examine the old fabric, and speculate upon the restorations which it required, when his cousin Laura, bent upon having him a little to herself, a privilege which as yet she had failed in obtaining, accosted him.

"You have been here before, I think?"

"Only for a day or two. How happy you must be here, Laura? Edward does things so nicely. He wants a little more of the æsthetical element. This church might be improved so very much outside. I like what he has done to the inside; but just look at this wretched porch!"

"I am afraid he can't afford to do much at present; his school has cost him a good deal."

"Do you mind walking round with me? I see that Edward and my uncle are going off together, and I don't wish to interrupt them, as one of my objects in coming down here was to get them together."

"I had not seen him before, unless it was a great many years ago at Cawthorne. He seems very silent."

"Well, I suppose you would scarcely wish him otherwise? I do not much admire conversational penitents."

"I so long to hear about your travels?" she said, changing the subject.

"It is a long story."

"Have you kept a journal?"

"Yes, but it is scarcely readable."

"You will let me see it?"

"Very well, but upon condition of keeping it entirely to yourself;" and then it flashed across his memory that it might contain certain little incidents which he should not like even Laura to know. "On second thoughts, you must let me look it over before I send it to you."

"You met Frederick Morden in the East?"

"Yes, and young Elliott. Do you remember his coming over to Carrowsby last summer when I was with you?"

"Perfectly; and that reminds me," returned Laura, "that you will meet his sister to-morrow, for Mary has accepted an invitation to dine at Lockwood, where Lady Elliott and her daughters are staying."

"Oh! I know the Elliotts well. I met them some years ago in Italy."

"And tell me, Herbert, about Miss Seymour," continued Laura, endeavouring to assume a boldness which she did not feel, but burning with curiosity.

"Oh!" and Herbert could scarcely conceal a momentary confusion: "the Seymours are charming people—that is, in a worldly point of view. I am not sure, Laura, that *you* would like them."

"Tell me about Miss Seymour. She is very pretty, is she not?" There was a latent irony in the intonation of her question.

"She is certainly lovely—very lovely, and most agreeable."

"And very clever, I am told, and accomplished."

"She is unlike any woman I ever met with," rejoined Herbert.

"She would make a good mistress for Cawthorne, perhaps," returned Laura, with a slight expression of pique; so slight that her cousin could not possibly perceive it, or only mistook it for feminine satire.

"No—I think not, Laura," replied Herbert, in a tone of confidence, which found an echo in his companion's breast: "I think she is scarcely suited to me. She is my superior in every way, and, I should worship her—that would be the danger."

"Are you afraid of having one too good for you?"

"I am afraid of influence, where I am not certain of its direction. Her family are not religious people."

"And is not she?"

"Scarcely what you would call so. She has been brought up almost a Unitarian."

"How shocking!"

"I should not say that she was exactly that

now, but she is not entirely changed. I could not, conscientiously, link my destinies with hers."

"Oh, Herbert, certainly not in that case! Cannot you influence her?"

"Not without running the danger of being influenced oneself. She is a syren whom it is next to impossible to resist. Sappho, Aspasia, Corinne, were nothing to her! There is no one like her," and Herbert relapsed into silence, during which his thoughts reverted to Elsie.

"She must be charming!" exclaimed Laura.

"Dearest Laura," pursued Herbert, after a pause, "do not say a word of all this, and, do not often remind me about her—pray do not. I almost wish I had never met her."

Thus talking, they had crossed the meadows bounding the village, and had come to the stile which separated one of these green fields from the vicarage garden.

"How pleasant such an English evening is !" said Herbert: "I think I hear a nightingale in those trees."

They stood and listened. Laura felt very happy as she hearkened to the notes of philomel, and wished that those moments might be prolonged.

"Do you know, Laura, I should like you to be acquainted with Elsie—Miss Seymour, I mean. I think you might benefit each other."

Laura made no reply.

"She is a singular mixture," pursued Herbert, who, notwithstanding his professions to the contrary, felt relieved by unburdening his heart to others: "for instance, she has established a sisterhood, in London, to provide nurses for the sick, and intends devoting her life to that object. Oh ! If she could be led to right views ! I think you might insensibly influence her."

"Not if you are unable," returned Laura,

somewhat too drily; and then, as if to correct her mistake proceeded: "I am afraid I am so little able to influence others."

"You underrate your powers, Laura. You are, of all others, the person to influence an imaginative being like Miss Seymour, you are so practical and earnest."

"You flatter me, Herbert; you ought not."

"No, but I do wish I could bring about an acquaintance between her and you, without coming forward myself in the matter."

"I fear it would be impossible!" answered Laura, who evidently did not long for such an introduction. After a silence she again fancied that she had not sufficiently responded to Herbert's confidence and felt dissatisfied with herself about it, and, anxious to prove her friendship, she continued: "but I suppose that if Miss Seymour devotes herself to this sisterhood, she will have to give up society?"

"Entirely!"

" And never marry."

" Perhaps not. She is too good to marry ; I mean too ideal. She ought to become a saint."

" There are married saints, I hope ?"

" A few, I suppose. But she would never find any one to suit her, any one worthy of her, I am sure !"

" But tell me, Herbert, seriously," pursued Laura, more reassured since she had heard about Elsie's devoted life, and half repentant at her former coldness: " how can I become acquainted with Miss Seymour ? I do not see that it is possible."

" The Mordens are intimate with her. You may go and and see her sisterhood in Blooms-bury ?"

" Is it exhibited then ?"

" Oh, no ! But I suppose you might go there with Miss Morden. I always imagine that you will end by turning sister of mercy, and I don't see why you should not ally yourself with Miss Seymour, dear Laura, and lead her into that narrow way, which I fear she has not yet found."

This was spoken very tenderly, but, nevertheless, it grated upon Laura's heart.

" And so you destine me for a sister of mercy, do you, Herbert ?" she asked, in a half-laughing voice, to conceal her inward feelings.

" Well, I don't know, but I always think of you, as I said of Miss Seymour; I think you too good for the world."

" How little you know me !" she said, and, after a moment's thought, added : " but you may be right after all, about its being better for me to give up the world ; not because I am too good for it, but because its temptations are too strong for me."

It was getting late, and Laura suggested that they should return to the vicarage. They had been sauntering through the meadow adjoining the garden, and now crossed the stile and approached the humble parsonage, with its rough-cast front and bay windows. The parlour casement was open and, Mary having disappeared to look after the children, Edward and Mr. Winslow were alone in the room. The conversation now became general, and Herbert was forced to give a graphic account of his eastern pilgrimage, which amused the party until bed time.

When alone, Laura recalled and dwelt upon the words, 'I always fancy you will end by turning sister of mercy.' Poor Laura!

CHAPTER IV.

LOCKWOOD.

LOCKWOOD was a square stone mansion with a portico in front, and a colonnade alongside. It was surrounded by a park without any deer, but containing some tolerable timber. Nothing could exceed the monotonous beauty of this undulating plaisaunce. It was all green up to the sunk-fence and, within this, all green again, with the exception of the gravel-walk, up to the walls of the house. The owner had the satisfaction of being lord of all he surveyed from his windows, which is a great desideratum and one which weighed strongly with land-scape gardeners of the old school. That particular pupil of capability Brown who had laid out the grounds at Lockwood, had succeeded admirably in so marshalling his clumps, as to shut out every hillock or wood belonging to any one but the squire of the place. Enclosed in this green domain, Mr. Reginald Elliott was able to indulge in the most agreeable reveries of proprietorship and to feel himself the greatest man in the visible creation.

However delightful this may have been to the landlord, it was less entertaining to his guests, and Katharine was tired to death of gazing upon the sea of green which lay before her windows and ventured to think that she preferred the landscape gardening at Thornwood, where a totally different system had been pursued, and where, in the place of harmonious monotony, the artist had aimed at bold and striking contrasts.

The family was scarcely less harmonious than the place. Mr. Elliott was an off-hand man accustomed to have his own way and Mrs. Elliott was accustomed not to have hers, at least with him, and so, things went on very smoothly. The

children, that is the two eldest girls, both very
quiet and docile, were educated at home, by
the German governess, Madame Hoffner. The
boys were at school, at Harrow.

Reginald Elliott was a younger brother of
Sir Ralph, who had been knighted for his dis-
tinguished services in India and with whose
family the reader is already acquainted. Re-
ginald had practised for some years as a bar-
rister on the Western circuit, until he had
fallen in with Miss Blantyre, a rich West
Indian heiress, whom he had married and with
whose money he had purchased Lockwood,
where he lived in tolerable style and had grown
as intimate with the neighbouring squirearchy
as an interloper can ever become.

Lady Elliott had been prevailed upon to
visit her brother-in-law chiefly from a consi-
deration that the change would be beneficial
to Katharine, for, although she would some-
times give way to selfish impulses, at heart,
she was devoted to her children and would have

made almost any sacrifice for them. She had only awaited Frank's return to leave Brighton, and had contrived to meet him in London on her way down.

In addition to his own private affairs, Frank found that a good many family matters had devolved upon him in consequence of Godfrey's death. Their father's fortune had been almost entirely made in India and the money invested in Indian securities. The greater part of it was in trust for Lady Elliott during her life and for Sir Ralph's sons in succession, a legacy of twelve thousand pounds having been left for younger children. Godfrey had been made a trustee and, upon his death, Lady Elliott had nominated Frank in his stead. He consulted experienced persons upon the several items and was recommended, as much as possible, to withdraw the capital from India. These transactions took up a good deal of his time, but he devoted himself assiduously to the task.

F 2

Godfrey's death had thus considerably improved his prospects, although, during his mother's life the only benefit which he would derive, was the increased allowance which Lady Elliott did not hesitate to make him in consequence of his having become the eldest son. At the same time, it must be said in justice to Frank, that he deeply felt the loss of his brother and seemed unwilling to take advantage of his improved fortunes, at least, in the manner so judiciously marked out for him in the imaginations of Lady Morden and her daughter.

Kate had, as yet, seen very little of him, for when they met in town his time was absorbed by Lady Elliott and by the numerous matters of business which they were called upon to transact together. She was longing for his promised visit to Lockwood in order that she might open her heart and exhibit those wounds to him which she had so carefully endeavoured to conceal from all the world beside. It is not certain that, when the time came, she would really have made them known to Frank. Her doing so depended upon a thousand circumstances, but it was a relief to her to fancy that she should at last have one confidant who would know of all the anguish she had suffered and of all that she was still prepared to undergo. No sooner had she speculated upon her intended confidence than it flashed across her that it might be treason even to reveal her feelings to her brother, for, supposing he were to cast off Montagu like the rest, how much more humiliated she should feel than if she had kept her secret entirely to herself.

Kate had so dreaded her visit to Lockwood that, as is often the case, she found the reality far less awful than her anticipations. She had gone fortified with a determination to keep every body at arm's length, and not to suffer any one to discover her feelings upon the subject of Mr. Montagu. She foresaw that her

uncle and aunt might attack her upon that
topic, and she sought to prepare ready answers
for all conceivable emergencies. Above all, she
looked forward with especial horror to meeting
the governess, who had caused the breach
between herself and her lover. Having been
given to understand that she had been ac-
quainted with Montagu, she made up her mind
to treat all overtures from such a quarter with
freezing coldness.

Happily for Katharine's peace of mind, Lady
Elliott had also felt some alarm lest her
daughter should be plagued by allusions to her
attachment, and, although she never commu-
nicated with her upon this subject, she ex-
pressed very decidedly to Mrs. Elliott her
wish, that nothing might be said to pain her
child by reviving bygone sorrows. Perhaps
their own delicacy or good nature might have
forestalled their sister-in-law's request, but
Kate found that her uncle and aunt were

scrupulously careful in avoiding the one topic which continued to form the centre of all her thoughts and dreams.

The German governess only appeared at breakfast and luncheon, or in the evening after dinner, and Kate did not cultivate her acquaintance or enter much into conversation with her. Her time had been spent almost in as complete solitude as at Brighton, excepting that she enjoyed some of her old rides with her uncle, and found pleasure in perfecting herself in an exercise, which Montagu admired so much.

Mr. Elliott was anxious to afford his niece the opportunity which he had promised her, of meeting the brilliant *parti;* but felt a delicacy in inviting guests, as his sister-in-law had only been induced to come upon the understanding of a perfectly quiet visit. The meeting with Laura Lisle seemed to offer a chance of breaking through the present monotonous routine. The ice once broken, he might proceed to ask others, and among them the wealthy neighbour whom he designed for Katharine.

"We have not asked any one to meet the Barings to-night," said Mrs. Elliott to Kate's sister Mary, as they were seated in the drawing-room after breakfast, "as we did not feel sure whether your mother would like a large party so soon, but Mr. Elliott is very anxious, some day, to invite a very agreeable neighbour of ours, a Mr. Grant, a widower, who, we both fancy, might suit Katharine. He is very rich, and has a charming old place. I should like to take you to see it."

"A widower, dear aunt! I don't fancy that a widower would do for Kate. Has he any family?"

"Only one child, a little boy. That is the only drawback for he is a most agreeable person when you get to know him. Not strikingly handsome, perhaps, but that is of no consequence you know."

"Oh! I am sure he is not good enough for Kate! I would never give my consent to it."

"Nonsense, dear Mary. You must see him before you reject him so decidedly. She would be a neighbour of our's too. It would be a charming marriage, I think. But if that does not do," she continued after a pause: "there is this Mr. Lisle, who is coming to us to-night. I am told that he has a large fortune, and is a delightful person in every way. But you all know him, I think?"

"Yes, we met him in Italy, and Kate has seen him since."

"Does she like him?"

"I think she does."

"Now, why should not that do?"

Mary drew a long breath.

"I wish she was well married," pursued the aunt.

"So do I, but I am very much afraid that she will never love any one as she did him."

"Don't think that, dear Mary. Why should

F 5

not she? She is young and does not look to me
at all heart-broken. Depend upon it that
people always console themselves. I never yet
saw an instance to the contrary, and I have
seen a great many."

"Well, I hope you are right, and I think
Mr. Lisle would suit admirably, if she happens
to fancy him."

    *　　　*　　　*　　　*　　　*

Katharine had ridden with her uncle, and
upon her return, met her eldest little cousin to
whom she had taken a great fancy, and who
entreated her to come and look at some flowers
which had made their appearance in her
garden.

The child's flower bed lay at the farther ex-
tremity of the kitchen garden. On arriving there
she found Madame Hoffner seated with a book,
while the youngest girl was in front of her,
watering the plants. Katharine had occasion-

ally addressed her in German, and Madame Hoffner availed herself of this to speak in her own language.

"You have been much on the continent, Miss Elliott, is it not true?"

"Yes," returned Kate, in a voice as if she did not desire to pursue the conversation.

"You have been in Germany. You speak German very well."

"I have been a little in Germany, not very much."

"In Italy? You speak Italian?"

"Yes, I was for some years in Italy," she replied drily.

"I too have been in Italy. You were in Rome, I conclude?"

"Yes, and Naples," rejoined Kate evasively.

"I suppose you are fond of the arts? I knew a great many artists," continued the talkative woman as if determined not to lose her opportunity; "and it occurs to me to have heard the name of Mr. Lisle, whom Mrs. Elliott is expecting to dinner to-day. If it was the same he was a great patron of the fine-arts and ordered several pictures by countrymen of my own, of the school, you know, of Overbeck. I suppose you went to Overbeck's studio?"

"No, I missed going there, but I know many of his works."

"Ah! from prints, no doubt? Everybody knows him thus. There was a young painter named Arnstein of the same school, who was a great friend of mine. I suppose you never saw his studio?"

Kate had heard the name, and felt that she was fairly in for something which she had longed to avoid. Without seeming to remark her confusion the inexorable German continued:

"Yes, he married a poor English girl who was confided to my care, and whom he left a widow after five years of marriage. Poor thing, she is now deranged, I am told, and wanders about, quite out of her mind."

Kate felt interested inspite of herself.

"You know Mr. Montagu, I think?" enquired the governess, in a tone of seeming indifference.

"That child will wet herself with the watering-can!" said Kate, turning hastily towards the children.

"Oh, no! they are accoustomed. But I was saying, Mr. Montagu was an old acquaintance of mine. A man of great taste. He has a beautiful house and domain in the county of Surrey. He invited me to go abroad with Miss Dolby. Having been in Italy before, he could repose full confidence in me and, believing him engaged to the lady, I willingly undertook the task."

Katharine felt most awkwardly placed, for she could not fail to be interested in what she heard, and yet dreaded hearing more. She ended by counterfeiting a look of indifference, and patiently awaited the completion of the history.

"I do not mean to say that I think he was engaged to Miss Dolby, not by word of mouth that is, but he had certainly given her every reason to think he should marry her I am quite sure, for he had educated her precisely according to his own tastes and in strict retirement, where she was visited by no one but himself. I am certain that during the whole time she spent with me, her one thought was of him. Poor girl! I can never forgive him."

"It is late!" returned Kate, with a sudden movement, as if she desired to go.

"Forgive him for his conduct to myself of course I can—but to her, never! It is true, she married Arnstein, a countryman of my own, and I was very glad of it, a most worthy man; but her mind was quite gone then. I am sure of it! She never recovered that shock. Poor Ann Dolby! she was such a gentle creature, and so full of high feelings of romance and poetry, and I hear that she has become a maniac. But I dare say she is not the first, or only one, he has ruined."

Kate, who had listened with ill-concealed interest to the history of the mad woman whom she had twice met at Thornwood, for she felt convinced of the identity, was angry at the conclusion of Madame Hoffner's remarks, which struck her as a voluntary insult. She turned rather abruptly, saying she was late and, vexed with herself for having listened so long, returned out of spirits to prepare for the arrival of the Lisles.

When she reflected upon the circumstance of her last interview with the maniac in the glen, and recalled her words, she could not doubt the truth of Madame Hoffner's narration, although she would have given worlds never to have heard it. There were many things to bring back Montagu to her recollection, and the very prospect of meeting Mr. Lisle reminded her of one who had succeeded in erasing from her heart the impression which he had once left there. She had liked Herbert whenever she had met him. At one time it seemed uncertain whether she might not prefer him to his more animated rival, but now, the heart which had once been fully given to the other, loathed a return to its earlier dream. On the other hand, he had not only been her brother's fellow-traveller but his attendant in sickness, and she felt a desire to listen once more to his agreeable and clever conversation.

She endeavoured to banish the unpleasant *souvenir* awakened by Madame Hoffner's remarks, but was not able entirely to efface the sorrow from her brow, over which an almost imperceptible cloud continued to hover even when she found herself seated by Herbert Lisle, conversing about his eastern travels and a hundred other subjects, upon which he discoursed with his usual originality and eloquence.

The party from West-Langton consisted of Mrs. Baring, Laura and Herbert, and these formed the only addition to the family circle.

"I wish my son had been here," said Lady Elliott to Laura : "he would have been so glad to have met Mr. Lisle. I cannot tell you how much I feel indebted to him for his kindness to Frank in his terrible illness."

Katharine overheard her mother's remark, and said to her neighbour :

"My brother wrote to tell us how kind you were to him when he was laid up with fever. I need not say how grateful we feel to you for nursing him."

"As to nursing him, I am afraid I cannot claim much merit. His devoted nurse was Miss Seymour. I suppose he told you ?"

"Miss Seymour ? He did not say very much about her having nursed him," said Kate, doubtfully.

"Why, how ungrateful of him ! I shall tax

him with it when I meet him. She was his nurse during the whole of his illness."

" Did you see much of her ?" enquired Kate, wondering at her brother's silence upon such a subject and anxious to change the theme.

" Yes—a good deal; but your brother travelled with them all through the desert."

" I heard that. She is very clever and agreeable, don't you think ?"

" Very. You know her well, I suppose ?"

" I made her acquaintance at the Mordens' last year."

" That was at the time I had the pleasure of meeting you, I suppose, at Carrowsby ?"

" And you shewed us the church. How full of interest you must have found your eastern journey ! I envy your visit to the Holy Land."

" You should persuade your brother to go again and take you."

" A lady must be very much in the way."

"You do not expect me to say yes, I suppose, even if I could think anything so treasonable, but, I assure you, that my experience is quite the opposite."

"I suppose Miss Seymour is a very good traveller !" said Kate, jumping at conclusions.

"She delights in it, I think," returned Lisle, evasively; and continued, inattentively :——"have you never met her since you saw her at Alfreton ?"

"Yes."

"Have you ever heard of her sisterhood ?" enquired Lisle, in a lower voice, and with considerable interest.

"I heard something about it——from Lady Morden !"

"Not from herself ?"

"No——I have not seen very much of her."

"I think your brother said he met her at Mr. Montagu's. Do you know him ?"

"Yes——we both met her there."

Herbert was anxious to discover whether

Cecil Montagu had been an admirer of Elsie's, and, in his eagerness to find it out, did not perceive Kate's hesitating and confused manner.

" And pray tell me, what sort of person is Mr. Montagu ?"

" What a question !" exclaimed Katharine, with a convulsive laugh ; " I can't exactly describe—it is so difficult !"

" I mean—he is very clever, is he not ? and a great patron of the arts ?"

" Yes," returned Kate, colouring, as she looked up stealthily to see if any one had overheard her neighbour's observations.

" I suppose he is a great admirer of Miss Seymour's is not he ?" pursued Herbert, coming boldly to the point, and without being the least aware of the pain he was causing.

This was beyond all endurance, and Kate concealed her blushes by dexterously dropping her bracelet, and obliging her neighbour to make a search for it ; after which she turned to Mrs. Baring, and talked to her perseveringly, as long as she could.

Mrs. Elliott was charmed with Herbert, and made up her mind that he would suit her niece to perfection, and, before the gentlemen had made their appearance in the drawing-room, had informed her sister-in-law and her niece Mary of her opinion.

Madame Hoffner made her appearance, as usual, in the evening, but Katharine took care to avoid her, by seating herself between her sister and Mrs. Baring. Laura talked to Lady Elliott about her cousin's travels, and, at length, turning to Kate, she said:

"I suppose you have not been at Alfreton since we met?"

"No. How is Emmeline?"

"Very well; but when I saw her, more than a week ago, she was very impatient to get to London."

"What a charming place Carrowsby is!" said Kate, for want of something to say; "and that lovely church ! The people must be quite lost without you. I suppose you do not stay long away ?"

" To tell you the truth, I have too many irons in the fire for them to depend much upon me," pursued Laura ; " I have pets in two or three places."

" Do you mean cottages ?" enquired Lady Elliott.

" Yes," put in Mary Baring, who had been listening to the last part of the dialogue, " my sister is very general in her favouritism. But I, almost, think, Laura, that your greatest pets of all are at Cawthorne."

" Oh ! I don't know that, Mary ?"

" I mean the Dolbys. I am sure they are your greatest favourites."

Just at this moment Mr. Elliott and Lisle entered the room.

" Don't you think, Herbert," asked Mary, as he came up, " that the Dolbys are Laura's prime favourites ?"

"Most decidedly. By-the-bye, you must tell me about them, for I have forgotten to ask you about Madame Arnstein; you know who I mean."

"Madame Arnstein!" exclaimed the German lady, "do you know Ann Dolby?"

"Know her? She is the daughter of the oldest cottager on my property. Poor thing! She is out of her mind, I fear. Can you tell me anything about her?"

All eyes were rivetted upon Katharine, at least those of her family, who knew the particulars of Madame Hoffner's story, and she, although feeling ready to sink into the earth, made so strong an effort to appear composed as actually to succeed in assuming an air of indifference.

"I know her well! Arnstein was a countryman of my own; but, perhaps, she may not be the same."

"Oh, yes!" said Herbert, "Arnstein was

a Bavarian painter in Rome. Poor girl, have
you heard much about her history ?"

"A good deal. She was heart-broken."

"A bad business!" rejoined Mr. Elliott,
pulling Lisle aside, and adding, confidentially,
in a lower voice, "I believe she was led
astray by a Mr. Montagu. I have reason to
think so."

"Oh, no ! I can assure you that was not the
case," replied Herbert : "I have it from—from
her own lips. You may depend upon it that
he was not the person who led her into evil
courses."

The words were spoken in an undertone in
order that they might not be overheard, and
Mrs. Elliott had turned the conversation to
other subjects, but, notwithstanding all these
precautions, one ear caught the welcome sounds,
and they conveyed joy to the stricken heart.

Katharine was asked to play and sing. She
had formerly cared little for music, but Cecil
was so passionately fond of it, that she had

practised much of late, and had endeavoured to cultivate a voice which was naturally sweet and melodious.

Herbert sat beside her, and talked of Frank, and thence he led the discourse into some of his favourite topics. She was pleased to be near him since she had heard his vindication of Montagu from part of the charge brought against him, and felt that it might, perhaps, be in his power to unveil the matter more completely.

"I am very fond of sacred music," said Kate, in allusion to a speech of Lisle's: "I suppose you can sing something of that kind?"

"No—I sometimes take part in chaunts, but I am no musician, I regret to say."

"I daresay your cousin sings?"

And Laura was induced to join them at the piano, and sing some airs, which consisted, for the most part, of Christmas carols and ancient hymns of the church, such as the Adeste fideles or the Stabat Mater.

"I suppose you have good music in the church at Cawthorne?" enquired Kate, timidly, and burning to speak of the subject which weighed upon her mind.

"I hope it is improving.   It was wretched before, but there is a new curate now.   Do you know, Laura, whether he has been able to instruct the choir?"

"Yes—I forgot to show you Perdon's letter which Phœbe Elton sent me," and feeling her rudeness Laura turned laughingly to Kate to explain, "you must know that Phœbe Elton is another of the Dolby family, towards whom I was accused of such gross favoritism."

"Now or never," thought Kate.

"How is she related to the mad-woman?" she ventured in a low voice.

"You don't know the mad-woman, as you call her, Ann Dolby, I suppose?" asked Herbert, struck by the tone of her voice.

"I have seen her, I think.   I met her in— in Surrey."

" What? When you were at Mr. Montagu's, where you met Miss Seymour ?"

" Yes," rejoined Kate, alarmed lest the discourse should be overheard by others, "I met her by accident. She wanders about the country. She frightened me when I first saw her."

" Did she sing ?"

" Beautifully."

" I hope she has ceased wandering about," said Laura, " for I hear that she has been remaining very quietly in her mother's cottage nursing her old parents and watching over her children. Phœbe says she has turned quite religious, and that Mr. Penrose, the curate, believes that one Sunday she was almost miraculously cured of her madness !"

" How very wonderful !" exclaimed Kate, willing if possible to prolong the discussion, " but, perhaps, the quiet life of her home may have cured her."

g 2

And then she continued with sudden determination—

"I should like to hear her true history?"

"Her history is simply this," replied Herbert: "she was induced by a promise of marriage from one who is now, thank God, as much changed as herself, to quit her home and run into dangers which would have lost her for ever, had it not been for a kind young man of high enthusiastic feelings, who restored her to better thoughts by causing her to be educated in accomplishments, perhaps, only fitted for one of exalted birth, but, which succeeded in weaning her imagination to loftier notions. This young man, who called himself Allardyce, sent her to Italy under the care of an experienced lady. I have never been able to discover that he professed any attachment to her, or that he was actuated by any but the most romantic and chivalrous feelings. I confess that it appears singular to me that one so generous and true-hearted, as, from all accounts he must have been, should never have sought to soften her spirit to the holy influences of religion. But, as far as she is concerned, this may have been providential. Such characters as hers, which live upon the juice of the forbidden fruit, are not to be drilled into faith by any human discipline, and the Holy Spirit taught her lessons which her instructors had neglected. However, even the best of human attempts have their drawbacks, and poor Allardyce could not do good without receiving a benefit in return."

Kate breathed more freely.

" I mean," continued Lisle with a smile, " that she must needs fall in love with him ; a kind of return which he had never intended, I presume ! However, in this difficulty, he behaved admirably in my opinion. I judge as a man, perhaps ladies will not agree with me. Is a man bound to marry every one who falls in love with him, that is the question ?"

Laura turned aside her head not to allow her cousin's eyes to meet hers. Poor Laura !

"She would have been miserable if he had married without loving her. He gave her a dowry and wedded her to an artist who was passionately attached to her."

"Then you think it lawful to sacrifice women's hearts but not men's!" exclaimed Laura, with a slight tone of indignation.

"Well, but she was very happy with this artist and very fond of him—only, being as mad as a March hare, she always persisted in calling him Allardyce."

"Yes, but it drove her out of her mind!" returned Laura.

"Poor thing! I contend it was her own fault. What do you say, Miss Elliott?"

"I do not think, after all, that he was bound to marry her!" replied Kate, timidly.

"There, you see, Laura, Miss Elliott gives the casting vote in my favour. But to finish my story. I was travelling in Italy and stumbled upon Ann Dolby, this Madame Arnstein, at Verona and Milan, after she had

lost her husband, and induced her to return to
England where I got her into a house of mercy
in Gloucestershire. The chaplain there thought
her quite changed, but a fresh fit of insanity
came over her, and she escaped in pursuit of
her Allardyce and continued her wanderings
until she was seized with her present qualms
of penitence, more real and earnest, I trust,
than the former.

During the latter portion of the dialogue,
Madame Hoffner had imperceptibly approached
the music-stand, where she stood fumbling for
one of the children's song books.

Herbert saw that she was listening to the
conclusion of his story and said :

"Was it in Italy you knew her ?"

"Madame Arnstein ? yes."

"Did you meet her at Arnstein's ?"

"No. I travelled with her."

"What ! after she was married ?"

"No—before."

"Then you are the lady whom Allardyce
engaged to travel with her ?"

"Just so! Mr. Montagu chose to disguise himself in de name of Allardyce, and for some time, to deceive both of us, but I found out his real name from his valet, a German, whom I met lately in London. I was quite taken in, I confess."

"Well, it was a harmless freak after all!" exclaimed Herbert, laughing.

"Oh no!" returned the German woman, shaking her head, "my family is as good as his any day. It is older dan any in Bavaria, and dat, you must know is much better dan your English family. We count twanty quarterings. True, I am not so rich as I could wish, or I would not work for my bread; but to insult a lady of my birth by giving me a cottage—a peasant what you call—to take care of—Mein Gott!" She pursued wrathfully and with strong emphasis on her words: "he can be no gentleman. He insult me and tread me under his foot. I will be revenge, I will!"

She muttered the last words between her teeth, and seeing a smile upon the faces of her audience, stooped down to the lower shelf of the music-stand to hide her annoyance. She had spoken sufficiently loud to attract the attention of Mrs. Elliott, who perceiving there was some sort of scene going on, begged Kate to sing another song.

Her stock of music was not great, but she remembered one which had been a favourite of her lover's, and sang it with much spirit and feeling.

Herbert, in the meantime, seated himself by Mrs. Elliott and her sister-in-law and, when the fly was announced, left them all much pleased with his conversation, and anxious to renew their acquaintance.

Bright visions flitted around the couch of Katharine, and she rose with a lighter heart.

G 5

CHAPTER V.

A DIGRESSION.

THE Mordens were established in a house in Belgrave Square, and Emmeline was able to enjoy the gayest of the London season. Ladv Morden had a large circle of acquaintances and had the opportunity of taking her daughter to as many parties and balls as she could desire. Sir Edward was supposed to be living with them in town, but to be called away into the country by important occupations. Such was the fiction. The truth was that he came up to London once or twice during their stay, upon which occasions Lady Morden managed to have large dinner-parties every night, as well as a ball and concert. Frederick's presence was indispensable and he was pressed into his mother's and sister's service upon all occasions, when required.

He rode with Emmeline in the Park and often found himself acting the part of dummy, while she was enjoying the conversation of more amusing companions than a brother.

Lady Morden and her two children were seated in the breakfast-room. Frederick was apparently buried in *The Morning Post,* while his mother and Emmeline were talking over their plans.

"How is it, Fred, that we see nothing of your friend, Mr. Elliott?" enquired Lady Morden: "I cannot help fancying he is not well. Have you called upon him?"

"Oh! he is well enough. I saw him yesterday. You know his brother's dead, and he tells me he has lots to do. I don't suppose he'll turn up at present."

"He might call, I should think!" returned his mother.

"He told me he had called and did not find you at home."

"That is some days since. Being so great a friend of yours, and your fellow-traveller, too, I should think he might have ventured to call again?"

"Perhaps, he has reasons—"

"What do you mean, Fred?"

"Why, I don't know; perhaps he is afraid Emmie may lose her heart to him, or fancy that he admires her."

"How stupid you are, Fred!" rejoined Emmeline, pettishly.

"He talks nonsense," said Lady Morden, in a voice which scarcely implied she so considered it, "as if such a thought was ever likely to have crossed his mind! Besides, he did pay Emmie a good deal of attention, only unfortunately the admiration seemed to be all on one side!"

"Well, I am glad to hear that it is not all on the other now, for, to let you into a little secret about him, he fell desperately in love with Elsie Seymour, when he was in Syria, and I'm not sure that he is quite out of it yet. But I thought I told you all about that in my letter from Beyrout."

"And so, because he happens to have fallen in love with Elsie, he has given up visiting us. This shows, at all events, that he has a guilty conscience," said Emmeline, laughing. "I am sure I should not have been able to discover his admiration from anything he said. I wonder whether he was more eloquent with Elsie."

"He is a capital fellow after all! I was travelling with him for, let's see, six months, and we never had a squabble—not a word."

"That was rather dull—I think."

"Well, I should like the fellow for a brother-in-law," said Frederick, surlily, "if he chose to propose to Emmie."

"Thank you, Fred, for your permission. I don't fancy I shall ask you to select me a husband, exactly !" exclaimed Emmeline, laughing very merrily, " your friends are rather too slow for me, I fancy. Slow and steady and very good tempered."

There was nothing which galled Frederick Morden so much as to be called slow, and she knew it. At college, he had always aimed at the distinction of being considered a fast man, and, by dint of ponderous attempts, had attained the via-media of a slow-fast man.

Emmeline, perceiving that she had vexed her brother, immediately set about to smooth him down, for it would not answer her purpose to put him out of humour in earnest, as she was entirely dependent upon him for her rides in the park, and other amusements. He knew his power, and showed it, by growling out something about an engagement with a friend to dine at Greenwich, which would prevent his riding. Emmeline coaxed him round, and, after considerable waste of words, induced him to own that the promise had only been a vague one, to go down, some day soon, to a white-bait dinner.

"I wonder whether Elsie is in town?" said Emmeline, to her mother, when they were alone in the drawing-room.

"We should have heard, I think, if the Seymours had come up," replied Lady Morden.

"We might call and enquire at the hotel where they always stay."

"Very well. I hope Elsie will give up her whims about her nurses. I trust she will have thought better of it while she has been away. It is shamefully cruel to her father and mother. I am sure poor Mrs. Seymour will break her heart!"

"Oh! mamma—I don't think that. After all, if she married, she would be just as much away from them; at least, I am sure, if I were her husband, I should never consent to being long with such dull people."

"For shame, Emmie! It is quite different

marrying and setting up for a quiz, in the shape of an old maid, dressed like a nun. Do try and dissuade her from it, dear."

"The idea of my dissuading Elsie from anything! She would as soon think of flying as taking my advice. Why, dear mamma, I am the last person in the world to give advice. She would much sooner persuade me to turn into a little nun," pursued Emmeline, jumping up coquettishly to inspect herself in a mirror. "Should not I look pretty as a nun, with a black hood like a mantilla, and the white headgear underneath? That reminds me, by the way, that I never dressed up the doll for Elsie, as I promised. Mamma, I must go and buy a doll to dress up as an Elsine nun—I told her I would."

"What nonsense it is!" said Lady Morden, as she rose to leave the room.

Late in the afternoon, Emmeline and her brother rode in the Park. Her seat on horseback was admirable, and she was well-mounted upon a thorough-bred mare, which showed to advantage, among the generality of park hacks. It was one of the days when the band played, and they proceeded towards the open space, already crowded with equestrians. Several hats had been raised and recognitions exchanged, as they advanced along Rotten-row, but, nevertheless, Emmeline remarked :

"There seems nobody, to-day. I wonder how it is ?"

" Everybody is listening to the band, I suppose."

And, in truth, when they had stood, for a short time, in the vicinity of the music she exclaimed :

"Look there, Fred !—do you see ! No— not in that direction at all. Next to that man with moustâches, there !"

" Why, it's Montagu, I believe, let us go that way," replied her brother.

" Yes—we shall be nearer the music," re-

turned Emmeline and forcing their way through
the crowd of horses, they were speedily re-
cognized by Cecil Montagu, who, as soon as
he could pass the intervening equestrians,
joined Miss Morden, and Frederick.

"He was mounted upon the same Arab
which he rode, when Frank Elliott met him in
the glen, at Thornwood, and his whole air was
no less graceful and attractive than in the days
when Elsie and Katharine had yielded their
hearts to his magic thraldom.

At that very moment, while the crowd still
separated Morden and his sister from Mr.
Montagu, Emmeline chanced to glance at the
pedestrian throng within Kensington Gardens,
and among them, recognized Frank Elliott,
who, having caught sight of her, seemed rapt
in admiration of her lovely figure, for she
looked to perfection on horseback. It gratified
her coquettish heart to be seen by her incon-
stant lover as she made a circuit near the place

where he stood, and, after a slight nod of recognition, joined Cecil Montagu, and rode off triumphantly by his side.

"Have you been out of London?"

"I have been abroad. How are Lady Morden and Sir Edward?"

"Mamma is very well, and papa too when we heard from him, but he is out of town."

"I need not ask whether you are enjoying the season? We shall, probably, meet to-night, at Lady Charles de Vere's, for I remember that she is a friend of yours. Are you going first to see the new opera?"

"Oh, I so entreated Mamma to go, but we had an engagement to a stupid dinner party, and she would not be persuaded."

"And I ought to have recollected that I have not seen you," said Montagu, addressing Frederick, "since your return from the East. You look sunburnt. I hope you enjoyed it?"

"Oh! yes," rejoined Fred, loutishly and as if pondering for a fast remark.

"Fred had a charming tour," pursued Emmeline. "I cannot tell you how I envy him his wanderings. I intend to set off alone on some pilgrimage, if I can't persuade him to take me."

"What shrine shall you visit?" enquired Montagu, drily.

"You know I have never been to Rome yet. I do so long to go. We are dreadfully stupid, stay-at-home people."

"You have never even kept your promise of coming to Thornwood. I must try and persuade Lady Morden, to-night," said Montagu, who had turned several times to reply to the numerous recognitions of his friends, and who yet seemed anxious to bear a little longer with what, to him, must have been insipid conversation.

"Fred saw a good deal of the Seymours in Syria," remarked Emmeline, who was burning to say several things to her companion.

"Ha! are they in England?"

" I believe so."

"I am only just returned from abroad," said Montagu. "You were travelling with Elliott, were you not?" he continued, addressing Frederick with perfect self-possession.

" Yes, poor fellow, he only heard of his brother's death just before he got home."

" I had not heard of it," rejoined Montagu, with the same coolness, adding, in a tone of the utmost indifference: " I suppose then, of course, he is not now in London?"

" Yes, he is," returned Emmeline : " for I saw him in the park, just before we joined you."

" Ha ! riding, is he?" he asked, carelessly.

" No, he was walking in the gardens."

" Did you kill any crocodiles?" he enquired of Frederick.

" One tolerable sized one. It was the greatest chance in the world. We were coming down. I don't know whether you know the Nile?"

"Oh, that tiresome crocodile story, pray spare Mr. Montagu!" exclaimed Emmeline.

"Ha! your sister has heard it before," replied Montagu, good-naturedly, "and we must remember that ladies are not sportsmen. I am rather a crocodile fancier myself, so you must reserve the adventure until we are alone."

Emmeline was very anxious to detain Montagu by her side, for he was so universally known that it was pleasant, she thought, to be seen with him, and she might also have been desirous of making some discoveries touching his feelings towards Elsie or Katharine.

"The Seymours, or rather Elsie, was delighted with all she saw," returned Emmeline, boldly making a dash; "she wrote beautiful letters to her mother, who let us see one or two of them. I suppose you have heard of her scheme for the nurses?"

"Something about it, not a great deal," replied Montagu. "Stobieski met Mrs. Seymour the other day. I think you know him? I see Ellingham there. I am afraid I must join him presently, for I have not answered a note he sent me."

Making an excuse to ride away, he politely bade adieu to Miss Morden and her brother, to join some more congenial companions.

"Montagu! Why, where have you been all this time?" exclaimed George Estcourt, stopping him as he was approaching Lord Ellingham.

"Abroad. I came through Paris the day before yesterday."

"How are they going on there? I thought I heard you had been in Germany. Stobieski, by the way, told me he met you at Munich. What took you there?"

"I had not seen it for some years. It is a place which has been terribly over-rated; the arts forced into premature existence without

any foundation in the sympathies of the people.
No king can convert beer-drinking Bavarians
into Athenians, whatever amount of public
money he may lavish upon Glyptoteks and
Pinakoteks. Come and breakfast with me in
the Albany, to-morrow ?"

And he joined Lord Ellingham, a leading
member of the cabinet, a man of sixty, still
possessing all the vigour of youth.

"Did you get my note, Montagu ? We want
you to come in for Luxbridge. Mackworth's
death deprives us of a vote, and, unless you
come forward with your brother's interest, I
am afraid we shall lose the seat."

"And you require me to forfeit my inde-
pendence?" asked Cecil, laughing.

"You ought to be in parliament," rejoined
the minister: "you have no excuse in the
world. We want your services. I am sure
you will not refuse ; come, what say you ?"

"Very well. I suppose I am in for it. My
brother is not very well, I am sorry to find."

"He never has been, since I knew him."

"Even for him, I mean," replied Montagu.

"Nothing alarming, I hope?"

"It was anything but a good account. I must go down and see him to-morrow, unless I hear he is better."

"Where is he?"

"At Worthington."

"Then go on and canvass Luxbridge. We must have you returned."

Montagu assented, and, after some further conversation, took the opportunity of Lord Ellingham's meeting with an acquaintance, to join Lord Charles de Vere and some other friends. While he was in the neighbourhood of the band, he saw Francis Elliott and, keeping his eye upon him until the music had ceased, watched his opportunity to ride forward and beckon to him as he approached the gate. Frank had already recognized Cecil Montagu and had almost made up his mind to avoid him. Lady Elliott had informed him of the circumstances

under which the engagement had **been broken**
off, and, while the shortness of their stay in
town in addition to her brother's ⌐recent death,
had interfered with Katharine's intended ex-
planations, her careworn countenance and pallid
cheeks had not escaped his observation, and
had, not unnaturally, been attributed to Mon-
tagu's shameful conduct! Unfortunately he
felt he could not, without excessive rudeness,
avoid replying to the recognition.

"Elliott!" exclaimed Cecil, in a voice of ir-
resistible softness tinged with melancholy, as
the other approached: "seeing you here, I
ventured to call you, for I have many things
to explain. Where are you living? In your
chambers?"

"Yes—but I am not often at home, for I am
much engaged."

"You have lost your brother! A loss which
you must feel very deeply. Pray tell me, how
is Lady Elliott, and, how is—your sister?"

"They are quite well," returned Frank,

with a look of surprise, as if he did not know how to interpret the question : "as well as they can be under the afflicting circumstances of my poor brother's death."

"But I must not detain you, Elliott !" said Montagu, perceiving that he showed signs of impatience, as if hesitating to prolong the conference : "only tell me at what hour I may venture to call upon you to-morrow, or if any other arrangement will suit you better ?"

"I am much engaged," rejoined Frank, doubtfully, "and I fear I cannot fix a time."

"At what hour do you breakfast ?" asked Montagu, good-naturedly, "or, tell me, if your business calls you to this end of the town, would not you come and breakfast with me in the Albany ?"

Frank was touched with the extreme friendliness of his manner, and replied less coldly :

"Why, to tell you the truth, my business is in my own neighbourhood, in Lincoln's Inn. But I should, of course, be delighted if you

H 3

would give me the pleasure of your company at breakfast ; or, perhaps," he continued, after a moment's consideration, " I had better come to you."

" Very well ! Between nine and ten shall I say ?"

" Or I almost think I would rather call upon you later," pursued Frank, who prudently reflected upon the unpleasant predicament in which he might be placed in vindicating his sister's cause at the breakfast table : "shall I say twelve o'clock ?"

" At twelve, I shall expect you. I am delighted to see you looking so well after your travels. Farewell !"

Frank Elliott turned away from the interview pleased with Montagu, but half dissatisfied with himself. He saw him who a few months before had been the betrothed of his sister ride off in that pride of manly grace and beauty which had assisted him in his art of fascination. With all his secret distrust and jealousy, he found himself unable to ward off the magic influence of his spell, or to reject the being to whose unprincipled conduct he attributed Katharine's pale cheek and sorrowing heart.

Until he returned to England, Frank had judged Montagu more leniently than his mother's letters seemed to warrant. Whatever he might have felt upon first reading them, there had been one who had known how to breathe a genial balm over the asperities which the news of the breach had created in his mind. What a holocaust must *she* have made of her own sufferings who could sacrifice pique and jealousy upon the altar of *his* happiness whom she had loved! Yet so it was, that Elsie's words had led Frank to think more favourably of one whom all his friends, but Katharine, appeared to have condemned unheard.

It is possible that the fresh incident of Godfrey's death may have tended to disturb whatever resolutions he had formed, and may have lessened his opportunities of confiding his doubts to his sister. Upon his return he found his family plunged into deep grief and he was tempted to defer a confidence which seemed misplaced at such a time. Not but that he would have availed himself of a favourable moment had it occurred, but it so chanced that, during the single day when he was with Lady Elliott and his sister, his time had been absorbed by his mother's affairs. She had profitted by the hours during which they were thrown together to insinuate her version of the story and, in a great degree, to weaken his former impressions.

There was another circumstance which, in this interview had weighed more strongly with Frank than even his mother's anxieties, and this—to his shame be it spoken—was a feeling of jealousy, which had been awakened from the moment when he had beheld his once loved Emmeline ride off in scornful triumph by Cecil's side.

He had never seen Emmeline look more winning and lovely than on that day! He had been watching her for some minutes before she caught sight of him and all his earliest admiration returned, as he observed her merry laughter. It had been a cruel, but perhaps not unmerited, cut, when she had coquettishly thrown him over with a glance. At that moment he fancied that Montagu might have become his rival in her affections, and he sighed and cursed his sad fate, wishing that he had never met Elsie—beautiful perfection that she was, too exalted for mortal dreams! Oh! that he had called oftener upon the Mordens! How silly of him not to have done so. He lamented having walked out. It was the first time he had shown himself in a place of public resort since his return, but he had felt the want of exercise and had ventured where he was likely to see— Emmeline! He had seen her and he bitterly regretted it.

As he turned homewards he felt disgusted with life and sick at heart.

"Give me back the wild desert!" thought he: "oh, that I were once again in the defiles of Wady Wateer or among the rose-coloured temples of Petra! Give me back my sick-bed in the vale of Jordan, with Elsie watching, by my side!"

Such were his thoughts as he made his way through the parks towards the Oxford and Cambridge Club, where it was his custom to dine.

He was a good deal perplexed as to the course which he ought to pursue with respect to Montagu. He felt as if he had done wrong in consenting to a meeting without first communicating with his sister, and yet it would seem strange to break it off after having accepted it. These thoughts worried him as he crossed the Green Park and, by the time he reached Pall Mall, he had almost made up his mind to write a note postponing the visit, upon some plea or other, until he had corresponded with Katharine.

"Sir, there is a table by the window, yonder," said the officious waiter, as soon as Frank had inscribed his name for the seven o'clock joint, "the joint of lamb has gone round, sir, but you are just in time."

"Very well. Get me a 'Globe!'" replied Elliott, as he made for the vacant place.

"Elliott, I think! How do you do?" was the greeting addressed him by a youth seated at the next table.

"I beg your pardon!" returned Frank, who did not instantly recognise his friend: "ah! Spencer, how are you?"

"Been with Fred Morden to the East, have not you?" asked the other.

"Yes, we returned ten days ago."

"Fred looked me up the other day, but have not seen very much of him. Looks very jolly, rather sunburnt, perhaps."

H 3

"I hope your sisters are well?"

"When I heard from them. I don't often hear—fact is I don't trouble them much with letters."

"You are living in town?"

"Yes—reading law, or eating it."

"In Lincoln's Inn?"

"No. Temple—Inner Temple. Suppose you keep your chambers?"

"Yes—I intend to keep them and I hope to be called next term."

"Hope Fred will look me up soon. Like to come and meet him, perhaps, at breakfast. Shall be glad if you would?"

Edmund Spencer, whose sisters Grace and Agnes shared Fred Morden's heart between them, was naturally shy, and this may have led to his falling into the habit of dropping his pronouns, and jerking out his words as if he were sharp-shooting from a place of ambush. His awkwardness was, perhaps, made more conspicuous by a certain juvenile vanity to shine and be considered.

"I shall be very happy if I am in town," replied Elliott to his last question, "but I am not certain about my movements. I may possibly go down into the country in a day or two. I have had some matters to settle, for we have been in great affliction." The latter part was mumbled in a low voice.

"Heard of it—yes — sad loss," rejoined Spencer. "Fred Morden told me."

After a pause, Edmund continued :

"The Mordens have a box at the opera. Often go to the opera ?"

"No : I have not been this year."

"No—of course —forgot !" replied Edmund, nodding his head with the approved expression of melancholy.

"Is there any new opera ?" enquired Frank.

"Law ! of course. To night's the new opera !"

"Are you going ?"

" No ; going to a party—two parties in fact, and so never took a ticket—great bore !"

" I hear it is an unusually gay season ?"

" Yes, very tolerable," returned the youth, who had only just left college, and had never seen a London season in his life before; " go out a good deal—going to Lady Charles de Vere's ball—know Lady Charles de Vere ?"

" Yes !"

" Not going, I suppose ?"

" Oh, no !   No, 1 don't go out at all."

" Seen much of the Mordens ?"

" No—to say the truth, 1 have been quite out of the way of seeing anybody.   I called, but without finding them at home."

And Frank turned, with longing eyes, to the evening paper, vainly hoping that his friend would leave him to his own meditations.

" Not seen Emmie then, I suppose ?" continued the other, in a tone which inspired Elliott with a secret desire to knock him down: "looking uncommon well, Miss Emmie. What a jolly nice girl she is! do you admire her?"

"Eh?" exclaimed Frank, feigning an absent fit. "Who do you mean?"

"Emmie Morden—you know! great friends, you know, of ours—brought up together almost. My sisters always will have it there is something in it—very thick, together, you know, but nothing more—always great friends, and that sort of thing. Ah, she is a jolly girl, and no mistake, is Miss Emmie!"

Frank almost groaned under the infliction, and, pretending to see something of interest in the paper, bent over it in hopes of discouraging any further discourse. This only succeeded for a short time, for, at the very first opportunity afforded by his raising his head, the youth re-commenced:—

"Almost time to be going—any message to the Mordens? Shall meet them to-night, I

expect, at the de Vere's.   No message to Fred,
eh ? or to Miss Emmie ?"

Luckily this was a sort of farewell speech,
for he soon took his departure, and left
Elliott to ruminate in disgust upon his
audacity in using, with familiar profanation,
the name of one, to whom, an hour or two be-
fore, he had felt himself unworthy to aspire.

Feeling very wretched and out of sorts,
Frank strolled homewards, to Lincoln's Inn
Fields.   There, seated in his old chambers,
amid his white calf bindings, he indulged in
melancholy reflections and made wise reso-
lutions.   He need not have been so miserable
all things considered.   His prospects in life
were better than they had ever been before.
At his mother's death he was entitled to a good
fortune and, during her life, was to receive an
increased allowance.   He had wisely deter-
mined to prosecute his studies with diligence,
and to embark bravely in his professional career.

He possessed talents which might not only ensure success, but would afford him a reasonable prospect of distinction. Considering all these advantages attending his lot, it might seem unaccountable that he should give way to despondency, unless allowance be made for that perversity of the heart which scorns the daintiest foods in comparison with a single particle of the ambrosia which nourishes its self-esteem. Elsie had refused, and Emmeline had slighted him! How much better than this, to have been drowned in the Cataracts, or to have died at Eyn-Sultaun, with Elsie at his side!

"And then, after all, to be jilted and despised by Emmeline!" he thought; not remembering how faithless he had proved to her.

CHAPTER VI.

POST NUBILA PHŒBUS.

It occurred to Elliott, when he awoke on the following morning, that he had omitted to decline his visit to Montagu, but, upon reflection, it seemed to him that perhaps after all, there might be no great harm in going. There was something strange in Montagu's having allowed so many months to elapse without seeking an explanation, but then Frank's own absence may have been, in a great degree, the cause of this delay.

"And yet," Elliott asked himself, "why had he never taken a single step towards giving a favourable construction to those passages in his past life, which had been brought up against him? Why had he allowed the blot to sully his fair name, if it was in his power to efface it?"

All these circumstances might have appeared conclusive against him, if there had not been a something in his voice and frank address which almost convinced Elliott that he still loved Katharine. If so, it seemed probable that he sought this interview with the object of affording some explanation, which could, perhaps, only be offered to a brother.

But then there was a second difficulty. Supposing the explanation satisfactory, would Kate still be willing to accept him? It seemed possible that her heart might no longer be free, after so long an interval! And yet, to judge by her pale cheek and cheerless look, not very probable!

The question was, whether it would be safer to call then, or to defer until he could hear from his sister.

At breakfast-time the post brought a letter from the country, which we transcribe:

"*Lockwood, Tuesday,*
"*June 2d,* 18—.

"MY DEAREST FRANK,

"Although you have not kept your promise of writing to me, I, at length, venture to attack you with a letter. Mamma begs me to say that you have never answered hers, and wishes to know whether the business with Messrs. Scott and Payne proceeds satisfactorily. She wants you to write to her about it soon if you can't come down here for a day, which she thinks would be the best plan, as things are so much better explained in conversation than by letter. I can only add my entreaties to hers, and beg you will do your best to come, dearest Frank, as I have a very great many things to tell you. I had no time to talk with you in London, and now I scarcely regret it, as I have

heard something which, I confess, adds greatly
to my happiness, although not to my confi-
dence in ———, for that was never shaken. Do
you ever see ———? Is he in London? He
has, of course, forgotten me now, and, if so, do
not think I blame him. My conduct towards
him showed such an entire want of that trust,
which I have never once ceased to feel, that he
was justified in forgetting me. Whoever he
may marry, or whatever becomes of him, he
shall always have my prayers for his happiness!
I longed to tell you my feelings about him,
and I am now happy to add that his innocence of
the charges brought against him is proved
beyond a doubt. That wicked woman, Madame
Hoffner, who prejudiced Uncle Reginald against
him, was forced to own to her exaggerations
(not to say more), when Mr. Lisle explained
the true story, as he had heard it from the
mouth of the principal person implicated. I
have written very hastily, having been out

riding with my uncle, and it only wants a few minutes to post time.

"Adieu, dearest Frank, with mamma's and Mary's best love.

"Your much attached sister,

"KATHARINE."

This letter decided Elliott to call on Montagu and, after repairing to the solicitors to whom Kate alluded in her letter, he returned to his chambers to prepare for his visit to the Albany.

In his letter-box he found two notes, the first from Montagu, expressing his extreme regret at being obliged to postpone an interview which he desired so ardently.

"My dear Elliott," he wrote, "I cannot tell you how vexed I feel at being forced to defer the engagement which I made with you for this day; but I have just received accounts of my brother's illness, which oblige me to start off without delay. Excuse my hasty note.

"Yours sincerely,

"CECIL MONTAGU."

The second epistle was a polite invitation to a perfectly quiet family dinner at the Mordens' for that day, apologising for the shortness of the notice.

Frank accepted it and went.

With a beating heart he drove to Belgrave Square at the appointed hour, dreading the reception which he should meet from Emmeline. For a moment he might have hesitated to accept the invitation, but his hopes soon prevailed over his jealousy, and determined him once again to embark upon his earlier enterprize, as valiantly as if he had never been attracted from his course, or, like the Arabian in the tale, made shipwreck against the magnetic rock.

His palpitations became intense when the cabman rang the bell and overwhelming, when the powdered footman ushered him into the handsome drawing-room, but, in a measure calmed, when he found the room empty. He walked about and looked at the books, ornaments and pictures.

Presently Lady Morden made her appearance and was extremely gracious, asking very warmly after Lady Elliott and Katharine.

"I wish I could persuade them," she said, "to come and spend a few weeks quietly with us at Alfreton, as soon as we return. You must promise me, Mr. Elliott, that you will do your best and endeavour to bring them—because, you know, we count upon you, at all events."

Frank was evidently supposed to be an eligible, and he could not help perceiving that his brother's death had made a slight difference in Lady Morden's manner towards him.

Frederick soon followed, and Frank began to

feel perfectly at ease, and as if he were one of the family. All depended upon Emmeline! He dreaded *her* arrival.

"Mother, it's very late," said Fred, "I don't know why they don't announce dinner."

"Emmie is not down."

"Why she was in from her ride long ago. I have been round to Mavor's to look after the brown mare since then."

"Perhaps she does not know the time," and Lady Morden rang the bell.

Frank began to feel ill at ease. It was all very well to be on familiar terms with Lady Morden and Fred, but what was it all worth if Emmeline should be cold and distant?

At length the door opened, dinner was announced, and at the same instant Emmeline entered the room. She spoke indifferently to Frank, who had offered his arm to Lady Morden.

"How late you are, Emmie!" said Frederick.

"Am I? I didn't know," she replied.

Frank who was in front, heard this as he was proceeding down stairs.

"It is so awfully slow, Emmie, not to be down when one has anyone to dinner!" returned her brother, in a tone of displeasure.

"I did not remember that you had one of your friends dining here; how am I to recollect?"

"My friends indeed! You are enough to provoke a saint."

Emmeline burst out laughing, and exclaimed :—

"Saint Frederick the martyr! What a good idea!"

Frank only overheard a part of the foregoing dialogue, for Lady Morden had drawn off his attention by other remarks, but, when they were seated at the dinner-table, he saw the laughter upon Emmeline's merry face, and, although he half believed himself the subject of her mirth, he felt that he admired her quite as much as he had done nine months before.

During dinner Elliott observed that Emmeline never joined in his discourse with Frank or Lady Morden, and that when he talked to one, she immediately turned to the other, and always endeavoured to hinder the conversation from becoming general. Occasionally, he addressed himself directly to her, but she speedily threw him off upon one of the others, and succeeded, by her skilful generalship, in making him as miserable as she could have desired.

"'I suppose I need not ask you whether you are going to Lady Balclavis's ball, tonight. You don't go out to parties yet, I understand?" remarked Lady Morden.

"I have not liked to go out so soon!" rejoined Frank, who was, reminded of his companion of the previous day, and continued, after a pause, "yesterday, at the club, I met, Mr. Spencer."

"Oh! ah! Edmund Spencer!" exclaimed

Frederick. " He told me he'd seen you. He was at a ball we went to last night. Capital fellow he is !"

" Well, I wish he would stay at Walcot among his dogs and ferrets !" replied Emmeline, in a merry tone of irony, " he is quite out of his element, at a London ball. You made me dance with him, Fred, and he waltzes atrociously—dreadful creature ! I was quite ashamed of him !"

Frank was pleased with her satire upon one who had so recently excited his jealousy and wrath.

" Oh ! He is a right good fellow, say what you will, and I am sure you often used to dance with him at Alfreton, and ought to have known, by this time, whether he could waltz or not," was Fred's hasty rejoinder.

" Perhaps I ought, Fred !" returned the girl, with a comical expression, " but, at Alfreton, one is glad to get an arm chair on castors, to waltz with, and my choice has usually been between Mr. Edmund Spencer and yourself, you know !"

" He is rather too provincial in his manner, I certainly think," observed Lady Morden : " one's good friends from the country, do not always shine in London."

" No," replied Emmeline, cruelly, " I would give the world to see Grace and Agnes at a London ball, with their dowdy dresses and stupid country airs. It might improve them, but in the meantime, by-the-bye, it would be awkward to be seen talking with them. I can't fancy them at anything beyond a Loughborough ball—poor girls !"

Frederick was ready to burst with rage, and secretly vowed revenge.

" You are hard upon them, Emmie !" answered her mother, who, although she was pleased at anything which might lessen her son's dangerous admiration for the provincial beauties, dreaded an explosion on his part.

I 2

" They are pretty girls. Did you see them, Mr. Elliott ?"

" Yes. They are very pretty !" in a tone which implied that beauty was their only *forte.*

" Not much besides, perhaps. We have always found them good neighbours, though," replied Lady Morden.

Emmeline perceived that she had inflicted a wound upon Fred, a nd felt that she must set about to heal it before it rankled into any hostile demonstrations, and this may partly have accounted for her sudden amiability to Mr. Elliott, of whom she began a series of enquiries about his travels, and finally expressed her anxiety to see his drawings.

When the ladies had left the room, Elliott felt sufficiently happy to be able to soothe Fred, who had been a good deal ruffled in the first instance, by his sister's coldness to his friend, but who was allowing his wrath to simmer down to a milder temperature, under the influence of her subsequent attentions.

When they went into the drawing-room, Lady Morden was alone, but Emmeline shortly made her appearance, dressed for a ball, to which she was going. In the meanwhile, her mother commenced a catechetical conversation with Elliott.

" Did you know much of your poor brother ?"

" Oh, yes, but it is several years since I saw him."

" I suppose he was a good deal older than yourself ?"

" Nearly eight years."

" He was in the civil service, I think I understood ?"

" Yes."

" How I feel for poor dear Lady Elliott ! I suppose, now, your brother must have been very well off with his Indian appointment, as well as being the eldest son ?"

" He had a very good appointment up the

country, but his being eldest son did not make much difference, during my mother's life."

"No; exactly," returned the catechiser; "of course Sir Ralph would leave everything to your mother, for her life, but then it would have gone to him at her death, or, at all events, she would perhaps, have left most of it to him?"

"It would all have gone to him. It was in trust for the eldest son."

"Ah, yes! For you, now, I suppose?"

"Yes."

"It is a poor consolation for the loss of a brother!" said Lady Morden, as she secretly chuckled over her discovery: "but, of course, you will give up your profession now?"

"No; I intend to go on with it."

"I should have thought that now you are an only son, Lady Elliott would enable you to give it up, perhaps?"

"So she would, I think; but I fancy it is wiser not to do so."

"Why, certainly, it might facilitate your obtaining some appointment. If you are ambitious, you should go into parliament."

All this was said by Lady Morden, in such an easy, off-hand manner, that it did not, in the least appear like over solicitude about Elliott's family or private concerns.

When Emmeline returned, she addressed him nearly as graciously as she had done before she left the dining-room.

"By-the-bye," said Lady Morden, "will you come with us to the opera, to-morrow?"

Frank was in ecstasies.

As he returned to his chambers, he felt jealous when he thought of Emmeline, at the gay ball, surrounded by handsome and agreeable partners.

On the following day he went to an earlier dinner at the Mordens', in order to accompany them to the opera.

"Mamma!" enquired Emmeline, in the drawing room, "did you see that paragraph in the *Morning Post* to-day, about Lord Alcester ?"

" Yes ; I am afraid he's dying."

" What does, it say ?" asked Frank, rather eagerly.

And he looked into the paper which was lying upon the table, and found this paragraph :

" We regret to announce that the Earl of Alcester is seriously indisposed, at Worthington Park, his lordship's country seat. The state of his lordship's health is such as to cause considerable alarm to his numerous family circle."

" That accounts for our not seeing Mr. Montagu, in the park !" said Emmeline.

" He will be Earl of Alcester before long, I should think," remarked Fred.

Frank thought it better to be silent upon the subject of his interview and the note.

Notwithstanding these assurances, he could not help feeling a little disturbed by Emmeline's enthusiastic way of mentioning him.

Miss Morden was much more conversational during this evening than the last. Frank had brought his drawing-books and she looked at them with evident pleasure, until they were summoned to dinner. Elliott's happiness increased as the evening advanced. In going to the opera, he sat opposite to her in the carriage, and thought himself perfectly happy at being in the presence of one so lovely, and in truth, she did look very bewitching, as she said a thousand sharp and witty things, and kept them all up to her own pitch of merriment.

Between the acts there were opportunities for conversation, and Frank had selected a seat, in the box, next to his beloved.

" So you saw a great deal of my friend Elsie Seymour ?" said Emmeline.

15

"Yes, that is," returned Frank, uneasily.

"Yes, that is a very great deal!" pursued Emmeline, mimicking him; "don't you think her very charming?"

"Very well."

"I dare say you mean that. Are not you ashamed to pretend not to admire her? I am quite sure you did."

"I admire all beautiful people."

"I suppose you do, that is the very thing I complain of."

"You shall have no reason to complain, in future," returned Frank, delighted at the opportunity thus offered him. Emmeline perceived her mistake, and looked serious for once.

"I did not mean 'complain,' in that sense. I do not, of course, pretend to any right to criticise your actions."

"Oh, Miss Morden, do not say so. It is cruel to retract the remark."

"I don't know what you mean."

"I hope you will allow me to submit my actions to your criticism ?"

"I shall be a very harsh and unpleasant critic. You had better not."

"Be as severe as you like, but consent to be my critic."

"I don't see how that will advance you !" said Emmeline, in a comical tone, which rather threw Frank out in his attempt to make a declaration of his feelings.

"How your consenting will advance me ?"

"How my criticizing and ridiculing your actions will advance you."

"Should you be very severe ?"

"I have not consented to such a thing, so I cannot possibly tell. Pray did Elsie Seymour consent to be your conscience-keeper as well as your nurse ?"

"What do you mean ? Oh no !" replied Frank, with a slight expression of indignation.

"She did not? Perhaps I may see her to-morrow. Can I take any message from you?"

This was said in a confidential tone as if she thought he were an admirer of Elsie's, and this vexed him still more.

"Is she in London?" he enquired.

"Oh! don't you know? I should have fancied you would have known."

"No."

The rising of the curtain interrupted their further dialogue. During another interval in the opera Emmeline said :

"I declare, mamma, I have seen that odious man, Mr. Bateson, looking at us through his glass, and now he has left his stall and is coming to us, I am certain."

"What an infliction!"

"That reminds me of our walk in the Zoological Gardens," said Frank.

"Do you remember that walk?" asked Emmeline.

"Oh! perfectly," he returned, with a slight sigh.

"And all you said?"

"All you said," he rejoined.

"Yes—but do you remember your abuse of Elsie?"

"No, no—but—"

"But—but you have nobly cancelled it—have not you?"

"I don't know what you mean?"

"Will you tell me the truth?"

"Of course."

"You have proposed to Elsie Seymour."

Frank blushed up to his eyes, and, while he was pausing to concoct a reply, in came Mr. Bateson, and he thanked his stars for the reprieve.

"I am delighted to see you all here," said Mr. Bateson, "enjoying this charming opera. Is this your own box, Lady Morden?"

"I have taken it for a month."

"Well, I confess I am like a horse," re-

turned Bateson, " for I prefer a box to a stall.
I don't mean a loose box, although there are
some such.   I shall often venture here if you'll
allow me."

" To say the truth, we have not availed our-
selves of it very much," replied Lady Morden,
evasively, and not feeling anxious to have Mr.
Bateson's society thrust upon her every night,
" and have generally let our box."

" Is not Sir Edward in town ?"   enquired
Mr. Bateson, wondering why he had never been
asked to dinner.

" No, he remains at present at Alfreton."

" And your household, how is it divided ?"
asked Bateson, thinking about the cook.

" Sir Edward is almost alone.   We have
nearly the whole establishment in town."

" And the cook ?"

" No, we hire a Frenchman, Mr. Bateson,
while we are in London.   Is not that creditable
to us ?"

" Indeed it is—a Frenchman ! ah ! ha !" he

said, reflecting how he could get invited to dinner : " I hope to do myself the pleasure of calling upon you to-morrow, Lady Morden."

" Call at luncheon."

" Very well, I will do myself that pleasure, although I suppose luncheon is scarcely a meal at which to see the Frenchman in perfection."

" Would you rather dine with us ?" asked Lady Morden, who had not strength to resist his pressing attempts.

" I should, indeed, much like it—very much," he replied, eagerly, " I will do so with pleasure. By-the-bye, you two gentlemen are just come back from the Nile. How did you like it ?"

" Pretty well," said Fred.

" It is lucky you were not *annihilated* on the cataracts."

" How tiresome he is. I wish he'd go," said Emmeline, in a low voice to Frank.

" And then you would teaze me again."

" Teaze you, indeed !"

" I deserved it, I admit."

" What ! you confess to my accusation ?"

" No—I don't know.   If I did, could you forgive me ?"

" There's nothing to forgive, nor do you require my forgiveness."

" I am the best judge of that.   To be happy I require it."

" Do you remember once promising never to flatter, or talk nonsense to me ?"

" I do remember.   I am not flattering. For my happiness I require it—pray grant it me ?"

" What !"

" Forgive me for ever thinking of any one but you."

This was said in a low voice, while Mr. Bateson was talking aloud to Lady Morden and Frederick.

" Supposing, for fun, I say ' yes.' "

" I should take your yes in earnest."

" How in earnest ?"

"As a final 'yes.'"

"You would have no right to do that."

"I should assume the right."

"Well then, I think I shall say 'no!'"

"I should not believe it."

"Oh come! you are driving me into a corner."

"Very well. Will you say a yes or no that shall decide my fate for ever?"

"Well, I must think—for the fun of the thing I shall say 'yes'—I hate being a young lady. You must promise to take me to Italy, and any where I like to go, and to do everything I like, and not require me to vow the obedience clause. I'll leave out that—I could not keep it if I tried, so it's no use pretending, is it?"

"No—Emmeline! my be— Miss Morden!"

"Oh, for Heaven's sake, don't make a scene, or I shall break it off!"

"Tell me, may I call you Emmeline?"

"Well, I am not sure—I have not quite

said ' yes' just yet.   You must come and ask
me to-morrow.   Come and meet me in the
Park.   Fred can mount you on one of our
horses if you have none.   So don't teaze me
any more now, or they will be sure to over-
hear us."

Thanks to Mr. Bateson's disquisitions, their
flirtation passed off almost unobserved.   When
the curtain was again raised, Frank's thoughts
wandered beyond the Tyrolese mountains there
depicted, to a fairy-land of his own, of which
the lovely girl by his side was queen. When he
came to reflect upon what had passed, he felt that
he had been hurried forward beyond all his anti-
cipations, and that he had actually made an offer
without intending it.   He wondered at his au-
dacity, but had only to look upon the sparkling
countenance which he had admired from the
first moment he had seen it, to congratulate him-
self upon his unexpected good fortune.   Had
he forgotten Elsie Seymour now ?

  When there was another opportunity for
conversation, Emmeline addressed Mr. Bate-

son, and thus prevented Frank's monopolizing
her society.

"We were shocked to see Lord Alcester's
illness in the paper."

"Little hope, I am told, of his recovery.
A great hypochondriac all his life ! Our friend
Montagu will come in for a good thing there,
and do it in good style. He is standing a con-
test for Luxbridge, so we shall have him in
Parliament again, if his brother recovers."

At length the *ballet* was over, and Frank
was delighted to find that Mr. Bateson's offi-
cious politeness induced him to hand Lady
Morden to the carriage, and thus left him with
Emmeline.

"You will tell me to-morrow whether I
may say ' Emmeline,' dearest Emmeline ?"

"Oh, you naughty, quibbling creature !
you have studied law to some purpose, I de-
clare !"

"Good night—Emmeline !"

"There again! you have no right to call me so yet."

"How cruel! Why even that Mr. Spencer, whom I met the other night, has the impertinence to talk of you as Emmie."

"What a wretch! Well, you shall call me Emmie if you like."

"Dearest Emmie!"

"I never gave you leave to call me dearest."

"Emmie! Good night."

"*Au revoir*, to-morrow at five in the Park. Fred shall send a horse for you. I'll make him."

CHAPTER VII.

NOT OF THIS WORLD.

In a small, close room on the third floor of a house in a narrow court in Westminster, lodged Phœbe Elton, who had been busily engaged in preparing for her examination at the National Society's Training-College. She had not only been unfailing in her daily attendance at the school, but had worked almost without cessation during her spare hours, at home. Latterly she had even given up writing to her friends at Cawthorne, unless it were an occasional note in answer to the long epistles which she received from William Perdon. The poor girl was bent upon a success which was to be crowned by no less a prize than the hand of

him whose heart had been so long and earnestly
devoted to her.   Many a time, as she sat in
the close dirty lodging, with its smoked walls
and ricketty furniture, her books before her,
and her head aching with incessant study, she
would encourage herself to proceed by the
thought of the little school-house and its tidy
garden.

As the day of the examination approached,
she redoubled her efforts and often sat up at
night and, by the light of a dip-candle, poured
over her books and arithmetic, with a determin-
ation that, if she failed, it would be from no
lack of pains on her part.

The time came, and notwithstanding a vio-
lent headache brought on by sleepless nights,
she succeeded to admiration.   The nervousness
which she had dreaded, seemed entirely to
vanish, and her endeavours were crowned with
success.   She was complimented by the exam-
iners and bright appeared her prospects, when,
for the last time she threaded her way from

the school in the sanctuary towards the narrow dusky court, where she lodged. Inspite of her aching brows and fevered pulse she could picture the dear old lane with its black and white cottages, its church where she should so soon be wedded, and the tidy school which was to be her home and the prize of all her labours.

William Perdon had, at one time, intended to come to London, to be present at her examination, and if successful, to conduct her down in triumph, or, if not, an alternative which he did not anticipate, to console her in a failure, which would be *his* as well, for the good school master had no intention to relinquish her, and would rather have thrown up his situation and have betaken himself to some more menial craft.

As soon as Phœbe reached her little room, she closed the door and kneeling down against the bed, sobbed hysterically until she could

weep no longer.   Her head ached violently, and
she lay down and fell asleep.

It had been her custom to go out to buy
her provisions, for she had no one to do it for her.
She had scarcely made acquaintance with any
of her fellow lodgers, excepting a good natured
widow upon the same floor, who would often
supply her with boiling water when her fire
was out, and bring her some things from the
shop when she went out for her own.   The only
other acquaintance she had, besides her school-
fellows, with whom she was not very compan-
ionable, was a relation of William Perdon's,
a kind old woman, who lived over the water, and
who came from time to time to see her.   Upon
the day in question she had made no purchases,
intending to go out and get some little dain-
ties for her evening meal, after her return from
the school.   Her intention had been to travel
down by railway to Cawthorne upon the fol-
lowing day.

When she awoke from her sleep the room was in darkness. She felt a chill upon her and, when she got up to grope her way to the mantelpiece for the matches, her limbs trembled to such an extent that she reached it with difficulty.

She felt so ill that she ventured to creep to her neighbour's door and summon the good-natured little widow to her assistance. The old woman lighted her fire and put some water to boil, in order that she might make her a hot cup of tea, in the meanwhile sending her to bed. Notwithstanding these precautions, when the woman returned to her room in the morning, she found her so much worse that she was at a loss what course to pursue with her. She was herself obliged to be out all day, having employment as a charwoman, and felt distressed at the prospect of this poor creature, in a high fever, being left all alone. What made it the more perplexing for the kind-hearted old thing, was that Phœbe was not even in a state to think for herself. She was evidently in great pain, and constantly uttering groans and moanings.

Luckily the little widow knew that she was a pupil at the Westminster Training-school and determined to call upon the superintendent of the establishment, on her way to her work. The person to whom she addressed herself was utterly at a loss how to befriend Phœbe Elton, when she suddenly recollected her friend Mary Thompson, to whom she immediately despatched a note.

When the note reached the House of Mercy in Bloomsbury, sister Mary was unfortunately out, but the messenger was directed to request that, in such a case, it might be opened by any of the other sisters.

Pale and beautiful, in the simple dress of the sisterhood, Elsie sat in her private chamber busied once more in the toil of her own creation. She had only returned within the last few days to London, after a painful struggle with herself about leaving her home. This time her parents had made no resistance, and she felt it the more keenly. Was it right after all ?

Her house of mercy was increased in its design, and included a hospital for the sick. The number of sisters was augmented, but, in her absence, she found that Mary Thompson had taken an ell where she had allowed her an inch, and had greatly increased the religious discipline of the establishment. Whether Elsie's own ideas upon this subject had undergone any change or not, it is certain that she seemed more distinctly to perceive the necessity of what had been done, and also the expediency of doing it still more effectually. At the moment when they knocked at her chamber-door with the note, she was engaged in writing a letter upon the subject of a chaplain for the institution, and after long balancing, had actually, addressed herself to Herbert Lisle.

The reader will excuse our lengthening the parenthesis in order to copy it verbatim.

> "*House of Mercy, Bloomsbury.*"
> "*June,* 18—.

" DEAR MR. LISLE,

       " You will be surprised at my writing to you, but I think our friendship might plead my excuse, even were the subject of my letter not in itself sufficient. I am busy in extending my little establishment, and have determined, at last, to have a chaplain. I am too proud to confess that this is owing to any modification of my principles or views. These have had to succumb to practical necessities in various instances, and I feel that it is better to yield with a good grace and to appoint an earnest chaplain at once.

" Now, Mr. Lisle, seeing how far I have given way upon this point, to what an extent the dreams of Mount Sinai and Jerusalem are influencing my judgment, you must also make an effort. It is only upon this condition of a compromise that I venture to consult you. You must lay aside for a moment your high-flown notions, and choose for me a really sober-minded, earnest, hard-working clergyman, as a chaplain. I know of no person in whose judgment I could trust so well, or of whose sense of devotion, in making the choice, I could feel so confident.

"When I speak of a compromise, I am not alluding to any desertion of principles, but rather to a modification of practice, and so long as the object of your choice is discreet and con ciliatory, as well as earnest, I shall be satisfied, for I do not pretend to investigate or controul his private theories or opinions. I am sure I may leave this in your hands.

"So much for the purport of my letter. I do not suppose that there is any inmate of this institution who more needs the advice of such a chaplain as I have described, than myself. At

times the distinction between right and wrong
becomes so hard to perceive, that I feel the
want of some one to point it out. Sometimes I
long to conjure back the days in the desert
when we conversed of such things. I feel more
than half inclined to consult you and, after all,
why should I not? I have long despised con-
ventionalities and can now afford to lay them
completely aside. We are old friends and can
never be anything more. My lot, please God,
is cast for ever. I have undertaken, in true
earnest, a toil which I will never forsake, and
why should *I*, thus freed from the world's law,
again place myself within its bondage? This
being so, I will venture to put the case to you:
last autumn my father entreated me, for awhile,
to forsake my institution in order to travel
abroad with him, and I consented, intending to
rejoin it upon my return to England. Upon
first coming back, I went home and spent a
short time with my parents, and now I have
left them to recommence what I must regard

as the purpose of my life. They said nothing
to deter me from my scheme, but always spoke
kindly when I ventured to mention it. This
silence was, nevertheless, more eloquent than
words, and I could easily perceive how dis-
tasteful my departure was to both of them. I
can never efface from my memory the last
evening at Dorrington, as my father sat and
poked the fire to hide his emotions, and my
mother occasionally left the room and returned
with her eyes reddened with tears. Oh! that
dear, dear mother, how she wept as she em-
braced me upon the morning of my journey
and yet, I had the heart to go! I had arranged
to go, and I went. I promised to return for a
visit, as soon as I had placed everything *en
train*, and I hope to fulfil it soon.

"Such is my case. Am I right or wrong?
or is there any middle course I can pursue?
Tell me candidly, as the best friend I have; for,
as such, I venture to consult you.

" I need not tell you that I write all this in

the very deepest confidence, since you will
understand that it could not be otherwise.

"Believe me always to remain

"Yours most faithfully,

"ELSIE SEYMOUR."

She had just concluded the letter when the
message was brought her. She did not wait to
address her epistle to Mr. Lisle but, finding
there were no sisters disengaged at the mo-
ment, immediately started off to the humble
lodging in Westminster, where the Cawthorne
maiden was languishing under the effects of a
violent fever.

The bearer of the note having been allowed
to accompany her to the lodging, she was able
to send her back to the House of Mercy for a
supply of such remedies as she deemed neces-
sary, and for the medical attendant as soon as
he could be despatched.

Elsie smoothed the sick girl's pillow and

watched by her side, awaiting the advice of the doctor. When he had seen her and prescribed, she continued to sit by the couch, giving her, from time to time, the cooling draughts which he had recommended.

Phœbe spoke wanderingly and called for William, and exclaimed :

"O save me, William, save me from Johnson !" and then she said rapidly, "take me home to Cawthorne !"

"Cawthorne !" said Elsie : "Cawthorne is in Gloucestershire !"

"Gloucestershire ! Yes ! yes !"

"To Mr. Lisle."

"Mr. Herbert, good gentleman !"

And two little tears trickled down Elsie's cheeks as she heard his praises uttered by the sick girl in her delirium, for her heart assented to the truth of what she said.

Late in the day another sister came to relieve Elsie, who walked home on foot to the House of Mercy, protected from recognition by her

K 5

dress. As she crossed a street in the vicinity of Covent Garden, a gentleman on horseback nearly rode over her. It was Frank Elliott starting off to meet Emmeline in the Park. Forgetful of the humble sister who nursed him in the tent at Eyn Sultaun, he was now radiant with health and spirits: she was pursuing her life-long toil.

On returning home she added a postscript to her letter to Herbert Lisle, informing him of the condition of the Cawthorne girl whom she had nursed.

Her hours were fully occupied with her various duties which even intruded into the watches of the night, but nevertheless there were moments for calm meditation. Oftentimes as she sat, at midnight, by the bed of sickness she was incited to reflect upon herself and her condition. Death is a monitor which she was frequently required to witness. Her occupation was too entirely religious in its character to be long severed from faith.

When she came personally to attend day and night, by the beds of the sick and dying, she was led to understand the urgent appeals of the sisters for an increase of religious discipline. She was often called upon to read and pray by the bed of some poor penitent panting for reconciliation with an offended God and only faintly apprehending the mediation of the Saviour.

" Tell me something about Jesus Christ and His dying for poor sinners ?" was the request which once met her ears : " will Jesus Christ save me ?"

And she felt utterly bewildered in the presence of that poor dying sinner, for she could not answer. She read and prayed, but the poor creature was seeking words of consolation from her own heart and she discovered that she had not herself yet learnt the great mystery of the cross. The penitent died calling upon the Lord to save her, and, no doubt, as once upon Mount Calvary, He again heard the prayer of agony, but how terrible to the sister who had watched beside her couch without the power of affording consolation! Poor Elsie knelt by the death-bed and prayed from the depths of her soul that God would guide her to the truth.

For days the impression dwelt strongly upon her, and, whenever she sat watching by sick-beds, she spent the hours of silence in meditating and beseeching God to enlighten her by Hi Spirit.

She returned daily to the lodging of Phœbe Elton, whose fever abated under the treatment she received and the constant care bestowed upon her by the sisters.

Elsie was surprised at not receiving an answer by return of post from Herbert Lisle and made up her mind that he was not at home.

Her time was now so apportioned that not a single moment was lost. When not called up in the night she would be dressed by six and, after devoting a short time to meditation and prayer—which was her newly acquired habit—she would transact the business and plan the daily routine of the establishment. She placed everything upon the most methodical footing and made it her endeavour that all the machinery should be as regular as clock-work. Ever since her return to England she had been occupied in the extension of the institution. In her absence she had been content to let it smoulder on in a modest unattractive form, but now that she was once more able to overlook its details and, by her genius of rule, to command success, there was no farther reason to limit the undertaking.

When she had devoted a certain time to these general affairs of the society, she spent the rest of the day in qualifying herself for her task and, in pursuing her laborious duties. As a means of fitting herself for her employments she was wont to attend the hospitals and not only to examine every form of disease but to witness complicated and painful surgical operations. She

learnt the art of dressing wounds and binding
amputated limbs, and so brought her amazing
powers of mind to master those various details
to which ordinary hospital nurses only become
inured through years of constant practice.

After this severe initiation, the hours spent
in visiting sick-beds came almost as a species
of relaxation, since in many cases they allowed
her time for calm reflection.   Few women
could have borne the mere physical exertion
which she daily underwent and, of those, how
small a number would have been able to endure
the close confinement and foul atmosphere of
the squalid sick-rooms, which it was her habit
to visit; at least, with the slight training which
she had undergone.

The desertion of her parents often rose be-
fore her mind, during the long hours spent in
these scenes of wretchedness, but she generally
contrived to banish the thought.   The life
which she had led, at home, had been one of
comparative uselessness and frivolity.   Her

mother's delight had consisted in paying a series of visits, displaying her daughter's talents and living, so to say, upon her accomplishments. During the short period they remained at home, the house was filled with guests, who courted and flattered Elsie, and almost hung upon her words. There were, certainly, schools to teach, and a few cottages to visit, but nothing to afford her any real, absorbing, occupation. It was a life of inanities and playthings, and she felt called to higher pursuits, and created for some more glorious enterprize. True, she might have married, but, in that case, she would have deserted her home as entirely as she had done now. She could have married and there was one whom she, possibly, would have married, had the choice been in her hands, but it was in God's, and she was still free! It was, perhaps, better so; but then she had left her parents, and, at times, the thought weighed very heavily upon her conscience.

One morning, she sat, as usual, in her little room, writing letters and giving orders, when sister Mary, happening to come in upon other business, ventured to ask whether she had thought any more of her suggestion about the chaplain. Elsie evaded the question, but felt vexed when she recollected that she had received no letter from Mr. Lisle.

While sister Mary was still in the room, one of the lay sisters came and announced that a gentleman had called to see Miss Seymour, and that he was waiting below in the public parlour. She went down, and was more pleased than surprised, to find that it was Herbert himself. He had never seen Elsie in the dress of her sisterhood, and failed to recognize her as she opened the door, but, the next moment, he thought that he had never seen that stately figure and Minerva face, look half so beautiful.

" Mr. Lisle !" she exclaimed, " I half

hoped that it was you. How very kind of you to come."

" I tried to answer your letter," he replied ; " I ought to have answered it, but I could not, and so I came myself."

Elsie stood before him graceful and dignified, as in days of yore, but with a shade of that humility which became the sister of mercy. Her auburn tresses were concealed, but the costume which she had adopted, set off, to advantage, the pale beauty which, to Lisle's eyes, seemed well suited to a heroine of the cross.

She did not invite Herbert to sit down, and both stood, as if hesitating, for an instant, to commence upon the subject of the visit.

" It was bold in me to write to you," she said, " and I certainly think I should not have ventured upon such a step, had I thought it would give you this trouble, and bring you up to London."

"Oh, Miss Seymour, do not say so."

"I am a sister here, you know. I drop the Miss Seymour. I am sister Elsie."

"Sister Elsie!" returned Lisle, with a slight thrill; for while he was admitted to call her by the cherished name, the barrier seemed stronger than ever between them; "how good of you to consult me. Do not call it troubling me. I would have gone to Mount Sinai upon such an errand."

"Can you tell me of a chaplain?"

"My brother-in-law would have suited you admirably, but, unfortunately, he has a living and is married, but I think I know of one, of the same devoted piety and zeal, and as conciliatory as he is, whose only fault would be his age. He has not been long ordained."

"That would be a fault," replied Elsie; "in a sisterhood where we may have young, and, perhaps, romantic girls, we ought to have a man of tried character and long experience.

But, tell me, before we go on; tell me how you have judged my case? I cannot any longer delay hearing your decision."

Herbert had, perhaps, longed to put off answering the question about herself, and proceeded, with some hesitation and after a pause, during which his eyes were bent upon the ground:

"Perhaps the chaplain, whose nomination you ventured to place in my hands, would be better able to advise you than I can."

"The chaplain? No—tell me *your* decision."

"Were there no home duties? No duties in the daily-life, to those who gave you birth and cherished you in your earliest years? To those around home, the tenants, the villagers, or the school? Duties, not great and ambitious, but obvious, humble and near at hand?"

"Listen to me, Mr. Lisle. My life was like one long scene of dissipation. I lived to shine

in brilliant and literary society.   I was courted
and flattered for talents which are utterly des-
picable in themselves.   I could write and com-
pose and might, as they told me, have earned
a reputation as a poet or an authoress.   As to
visiting the villagers, I did so, and superin-
tended the school, but these things are no
occupation.   My parents almost live upon
society, and I was taught to do so too.   The
line of duty was hard to perceive.   I had long
felt the emptiness of all my pursuits and the
need of some higher aim, and, by degrees, my
views seemed to centre in this particular design,
which suited the whole bent of my mind and
called its every faculty into active exertion.
Oh ! if you knew the happiness of such a life
after the vain frivolities of an aimless exist-
ence !"

    " There is something, no doubt, in what you
say," returned Lisle, " but do you not forget
your duty towards your parents ? a duty which
nothing can over-rule."

" I have their permission—it is not disobe-
dience ; but you mean that I ought to remain
at home with them.   Supposing I were married
—which is, perhaps, their wish, I could not
always be with them *then*."

" No," said Lisle, who involuntarily faltered
in a conscience-stricken tone, " no, but you
would often be with them.   As they get older
they will need a daughter's care."

" You are right," returned Elsie, in a sub-
dued voice, " I intended paying them frequent
visits.   Tell me what you would have me to
do ?"

" I would leave the decision in their hands."

" They would reply as they have done, and
beg me to proceed with my scheme."

" You have not laid it before them as I
mean."

" As I did before you ?"

" Yes."

Elsie was silent for a minute, and then conti-
nued in an altered tone :

"You must pay them a visit. My father will be so pleased to renew his acquaintance with you. Pray how is your uncle, Mr. Winslow?"

"He is very well. I brought him to London with me and he is gone with our Cawthorne schoolmaster to find your patient, our future schoolmistress. Will she be well enough to accompany her lover down?"

"In a day or two."

My uncle was too shy to come here, or I might have ventured to ask to see your intended hospital."

"He is most welcome. Pray bring him. Is he remaining in London?"

"For some time. Notwithstanding his age, he appears bent upon studying theology, in hopes of being ordained."

"When will that take place?"

"It will be sometime hence, I should fancy."

"Could my chaplaincy be supplied until then?"

"Would you think of such a thing?"

"Next to his nephew, I think he would be as good an adviser as we could have," she said, laughingly.

Herbert did not reply, and she seemed to regret her speech.

"Of course, I am not in earnest," continued Elsie, smiling: "however, if you should hear of a chaplain such as I described to you, pray let me know, for I am in immediate want of his assistance."

"I will write to my cousin to-night; he is certain to give good advice."

"And inform me of the result. Farewell, Mr. Lisle," she continued, seeing that he made a movement to terminate a conference which, however willing he might have been to prolong, seemed to be withdrawing her from her occupations. "I have not been disappointed in my appeal to you in my difficulties, and I cannot sufficiently thank you for your advice. I have kept the agate cross."

" And it has budded like Aaron's rod !" ventured Herbert."

" It points to a way which was new to me."

" And you are following the narrow path."

" Pray that I may be enabled to do so. Farewell."

CHAPTER VIII.

LUXBRIDGE.

It was the day of the Luxbridge election. The little town was hung with flags, and boughs of oak and laurel, to indicate the politics of the householders. Gay as was the appearance of the principal street of the usually quiet borough, it was as nothing at all in comparison with the noise and bustle of the market-place, where the polling-booths were erected. Of the two principal inns, where the committees of the respective candidates held their sittings, one was in the market-place itself, and the other in a street leading from it. The party colours of Luxbridge had been, from time immemorial, blue and pink, the conservatives having appropriated the former, and the liberals the latter colour.

The borough was placarded in all directions with the names of the candidates and their addresses, with squibs, and even caricatures. "Vote for Lord Lisle, the farmers' friend," for there was a large agricultural district included within the borough, and it was there that Lord Portaldowne's chief interest lay. "To the independent electors of the borough of Luxbridge," was to be seen on papers, white, blue, and pink.

The hotel in the market-place was called the Portaldowne Arms, and a gigantic blue banner, supported by huge branches of oak on either side, proclaimed the fact of its being the headquarters of Lord Lisle and his committee. Let us intrude for a moment within its sanctum and, entering the long room, of which the table was piled with registers, returns, squibs, handbills, placards, addresses and cards, see how the ground lies with the blues.

At the farther end of the room stood a good looking youth with fair hair and a faint attempt at moustâches. This was the young man who was willing to learn to be a legislator, but who did not appear to have much knowledge of the subject at present. Luxbridge was considered a good place upon which to practise representation. He rather hoped to take it quietly, and it was an easy constituency, as constituencies go now a-days. When his father had suggested his coming forward he had made no difficulties, for he knew that, however great a bore, it was undoubtedly the right thing to be in parliament, and he went through his canvass like a man.

He felt very anxious about the returns, and was making eager enquiries of one of his agents, who had just been occupied in getting up some ticklish votes. The fact is that there were some people who called themselves chartists, in Luxbridge. They were few in number, and were

L 3

so violently opposed to the rest of the liberal
interest as to be willing, for the sake of defeat-
ing it, to form what the whig paper termed an
" unholy alliance with the tories." The agent
in question, in whom the reader will recog-
nize an old friend, was the very party employed
to bring about this desirable result.

Mr. Alfred Johnson did not remain long
with his patron at Winfield and, having passed
his examination and found an opening at
Luxbridge, his father had established him
there. The election offered a noble field for
the exercise of his genius, and he showed him-
self in everyway worthy of the retainer, which
he received from the blues, by the activity and
unscrupulous zeal which he displayed in their
service.

" Have those fellows all polled ?" enquired
his lordship.

" Not all, my lord ! there is one of'em that
I couldn't blarney into coming, say what I

would, and he is a kind of leader among them. He sticks to the charter. I ventured to go the length of saying, you were for the charter."

" The deuce you did ?"

" The Magna charter. It is all one."

" Well, that is a joke, and what did the fellow say ?"

" He won't come without your lordship will tell him yourself, that you are good for the charter. I can't see any harm myself in your saying it."

" My good fellow ! I can't say such a thing as that."

" Can't you ? well I'll just try the fellow again. I've thought of a dodge. He believes me to be a chartist, I know. I'll tell him we'll stick up the five points on our colours, and I'll promise him a chartist speech, if we get in."

" How is the polling going on ?"

" It don't look quite so good; I hope we may get up a bit. If I had had my way I know how I could have shut up near two score of their votes. The register has been very badly looked after."

"I think I shall go back to the booths."

"You wont give in, my lord, and think better about these chartist fellows? It's no harm, ye know—all fair."

"No, no. I can't do that."

"Will you come and tell them you're good for the five pints, that's all I want."

"Five points?"

"Five pints, pints of beer or ale, you know; there is no lie there."

"The deuce take it! I can't do it, indeed I can't!"

And he left the room with a slight show of annoyance.

"I'll do it for him fast enough. Lor bless us! I'm not quite such a muff as all that!" muttered Alfred Johnson as he followed the candidate downstairs.

Within the precincts of the town the laurel

branches and pink flags certainly preponderated over the others, but, around the arched door-way of the Portaldowne-Arms and within its yard, was a throng of sturdy farmers, who cheered Lord Lisle as he descended among them, and who accompanied him with vociferous acclamations as he advanced towards the polling booths.

In front of these booths stood the hustings, and thither the liberal voters proceeded one by one from the poll, and received the courteous thanks of their candidate, Cecil Montagu.

The town clock was marking the hours, and its hands were approaching the decisive moment. The numbers of the rival candidates were sufficiently balanced to create an intense interest in all concerned, and the crowd of blues and pinks around the booths, stood cheering or groaning as each elector polled his vote.

There were several anxious faces at the

place where Cecil Montagu was conversing with his principal supporters. He alone looked as calm and unconcerned as upon any ordinary occasion.

"I received your note," he said to one of his committee, who was among the most influential of his supporters, "but I could not well arrange to go to Dorrington last night—to my regret."

"You must come to-night. We are quite alone. I regret to say that even Elsie is not with us."

"No? where is she?"

"In London, but it is a sore subject. If you do not mind a dull dinner with no one but ourselves? Or I will ask some of your supporters if you like?"

"No, no, I beg you will not. I would rather be perfectly quiet."

"In that case I shall wait and drive you back in my carriage."

"You look tired, Seymour, with your exertions in my behalf. I cannot sufficiently thank you for the trouble you have taken."

"So long as we succeed, I don't care!" rejoined his friend. "What are the numbers?" he enquired of a stout red-faced little man.

"This is the last return: a quarter past three."

Montagu 240
. Lisle.................... 229

"That's well! What a near run it is! Have you seen this return?" he continued, as he handed it to Montagu.

"They are getting up their votes now a bit," rejoined the red-faced gentleman, "they have got a lot of chartists, those fellows down in the Tanneries. That rascal Johnson has done a deal of work among those fellows, I'm told."

L 5

"Do you mean to say the chartists vote for the tory?" enquired Mr. Seymour.

"It ought not to have been so. It is bad management, no doubt, but it is so!"

"Bad job!" exclaimed Seymour, gloomily.

"I have not seen you," said Montagu, in a voice to cheer him in his despondency, "since your return from the East. I long to hear of your travels."

"Ah! I wish Elsie were at home, to tell you of them," returned Mr. Seymour, still more despondingly.

"I just saw the Mordens in town—Miss Morden and her brother," pursued Montagu, perceiving that his former attempt was unsuccessful, in dispelling the gloom from his companion's face.

"Ah!" but even they were so connected in his mind with Elsie, that he was forced to pause ere he could reply.

In the meanwhile, the little red-faced gentleman, who had been away, returned with a paper, saying :—

" Fresh return, sir ! Half-past three.

Montagu 244
Lisle..................... 241

" Bad business this. They've been getting up the chartist votes, I expect. I saw that blackguard, Johnson, with a lot of fellows, yonder. They've pretty near exhausted them now, I take it."

In the meanwhile, Lord Lisle had been walking among his supporters, and had returned towards the inn, when Johnson came and informed him that he had polled several of the chartists.

" A close shave, my lord, but we'll do it yet. Only let me look up the registration, next time, and see if I don't manage things better. I promise your lordship I'll make it a pocket borough. D'ye twig, eh, my lord ?"

His lordship understood that the knave wanted to supplant the present tory agent, and have the whole thing in his hands, but he felt loth to make a promise, which he did not see his way to fulfil.

"There are more votes, my lord, that no one can secure but myself; d'ye twig, now, my lord. Every one for himself, my lord, you understand, in this world! Look at yonder clock—eh?"

"D—— the fellow!" muttered the wretched candidate. "Hang you, my good fellow, I'll pay you well—any sum you like—only, by Jove, get up these votes, quick, quick!"

"Scarcely more than twenty minutes now, my lord!" returned Johnson, coolly pulling out his watch with one hand, as he scratched his head with the other: "like being hanged almost, ayn't it? Ever seen a man hanged, my lord?" he continued, in his free and easy tone.

"Confound the fellow !" muttered his lordship, in despair.

"Lord Portaldowne might manage it very well, you know, my lord," said the young attorney, in a calm, meditative tone, " he might—a word from him, eh ? I must go and see for the quarter to four return for your lordship."

"Come, I'll get you what you want, if you'll secure the election—no nonsense."

"Word of honour, my lord ?"

"Yes—I'll promise it."

"Done !"

And off he bolted, to secure his prey.

A quarter to four.

Montagu 249
Lisle.................... 243

"Capital !" said Mr. Seymour, as he brought the return to his friend : " we are all right now.   They have only polled two votes during the last quarter of an hour, and we have got up five.   We are secure !   All right, is not it, Timms?" he continued, as he turned to his little red-faced friend.

"Yees," said the little man, with a signifi- cant wink, "I'll get our fellows ready for a good hearty cheer.   I suppose, Mr. Montagu, you'll make them a bit of a speech from our committee-room window ?   It is usual."

The hand of the clock was rapidly approach- ing the decisive moment.   There seemed to be a good deal of bustle round the booth.

"Getting up a few votes," said Mr. Timms ; "but they won't catch us up.   We are all right !"

The clock appeared to go too slowly, but at last it struck the hour of four, and Mr. Timms had already taken off his hat to lead the glorious applause, when their ears were greeted by a deafening cheer from the blues around the polling-booth. Mr. Timms ran for the return, and, to Mr. Seymour's consternation it stood thus :—

Lisle............... 253
Montagu 2𝑈0
                   _____
Majority...... 3 for Lord Lisle.

Cecil Montagu showed not óne sign of annoyance, but, after shaking hands cordially, with such of his supporters as stood around, offered to make a speech from the inn windows, in order to mitigate the despondency of his party.

Arm-in-arm with Mr. Seymour, and accompanied by others, he walked towards the Flying Horse, and was well hooted by a small knot of blues, upon his way.

The defeated party congregated around the inn, and their candidate stood at the balcony, before the open window, to address them.

"Gentlemen," said Montagu, in the courteous flowing style of oratory, at which he was an adept, "I confess that the result has taken me by surprise. We were, all of us, confident of success; it may be, we were too confident, but let us not be disheartened by failure—defeat is, sometimes, the prelude to victory, and I am persuaded that it will be so with you."

His audience commenced a loud cheer, and one of his committee, who stood behind him, at the window, said :—

"Sir, it was hard upon you—we ought to have managed better."

"My good friends, I thank you for your welcome cheer. It has just been said to me by a gentleman standing here, one whose zeal in the liberal cause has been well proved, that he considers this defeat hard upon me. I feel his kindness, and in one sense, no doubt, he is right for, inasmuch as it is a blow to our party, it is a blow to me. In no other sense will I allow of his consideration for me, since if he intends to say that I am personally a sufferer beyond others, beyond you all whom I see around me, I must, with many thanks for his kind thought, decline the insinuation. Gentlemen, it is in conjunction with you that I must lament over the loss we have sustained this day; with you, who have struggled so bravely for victory, and at the eleventh hour, when success seemed within our grasp, have encountered defeat. Upon our part this was no wanton aggression upon a faction established in power. This borough has long been in the hands of the liberal party. We treated success as a certainty, and even deemed opposition an idle attempt. Our confidence in our own strength has proved our ruin. We have lost the day. Look yonder, how they cheer their new-fledged legislator, how they glory in the triumph of the hour! Let us not grudge them their delight, however, we may regret their victory. It is the first time, almost within the memory of man, that they have returned a member for this borough, and I believe, gentlemen, that you will bear me out in saying that it shall also be the very last. (cheers) Why grudge a satisfaction, which they have never known before, and will never enjoy again? (cheers and laughter) But, gentlemen, you will take a broader view of our position. The great party to which you and I belong, is the party of Progress, and when was Progress exempt from failure? From age to age, the battle of improvement has been fought. . Civilization has had to contend with the conservatism of barbarism and ignorance, and where has been the royal road to success? I reply through failure and defeat! There is no safer way to final victory, and no cause can bear defeat like ours. With them to lose is to be ruined, with us it is a mere postponement of what we *must* gain in the end.

" Our cause is like that for which, in days of

yore, the martyrs shed their blood, and in which
the failure of the hour was the surest prelude
to conquest (loud cheers.)

"I have done—I can only wish you better
luck for the time to come. It is possible that
our fortunes may, at some future day, be allied
for glory as they have now been united for
defeat—but, whether so or not, I shall preserve
a grateful recollection of your kindness to me,
and an affectionate memory of having shared
in your loss."

Montagu spoke in such silvery tones and
with such graceful ease of delivery, that we
strive vainly, by a mere transcript of his words,
to convey the effect which they produced.
As he left the balcony he was greeted with
long enthusiastic cheerings, which lasted until
the chairman of his committee came forward
to propose a vote of thanks. This obliged him
once more to display his eloquence, and he
succeeded this time in entwining so much

humour into his speech that he caused the
defeated electors to roar with laughter. Such
was their hilarity that a passer-by might have
mistaken them for the victors, especially if he
had previously seen the stolid patience of the
bluff farmers as they listened to the crude
oration of Lord Lisle.

CHAPTER IX.

THE DESERTED HOME.

As they drove towards Dorrington Grange, Mr. Seymour's place, Montagu was forced to sustain the conversation, and by his lively wit, to endeavour to arouse his companion from the gloomy melancholy which seemed to have come over him.

The house where Elsie's early years had been spent, was situated in a country entirely destitute of fine old timber. The plantations were making rapid progres, bnt there was nothing to supply the want of forest trees and woodland glades. The place was principally of Mr. Seymour's own creation, and the grounds were laid out with taste, and promised well for the distant future. The mansion was a happy specimen of the Italianized Elizabethan, in which large mullioned widows were harmonized with the balustrades and parapets of sunnier climes. The combined brick and stone of the structure set off the rich verdure of the cypresses upon its broad terrace walk.

When they drove to the door, it was already late and, after a brief dialogue with the servant, Mr. Seymour found that it would be absolutely necessary for him to consult his better-half before he could duly install his guest in an apartment, and sohe hastened to advise with the lady of the house.

"Why, my dear, I could not possibly tell that he would come to-night," said Mrs. Seymour, when she heard her husband's story: "so very inconvenient! I only wish you could have sent me a message. It had become absolutely necessary to have these rooms cleaned and the chimneys swept, the soot was actually falling down upon the best rugs."

"Well, darling, you did it for the best, I know," returned the meek husband: "but what is to be done?"

"Well, dear, there's Elsie's room, you know."

"Surely there must be some other?" pleaded the husband.

"Only those poky little west-rooms and the attics; you can't put him in those."

And, notwithstanding Mr. Seymour's objections, it was finally over-ruled that the stranger should occupy the apartment in question.

The spacious bed-room to which Cecil Montagu was conducted, overlooked the terrace garden. The windows opened upon a wide stone-balcony, enriched with marble vases. The small brass bedstead was of a classic design worthy of Thornwood itself, and the fittings and furniture of the room were in the same chaste style. Copies of Rafaëlle's Parnassus and school of Athens, Guido's Aurora

and a minute fac-simile of the ceiling of the
Farnese, were among the pictures suspended
around the walls.

In one corner was a low book-case, upon the
slab of which were arranged Greek and Etrus-
can vases of earthenware, glass lachrymatories,
bronze busts, statuettes and lamps, interspersed
with coins and broken fragments of marble.
Upon the chimney-piece were two bronze can-
delabra, copied from some of those found at
Pompeii, and, upon the shelves of a rosewood
chiffonier, were displayed mummy rags—
vitrified images of the dead—scarabœi—beads
—gold rings and ornaments—hieroglyphic
cartouches—rolls of papyrus—embalmed cats
—pieces of painted coffins—and various other
curiosities sent home from Egypt.

Notwithstanding all these reminiscences of
Elsie, there appeared to Montagu an air of
desolation about the room. It looked as if
years might have elapsed since it was last in-
habited.

While awaiting his servant's arrival, he could not refrain from glancing at the various contents of the apartment. The books especially attracted his attention. There were the Greek tragedians by the side of the Italian poets. Some of the books were dotted with pencil marks and notes, and one he found entirely filled with manuscript. He no sooner discovered this than he proceeded to close and replace it. He opened a second, which contained drawings, where he found a sketch from the glen of Thornwood, and underneath it the words of Petrarch, in pencil, half effaced:

> Aer sacro sereno
> Ov' Amor co' begli occhi il cor m'aperse."

Once, in the course of conversation during dinner, Montagu had spoken of Elsie to her mother, and she seemed frozen up by the accidental allusion. He was forced to turn to general themes, but it was hard to interest the parents who had lost their child.

"Perhaps you can tell me," enquired Montagu, "whether Lord Portaldowne is in any way connected with a family of Lisles who live in Gloucestershire?"

"Certainly he is," replied Mr. Seymour; "they are cousins of some sort. Lisle of Cawthorne I am acquainted with. I have some idea that Lord Portaldowne is one of the first in the entail for that Gloucestershire property."

"Ha! Is the Lisle you speak of a young man?"

"Herbert Lisle? yes, he is only just come into possession. His father died last autumn."

"Exactly. He is a man of great promise, I have been told. A man of fine feeling."

"Well! yes!" returned Mr. Seymour: "he is an odd fellow in some things, but high principled, and a thorough gentleman. An old friend of ours. We have known him a great many years. He is a high-tory and high-churchman, and all that kind of thing, but he is a good fellow in the main, and a man of considerable taste and information."

" Not like his cousin?"

" Our friend, the member for Luxbridge, you mean?" rejoined Mr. Seymour, who pursued, " well, I hear Lord Lisle well spoken of in the country. They are great tories. Lord Portaldowne is said to be a bitter politician, but we have always got on very well together, indeed, nothing can exceed his uniform civility, and, even kindness, I might say, whenever we have come in contact."

" I conclude, from what I gathered during the canvass, that his property might almost command the borough," said Montagu.

" It is terribly involved, though," answered Seymour, " the late man ran through the best of the fortune. They would not be sorry to get back the Cawthorne estates, which passed to the younger branch two or three generations ago, and would, I fancy, now revert to Lord

M 3

Portaldowne, if Herbert Lisle died without issue."

"My dear, you forget," ventured Mrs. Seymour, "there are those Lisles who live near Alfreton. They are near relatives of Herbert Lisle's."

"But I am almost sure," replied her husband, "that the Mr. Lisle you speak of has no sons. I think Morden told me so."

Montagu profited by Mrs. Seymour's lessened apathy to draw her out upon a subject which seemed, more than any other, to claim her attention. A mother is keen for a child's interests, and this may account for her feeling more lenient than her husband to any defects in that Herbert Lisle, who appeared to have a certain power of fascination over her whom Montagu had deserted. Cecil was conscience-stricken when he saw the cold rooms and colder hearts in this desert of his own creation, and struggled hard to enliven the discourse with his accustomed sallies. Having failed, he could do no better than touch a key which seemed to strike some hidden chord of sympathy.

"Herbert Lisle is not married?" he enquired of the mother.

"No," she returned, "I wish you could meet him, for although he may be peculiar in some respects, I fancy you would like him. Mr. Seymour met him abroad. He was in Syria when they were."

Montagu began to perceive the drift of her thoughts, and enquired minutely into all she knew of Herbert's history. He may have had a curiosity of his own to satisfy, for there was a tie which united their benevolence, and which gave him an interest in the village of Cawthorne.

"Who was his mother?" he asked among other questions.

"A Winslow."

"Winslow! Oh! I remember!" exclaimed Montagu.

"Yes," joined in Mr. Seymour, "that strange creature Arthur Winslow is his uncle. You must have heard of his so-called conversion?"

"I heard a story, but I confess I am sceptical about those sudden changes. However, he had run through all his property before he became a devotee. It was a wager, I am told, as to whether he first gave up the world, or the world him, and he won."

"He was travelling with his nephew. We saw a good deal of him," pursued Mr. Seymour, "I am inclined to think the man is in earnest. Those sort of fellows always rush to extremes, you know. 'The greater the sinner the greater the saint,' is the old proverb, and it must always be the case; but, at all events, he is now quite harmless, which is so far an improvement upon his former condition."

"Yes. I quite agree with you there. After

all, these conversions from one extreme to another show no change of human nature, but simply an altered taste and pursuit. The real conversion would be if you could transform an intemperate into a moderate man."

"Yes, indeed," replied the other, "that would be a miracle!"

The drawing-room looked very desolate. There were the forsaken piano and the dusty music-books piled upon the stand. Montagu had only once been at Dorrington in days gone by, but he had seen sufficient to feel that it had become like the body which the spirit has abandoned. Where were the songs and laughter which once echoed through its saloons and halls? Where the life and centre of all its festive merriment—the charades—the excursions—the music—the literature—the art—the philosophy enshrined in wit—the nightly dances and continual pastimes—where were they? A vacuum was what remained. It was utter dreariness, but, still more desolate than all, was the heart of the deserted mother!

"Are you now going back to Thornwood?" enquired Mrs. Seymour.

"Not immediately. I shall remain in London."

"You know that my daughter is—is settled in London," she pursued, in an undertone: "she is interested in a sisterhood of nurses for the sick. I don't know whether you have heard."

"Yes," replied Montagu, overcoming a momentary surprise at being attacked upon such a subject: "I remember her telling me of her intended scheme, but I never thought she would live there herself."

"Oh, indeed! Then she told you about it?" said Mrs. Seymour, eagerly jumping at anything concerning her child.

"She only said that she was much interested in an establishment of the kind, and, I must say that, I highly approve of such societies under proper regulations and restrictions. The plan she described to me appeared admirable. I did not suppose, from what she said, that she would do more than superintend it, as it were, from without."

"It did not go on so well until she took it in hand."

"But does she intend to remain long?"

Mrs. Seymour could not repress a sigh as she replied :

" I fear—I fancy some time."

The mother longed to say much more. She could have wished to interest the man who had once touched her daughter's imagination, fancying that it might yet be within his power to win her affections, but eloquence seemed to have deserted her.

"Surely she will return—the piano, the room, the whole place requires the presence of its divinity. It looks like a deserted shrine."

M 5

He spoke lightly though feelingly, but it was more than the mother could endure, and she turned to conceal a tear, and made an excuse to escape to her solitude.

Cecil Montagu felt ill at ease in his room. It came across him more than once that he had been the cause of all the desolation which he beheld.

"After all," thought he, "how beautiful, how divine was that Elsie, whose heart might have been mine for ever and all this sorrow spared!"

He rose early from his couch and went out into the grounds, endeavouring to fix his thoughts upon other objects, but he could not help recurring to the preceding autumn at Thornwood and wishing that it could be effaced from his existence. He walked long and, mistaking the breakfast hour, came in late. He looked forward with a certain dread to encountering once more the melancholy and soured faces of his good host and hostess, for however praise-worthy to share the grief of others, it is not amusing.

With trepidation he entered the dining-room and, to his surprise, found them both looking exceedingly cheerful and scarcely aware of his prolonged absence. He was suf-ficiently struck with the change to feel con-vinced that they must have had some good news, but he vainly endeavoured to discover what it was, until just before his departure, when alone with Mrs. Seymour in the library.

It was a letter, and ran thus:

"*House of Mercy, Bloomsbury,*
"— *June*, 18—

" MY DEAR FATHER,

" I would not lose a post and must, therefore, beg you to excuse the hasty manner in which I am forced to scribble

this note.   One of my greatest failings, dearest
father, and I am sure I have many, is pride. It
is well that I should occasionally be humbled
and I confess that I have been so to-day, for
there can be no greater humiliation than to be
made sensible of our faults.   I have discovered
that during the last six or eight months, I have,
in direct opposition to all precept, preferred
sacrifice to mercy, as well as overlooking my
positive duty to my friends.   I have done
wrong and I wish to make amends.   I almost
feel like the returning prodigal.   I must go
back to my father's house (to the old room and
forsaken piano) and ask him to forgive my
error !   I do not doubt but that I shall be as
well received as the son for whom the fatted calf
was killed.   Tell my own dear mother how
penitent I feel to-day and how I long to be
once more in her arms.   I must not take the
praise of my repentance ; I have seen Her-
bert Lisle who urged me strongly to this
course !

" Mamma said in her last letter that you both talk of coming to London. In that case may I remain here to organise a system until you return to Dorrington ?

" With best love to both of you, your own affectionately attached child,

"ELSIE SEYMOUR."

Montagu returned to London. If he had not owed allegiance to Katharine his thoughts might have been concentrated upon Elsie; but he felt more than ever convinced that Miss Elliott was in all respects suited to afford him that domestic happiness, for which he sometimes pined in secret and which he fancied that he could never enjoy so perfectly with any other upon earth.

He hastened to seek Frank but, to his disappointment, found that he had left town. The fortunate lover had gone to Lockwood to communicate his sudden bliss to Lady Elliott and his sister.

Cecil determined to spend the interval of his absence, in completing what he considered an act of justice to one who had repaid his former generosity by loving him too well.

BOOK SIXTH.

———

THE CONCLUSION.

CHAPTER I.

THE VILLAGE FEAST.

HERBERT LISLE was a great advocate for popular recreations and, for many years, had endeavoured to expand the school tea-drinking into something like a general holiday, but, upon the present occasion, he had combined it with a religious festival which was also that of the dedication of Cawthorne Church and thus, it came to pass that the peasantry were assembled around the Court to do honour to Midsummer-day.

The curate, Mr. Penrose, was zealous in the cause and, even Mr. Drislow showed more enthusiasm than could have been expected. All the farmers' families were persuaded, not

only to attend themselves but, to give a general
holiday to their servants and labourers, by
which means, the whole parish was congregated
upon the lawn in front of the old gabled
mansion.

Mary and Laura were both present, but
Edward had been unable to get away from his
parish in time. Herbert had, however, at length
succeeded, through Laura's instrumentality, in
inducing his uncle and aunt from Carrowsby
to pay him a visit, to meet Mary and their grand-
children.

The preparations had been commenced some
days before.   Tents were pitched upon the lawn.
May-poles, swings, see-saws, whirlabouts, and
various other contrivances for the amusement
of the children were scattered in all directions.
The villagers, who availed themselves of this
fête as an opportunity to welcome their new
landlord into his domain, had erected floral
arches in the lane, and had ornamented their
cottage gates with devices and leafy embellish-

ments. The lych-gate was gay with festoons and the interior of the sacred building had been decorated under the auspices of the curate.

A good deal of restoration had been effected since the preceding autumn, open seats having been substituted for pews, the unsightly tripartite edifice removed, and other improvements made in the chancel. That portion of the interior was still farther beautified by the introduction of stained windows, in memory of Herbert's father and mother. We mention this, because, in addition to the services of the holiday, the village festival commenced with a most auspicious event, which tended more completely to enlist the sympathies of all, on the happy occasion.

It was a bright and lovely June morning. The flowers perfumed the air with their fragrance, and the bees from the cottage hives were pursuing their busy task. Herbert and his cousins were waiting near the porch as the stable clock struck eight. Already a little

party of villagers had passed the lych-gate
and were wending towards the church, among
whom were Phœbe in her bridal attire and
William Perdon in a spick and span new suit
of clothes.   Old Dolby, in a clean smock, hob-
bling upon his crutches, and his wife, with her
best black bonnet and coloured shawl, leaning
upon William's arm, were almost foremost in
the throng and, in the rear, was a remarkable-
looking female in a plain print dress, with a
veil drawn over her face and the two children
by her side.   The widow had yielded to Phœbe's
request to be present at her wedding.

These were not all.   The villagers of Caw-
thorne were not indifferent to the event.   The
children came from every cottage to see their
worthy pedagogue married to their new school-
mistress ; and even Mrs. Welbourne, decked in
her Sunday best, and Mrs. Wales, whose truant
son was said to be improving at the S. Ni-
cholas Refuge, were among the spectators of
the event.

The bride was still pale from the effects of her recent illness, but William had fancied he could perhaps nurse her better than anybody else, and she was not disinclined to try the experiment.

The Lisles greeted the couple very warmly and accompanied them into the church, which was bright with floral decorations. The curate met them and concluded the sacred rite with the holiest act of Christian worship. After receiving the congratulations of all, the bride and bridegroom returned to the school and reposed before the various rejoicings in which they were expected to take part.

" You look pale, Phœbe," said William, " I almost think you should stay quiet here, *at home*, and not do too much. I fear you will be too much fatigued, my Phœbe !"

" I am so happy, William ! I feel quite strong now."

" You worked too hard. You did too much."

"Oh! don't say so, William! I would have worked ten times as hard to have won this."

"Say that again, my Phœbe! It was a poor prize for such self-denying hard work; but I will strive to make thee happy, and to be worthy of thee, my own wedded bride."

"A *poor* prize, William? a *poor* prize? *this home* and thy fond heart! Oh! I am too happy —so happy that I can't believe God Almighty will let it last. It seems like a dream. A short time ago I was all alone upon a bed of sickness, but that was better than the toil that came before, when I could only bear that dull, smoky room by thinking of dear Cawthorne and of you. And now it is all like sunshine, and I am in his arms—in William's arms!" And she burst into a flood of tears, the effect of the excitement upon her weakened nerves.

*   *   *   *   *

The farmers dined in one great tent and

their labourers in another, while their ladies paraded up and down in all their blaze of ribbons to do honour to the day.

The Greens were conspicuous among the guests. The yeoman with the moustaches, having kept his heart unscathed, was an object of general admiration and sympathy with the fair sex. The two Miss Greens were no less fortunate in attracting the attentions of the gentlemen. Letitia was fond of children and was an adept at superintending their games, especially when aided in the task by some eccentric youth of maturer age.

The spectators of the *fête* were not limited to the immediate friends of the Lisles or the parochial magnates, but included reinforcements from the neighbourhood, to which Winfield furnished its quota. Matthew Beakham had consented to attend and Mr. Butterworth and his family had, like all their neighbours, availed themselves of the joyous occasion.

In one direction there was a cricket match,

in another a quintain, and various other old
English games; in a third dances, in which
the farmers' ladies were conspicuous. Herbert
had taken care that every villager and farm-
servant should be regaled with a good dinner,
for our countrymen require that foundation to
their hilarity, and they were thus prepared
heartily to enjoy the subsequent games and
merry-makings.

The schoolmaster and his bride, partly owing
to her recent fever and partly to avoid observa-
tion, had shrunk from appearing in the grounds
until a late hour. His absence had, neverthe-
less, not prevented his health being drunk in
the dining-tents where much laughter had
been caused by the supposed reasons given for
his non-appearance. When, at length, he
slunk timidly on to the grounds, accompanied
by his blushing bride and anxiously hoping
not to be noticed, some merciless wag called
speedy attention to the fact, and, far and wide,

the cheer of welcome rang through the grounds of Cawthorne.

"Once again. One cheer more," and so on, until poor Phœbe felt ready to sink into the earth and devoutly wished herself back in her little cottage.

"Well, well!" said the stately Matthew Beakham, when he heard the cheer and had turned to Mrs. Baring and her mother to enquire the cause, "what's all this? what have we got here?"

"I think it must be the bride and bridegroom," returned Mary.

"Well, well! ha! indeed! bless me! who is that? when was she married?"

"The schoolmaster married a girl in the village, Phœbe Elton, who has been at the training school and is to be the schoolmistress."

"Ha! ha! Phœbe Elton? well, well! I should know her name."

"She is a grand-daughter of old Dolby's."

"Dolby! Ah, yes—gets three and four-pence a week from the board, or used to do! Know him by name. Well, well! Phœbe Elton, let me see?"

"Here comes Herbert," replied Mary Baring, "he will be able to tell you more about it."

"What is that?" he enquired.

"Mr. Beakham was asking me about the bride, Phœbe Elton that was."

"Don't you remember, Beakham," said Herbert, "that affair last autumn, of some clothes stolen by two boys, where Phœbe was falsely accused and in which the schoolmaster took a prominent part?"

"Ay! bless me! well, well; and she is married now to the schoolmaster; ah! well, well!"

"It took place this morning."

"Yes, yes! and I'm told that scamp (per-haps, however, I ought not to call him so) that young fellow, who didn't show very well, I thought, on the occasion you refer to, that Mr. Johnson, clerk you know to our friend Butterworth, has set up as a solicitor somewhere in the south and has made a very good start, so Butterworth tells me. Here he comes, let us ask him."

Herbert would gladly have escaped, for he knew that whenever the justice got upon magisterial topics an extra amount of patience was required. There seemed, however, to be no option. Mr. Butterworth was summoned to the conference and both were victimised.

" Alfred Johnson ?" rejoined Butterworth, when he had heard the question, "quite right ! I heard from him only yesterday ; he has been very successful, canvassing for your cousin, for Lord Lisle, won him the election at Luxbridge, and my Lord is so delighted that he has appointed him his principal agent. Likely to get on now, clever fellow, always thought so ; sure to make his way."

" Agent to Lord Lisle !" said Herbert. " Why what took him to Luxbridge ?"

" His father had some interest there and thought there was an opening, asked my advice, you know, and I thought it seemed a likely place enough, and he set him up and started him. I intended to have applied to you for an introduction to the Earl of Portaldowne, but, finding he got a retainer from my lord, I did not think it necessary to trouble you."

Herbert had no fancy to hear more particulars about one whose antecedents were so distasteful to him. He had not seen much of his cousin the Earl, but had been invited to more than one house in the neighbourhood of Luxbridge, and something in the name seemed to act as a spell upon his fancy.

There was a magnificent old elm in the park, beneath the boughs of which seats had been placed for such of the old people as chose to look on at the games and dances. Towards this spot Herbert directed his course as soon as he could escape from his Winfield friends. He found Laura already there, conversing with old John and Sally Dolby, while the newly-married couple were seated close by, too much busied in each other to heed the scene around them.

"I have not seen her," said Laura.

"No, Miss. Our Ann bain't come. She be keepin' house for we at home I 'xpects. Her little ones be here though. They be playin' along with the children yonder—enjoyin' themselves, I make no doubt."

"I am sorry Mrs. Arnstein is not come."

"May be it's better not," said old Sally, shaking her head oracularly, "ye know she bayn't quite the like o' we. She ha' been a fine lady like, and more's the pity, but she might n't bring herself to be stared and looked at—might she?"

"No!" returned John nodding his head, and fancying he had been addressed.

"Yes, I think she is right not to come, perhaps," rejoined Laura.

"Why, if it bayn't the squire!" exclaimed Sally, as Herbert approached.

"Ah! Be it?" said John.

Herbert shook hands with the old people and asked after the widow Arnstein, informing them that he was anxious to have some conversation with her.

His time had been so entirely taken up ever since his visit to Wiltshire, that he had not been able to question her upon the circumstances discussed at Lockwood, upon which he was desirous of obtaining farther information.

"She was at the wedding?" he enquired.

"Yes sure! I told her the squire be sure to see her."

"And won't she come here?"

"She be fearful to come among so many."

In the meanwhile Laura had addressed herself to the newly married couple.

She had only arrived late on the previous evening with her sister Mary, and had found no opportunities for conversation with Herbert. Indeed very few words had passed between them since we lost sight of them at West-

Langton. She had been much struck by her cousin's altered appearance. It might not have been noticed by a casual observer but there are some eyes which can read deeper than others and some watchful hearts which can guess the hidden sorrow. She knew that he had been in London, and earnestly longed to probe his secret grief. She was pleased, therefore, when after joining in her discourse with the Perdons, he said:

"Laura! Where are you going? I want to show you an opening I think of making."

She felt overjoyed at the idea of being consulted about the place, and at the prospect of a walk with Herbert.

Unfortunately, at that very moment, a footman came in search of his master.

"A gentleman is waiting and wants particularly to see you, sir. He gave me this card, sir."

"Where is he?"

"Walking in the grounds, sir."

" I will come to him."

And poor Laura's walk was deferred.

The stranger was one whose whole appearance offered a striking contrast to that of Herbert Lisle. His beautiful Grecian face beaming with vivacity and intelligence combined with a tall and graceful figure, were such as to please at first sight, but there was also much in the simple candour and earnestness of Herbert's expression, as well as in his manly address, to win the admiration of his guest.

" Mr. Montagu !" said Herbert making himself known.

"I have taken the liberty of thus introducing myself to you," replied Cecil, " and I fear I must have selected rather an inconvenient moment, but my object is to find out a person in your village of the name of Arnstein, formerly Ann Dolby."

"I will take you to her. I have already heard of all your kindness in befriending her. It is singular that at the very moment when your card was brought me I was talking to her old parents under yonder tree, and the thought had occurred to me to go and see her in order to discover some particulars about— in short about yourself."

" About me ?" exclaimed Montagu. " Why what in the world could induce you to take such an interest in my fate ?"

" Well it does sound strange considering that we have never met until now !" said Herbert, " but it strikes me that we must have many mutual friends."

" The Seymours, for instance !" returned Montagu. " I am just come from them. By the bye your cousin, Lord Lisle, beat me by a morjority of three votes at Luxbridge the other day."

" Ah yes ! and I am sorry to hear that he employed a dreadful scamp as his agent ; one Johnson, who was for sometime in this neigh- bourhood, and behaved very ill."

N 5

" I heard of him and was told that Lord Lisle was indebted to him for his election."

" No credit to him! I am sorry to hear it. But I think we must have some other mutual aquaintances," said Herbert "do you know the Elliotts ?"

" Yes.　Have you met them lately ?" enquired Montagu with considerable interest.

" I met them a fortnight ago or more, at Lockwood."

" That is Mr. Elliott's, I think ?"

" Exactly, and I was reminded of it by your coming to enquire for the widow Arnstein, for curiously enough, our conversation there turned upon that very subject."

Cecil Montagu, who took care to veil his anxiety for farther information under a tone of indifference, felt, nevertheless, that his journey would be more than amply repaid by the discoveries he was about to make.　During the above conversation they had been pacing up and down the terrace, when Herbert invited his guest into the house to partake of some refreshment.

"And I hope," he added, " you will take up your quarters here. You have brought your luggage, I trust ?"

" I left it at the station."

" I'll send for it. You must sleep here to night at all events, and I hope you will stay longer."

Montagu found himself unable to refuse the invitation for the night. He was delighted with the old Tudor mansion and its finely timbered park, enlivened by the presence of the festive crowd. Never was there a more complete contrast of style than between his own Pompeïan Villa, and this antiquated gothic structure, but he was fully able to appreciate the beauties of each and to acknowledge their various excellences. After conducting him into the dining-room for luncheon, Herbert proposed that they should proceed to the cottage and see the widow. He felt that, as long as Laura was there to superintend the games, there was no immediate necessity for his remaining.

Some time elapsed before Montagu saw a fitting opportunity to renew his enquiries about the Elliotts. He did not feel certain whether Lisle might be aware of the engagement which had existed between Katharine and himself. It is possible that some rumour of it may have reached Herbert for, after naming them it had suddenly occurred to him that there was some reason or other why he ought not to have done so, but any particulars which he might have heard had completely vanished from his memory.

"You must have met Frank Elliott in your travels?" said Montagu after a pause.

"Yes, but I have known them all for some years."

"His mother was abroad for sometime with her daughters," continued Montagu.

"I knew them first in Italy," returned Lisle.

"They where staying with me in the Autumn and that reminds me," pursued Cecil, "that Miss Elliott must have encountered this poor creature whom we are going to see, in my grounds. She came and stationed herself in a cottage near my property, and was accustomed, day after day, to wander through my shrubberies and walks. You must remind me to tell you her history. Perhaps you have heard a portion of it?"

"I heard her own account of it," replied Herbert, "from the superintendent of the Penitentiary at Beesleigh where I placed her, after her return from Italy."

"Did you meet her in Italy?" asked Montagu.

"Yes, immediately after the death of her husband."

" Exactly. I will tell you presently what I have done; but, before we go into the cottage, pray inform me whether Miss Elliott happened to mention meeting this poor woman at Thornwood."

" Yes, I think she did, but the way in which the conversation originated was through the governess at Mr. Elliott's, a Madame Hoffner—a German woman, whom you must know ?"

" Is that so ? And you saw Madame Hoffner ?"

" Yes, and, strange to say, when I defended the manner in which you have befriended poor Ann Dolby (for 1 cannot help calling her by her old name) she grew furious," pursued Herbert laughing. " I am afraid you must be in her bad books !"

" I wonder how I have offended her ?" said Montagu, joining in his laugh.

" I can't make it out," continued Lisle in the same merry tone, " but she declared, in

her wrath, 'that she would be revenge on you.'
By the way, I think, as far as I could discover,
her indignation was, in some measure, owing to
your having made use of a person of her ancestral
pride and dignity to act duenna to a peasant's
daughter. She said she could never overlook
such an insult."

"Then I am afraid she has revenged herself
by endeavouring to innoculate the Elliotts with
her views ?"

"She has certainly not succeeded there ;
at least I know that the young lady was most
warm in your defence."

This was, perhaps, as much as he required
to hear, for, having approached the cottage
gate, Montagu proposed that they should go
in and see the widow. Herbert knocked at
the door without receiving a reply, and upon
endeavouring to raise the latch found that it
was locked. Upon looking through the win-
dow he could see nothing but the empty kitchen
and could hear no sounds, but the vibrations

of the pendulum of the old clock. The neigh-
bouring cottages were likewise closed, and
they both came to the conclusion that she
must have yielded to the temptation to go
forth and join in the universal festivity.

Herbert returned to the Park by a different
road in order to vary the walk and, perhaps,
to impress his guest with a favourable notion of
the village and of his place. Proceeding along
the lane he conducted him through a small
gate into one of those wild woodland paths
which were among the chief beauties of Caw-
thorne. Mention has already been made of
these walks and rides, winding through forest
scenes among the extensive woods skirting the
deer-park. The latter seemed to merge almost
imperceptibly from open glade, carpetted with
fern, into plantation thickened by dense under-
growth. Passing through the tufted brush-
wood, they suddenly came upon a vista afford-
ing a glimpse of the old mansion and the groups
of revellers congregated in all directions around

it.   The opening, through which they obtained
this prospect also commanded a view of some
fine trees, among others an oak remarkable for
its size and picturesque effect.   Seated beneath
its branches was a female, whose back was
turned to them.   She appeared to be engaged
in singing while she contemplated the gay
scene.   A few of her words only could be dis-
tinguished.

SONG.

Dost thou ask me to sing a bridal-song,
   Of a Bridal far away,
Where the sun shone bright on the joyous throng,
   Which chaunted their roundelay ?

I remember a Bridal there
   In the long, long, time ago,
I remember the perfumed air,
   Of the land where citrons grow !

And balmy the breeze of that vernal,
   Which ever encircled my home,
When I dwelt in the City Eternal,
   As proud as a daughter of Rome !

I remember the joys of my Bridal !
  O teach me, my God, to forget !
And instruct this poor heart where to hide all
Its sorrows, and each vain regret.

They listened attentively for some min-
utes.

"She raves less than formerly," said Herbert
doubtingly, " but do you think it safe for us to
see her without our first ascertaining her con-
dition ?   I fancied she had given up this im-
provising which always appeared to me like a
symptom of her madness."

"She always sang, in her best times," re-
turned Montagu.

"However," replied Herbert, "if you have
a doubt we can ask Penrose the curate, who
will be sure to know.   To tell you the truth,
I am only lately returned home and have not
yet seen her."

"I am willing to risk it," rejoined Cecil ;
"her song is not that of a mad woman.   Let

us approach and see whether she recognizes me."

Montagu led the way, and they drew near the spot where she sat, without being observed until they were actually beneath the shadow of the tree.

The widow, who had now adopted a dress of the simplest character, only turned when they were close at hand, and almost instantly rose from her position upon the ground. Whether she recognized Montagu until she had risen to face them, they could not discover, but, at all events, she saw him then, and giving a sudden start, bent down her eyes upon the ground, and raised her hand to her forehead. She remained in this posture for more than a minute.

"We have been in search of you," said Herbert, "we went to the cottage and found it closed."

"I am come expressly to bring you some information, which will be of the greatest advantage to your children," pursued Montagu. "I am just come from Munich, where I have been to assert their rights to Arnstein's property. They have inherited a considerable patrimony."

"Oh! Mr. Allardyce—I mean—"

"Call me Allardyce, and forgive me my apparent harshness at Thornwood."

This seemed to bewilder her, and Montagu thought it better to proceed in another key:

"You must not allow your children—Arnstein's heirs—to be neglected. Their father's family is one of note in Bavaria, and I am sure his works are worthy of the name he bore. You must go to Munich. I have endeavoured to pave the way for you, in order that you and your children may be well received by the family. You will meet Steinbock there, who will present you to your husband's relations."

"Oh! Mr. Lisle!" said the widow, who appeared scarcely to have noticed Herbert until that moment, and whose voice, in addressing him, rather assumed the tones of Ann Dolby, the villager, than of the lady, Madame Arnstein; "what is to be done, if I leave my poor old father and mother? I intended to stay with them until they died. What do you think I ought to do?"

"You can return," said Herbert, "Phœbe will look after them in the meantime."

"But Phœbe is married and has left the cottage now, and the poor old people have not a soul to attend to them, if I go."

"Let us talk to them, and to Phœbe," suggested Herbert.

"And thank you, Mr. Allardyce, from my heart I thank you, for your kindness to me, a kindness totally unmerited, and which I can never forget."

Ann spoke these words in a voice of deep feeling, which rather alarmed Montagu, at the moment, but he soon perceived, from her constrained and bashful manner, that she was entirely free from her former symptoms.

Herbert persuaded her to accompany them towards the elm, beneath which the old Dolbys and the Perdons were seated. As they approached the spot, he went forward to prepare them for her coming. Montagu availed himself of the opportunity to address her.

" Do you remember all that has passed ?"

" No—not all.

" Do you remember Thornwood ?"

" Thornwood !"

" Do you remember me—Allardyce ?"

" Yes—yes—indeed."

" And your cottage, in Surrey ?"

" Oh, yes !"

" And your return there ?"

" My return where ?"

" To Surrey !"

" When ?"

" Lately—last year."

" Last year ?"

" You came to Thornwood, to find Allardyce."

" Ah, yes ! Did I ?"

" And you met a young lady in a wood—in the glen at Thornwood ?"

" No—I remember nothing," she replied, with a sigh.

" You don't remember ?"

" No—nothing—nothing ! I don't wish to remember anything."

" Do you remember singing songs ?"

" I often sing."

" Do you remember Madame Hoffner ?"

" Madame Hoffner ! Oh, yes !"

" She has been spreading reports to injure me."

" Madame Hoffner ! For what reason ?"

" I cannot imagine her object. But she has injured me. She has employed your name, and endeavoured to blast your reputation, for the sole purpose of inflicting injury upon me. Wherefore she should do it I cannot tell; but it is in *your* power alone to restore my fame, and to undo the evil she has done. Will you do it?"

"Oh, Mr. Allardyce! How can you ask me? Tell me what to do and I will do it."

"I want you simply to tell those whom she has misled, the tale of your life and the share which I have had in it. She has made them believe that I have been your evil genius."

"You, Mr. Allardyce! Oh, let me go and tell them my tale. Where are they? Let me tell them who has been my best, best, friend."

"You shall. You shall see them before you go to Germany, if I can so contrive it."

During this conversation, Montagu had diverged from the path which they had been pursuing, and had inclined in another direction. Finding they delayed to follow him, Herbert now came in pursuit, and shortly afterwards presented Montagu to the old Dolbys.

With his accustomed ease and elasticity of manner, he addressed himself to the aged couple as well as to the Perdons, so as to make them feel perfectly at home in his society. He introduced the subject of Arnstein's inheritance, and easily convinced the poor people that it was for their daughter's interest to start for Munich. Phœbe immediately offered to supply her place if her husband would permit it, and it was finally agreed that, during Ann's absence, the schoolmaster and his bride were to take up their quarters in the Dolbys' cottage.

While they were thus engaged, Laura came to inform her cousin that he was wanted to open the grand country dance. He introduced her to Cecil Montagu, who having vainly attempted to persuade her to join, accompanied his host, in hopes of finding some more willing partner.

VOL. III. o

The festivities continued until a late hour, and, long after the music had ceased, voices might be heard in the park and merry laughter resounded from the village lane.

CHAPTER II.

COUNSELS OF PERFECTION.

LISLE and Montagu had appeared, to any casual spectator, well suited to each other, and the contrast, offered by their characters, was perhaps, such as to ensure a good understanding upon first acquaintance.

Having accomplished the object of his journey, Cecil was anxious to lose no time in returning to London, in order, if possible, to achieve that reconciliation which seemed destined to form a bright era in his future life. His visit to Cawthorne had proved far more successful than he could possibly have anticipated, since, in addition to the primary object which he had had in view, he had almost satisfied himself

o 3

as to the fact that Katharine still loved him, and that she, at all events, did not doubt his honour. He remembered her solemn words at Thornwood, and felt almost convinced that she must have kept her word, and must have continued, amid good and evil report, to " trust him with all her heart, and without reserve."

He started from Cawthorne to meet an early train, leaving all the party enchanted with his easy and agreeable manners.

The Lisles of Carrowsby proposed remaining until the following day. Mrs. Lisle was too delighted with an opportunity of seeing something of her daughter Mary and her grandchildren, to tear herself away sooner than was absolutely necessary and, as Miss Pinsant was at home to take care of the house and deal out dry cake and sour wine to any chance visitors, she might feel perfectly satisfied upon that score.

After Cecil Montagu's departure the family party were assembled in the library. Herbert's uncle was always delighted to find himself at the old place where he had spent the happiest days of his life, those hours of childhood when the world seemed to lie before him like a vast field for romantic adventure, teeming with bright visions which, when pursued in after days, had fled farther and farther, until like "the bird in the story," they "bore the fair gem away."

Herbert found his uncle bent upon a visit to some of the older tenants, and offered to meet him in the afternoon, to accompany him to the more distant farms.

"I have some letters to write and one or two people to see," said Herbert, addressing Laura, who was standing in the oriel window, "and then I shall be delighted if you would come and see the opening of which I told you yesterday; or," he added, in a lower tone, "hear what I have to say."

Her heart fluttered and her cheek flushed as

she accepted his invitation, but he did not appear conscious of having excited any vain hopes, and returned to his affairs.

The elder Mr. Lisle, with his wife and daughter Mary, went out upon the terrace to enjoy the lovely day. Laura had been invited to accompany them, but did not appear. She was too much absorbed in the prospect of her walk with her cousin, and too fearful lest she should be out of the way when he was ready for her.

Poor Laura! Religious as she undoubtedly was, her heart was not closed to the woman's dreams, or blunted to the woman's cravings. She worked hard among the poor and was earnest in her work, but there was still, at times, the feeling of the mission unaccomplished, the vacuum unfilled. Perhaps she had not yet been perfected by trial, since she still clung to earthly hopes!

When her father and mother walked out with

Mary and the children, she retired to her room, and returning, after a time, in her bonnet and shawl, patiently awaited Herbert.

"Oh, my dear Laura! I am afraid I have kept you waiting!" he exclaimed as he re-entered the apartment, "the fact is, I have a good deal of business to settle upon coming home. I must work hard to get it done during the next few days, before I go away."

"Going away? Why where are you going now?"

"Will you come for a walk, and I will tell you all about it. It is a long story, and I am anxious to tell it you, Laura."

She felt rather less hopeful as she accompanied her cousin into the shrubbery walks and followed the direction which, in former days, he loved to pursue when bent upon meditation; the same which he had taken soon after his father's death, when he had heard the song of the mad woman in the wood.

"Laura!" he said, "the reason that I select

you as my *confidante* is, that I believe you will
not judge with the world's judgment. What
I am about to disclose to you requires to be
weighed in the balances of the sanctuary.
Will you promise me to endeavour so to see
it?"

"Herbert! Oh yes; but am I suffi-
ciently clever and learned to give you an
opinion, if it is a question of religion?" re-
turned Laura, perplexed, and not without a
self-conscious feeling of her own latent aspi-
rations.

"No, no. You shall hear my story. Of
course, it is in confidence."

"Of course. I promise never to disclose
what you tell me."

"Well. You remember I told you about Miss
Seymour when we were at West-Langton?"

"Yes," and Laura's heart sank within her.

"I told you that she was striving after, and
approaching better things. I have seen her
again, and I almost think she has attained

them. She seems so changed and purified—so like a saint."

"Is she still bent upon the sisterhood?"

"Completely! at least, if she could pursue her vocation without trenching upon her duty to her parents. They are old and, being an only child, she will, I fancy, determine not to be long absent from them in future."

"That will interfere with the sisterhood?"

"No, I think not! I feel convinced that a way will be opened for her to pursue the good work which she has begun and which, I am sure, she will never abandon."

The quicksilver of Laura's heart began to rise.

"Then do you fancy that if anything should happen to her parents, she would resume her vocation as a sister of mercy?"

"I don't suppose she will ever abandon it," returned Herbert.

"Unless she marries, I suppose?"

o 5

"I feel convinced she never will."

"Then you mean that all the while she remains at home she will be a sister of mercy at heart?"

"Yes. Oh, Laura! I wish you knew her," said Herbert, who felt a chill in her manner which discouraged him from proceeding as he had intended.

There was a pause, which perhaps led Laura to perceive that she had not allured him to open his heart in confidence.

"But tell me, Herbert, what is the story which you promised me?" she said at length.

"I can tell you in two words. She is pursuing the counsels of perfection. Born an heiress, she has forsaken lands and domestic ties, in order to follow her Lord and to win the heavenly treasure. She has hearkened to the Master's call, and what is more, she has persuaded me to do the same."

"To do the same? why what do you mean, Herbert?"

" To obey the call, and follow Him, who had not where to lay his head."

" What call ?"

" A thrilling call which I could not mistake."

" Addressed to you ?"

" Through her lips."

" Was that a call from God ? Remember that you occupy a station and have plain duties to fulfil.   What do you propose ?"

" Not to act rashly. I shall consult Baring."

" I don't understand you now," said Laura, " I cannot see your end or object ?"

"To become a clergyman in order to be chaplain to her sisterhood."

"And what is to become of Cawthorne ?" asked Laura : " Papa will be wretched when he hears of your intention. Poor dear old Cawthorne ! do tell me what you propose doing ?"

" *There* is the difficulty, what sort of person is Lord Lisle ?"

"Are you actually thinking of making it over to him ? Herbert, you must consider well about this. Remember the influence which God has given you for good, among your tenants and neighbours, in a thousand ways. I am sure Edward will never give his approval. It seems to me quite shocking !"

"Oh Laura ! Is that what you would have said if you had known those saints who have followed the divine counsels. Remember the words : 'when he heard this he was very sorrowful, for he was very rich.' I was meditating upon it this morning."

"But that young ruler was called; distinctly called," said Laura in a hesitating voice.

"And how are people ever called now-a-days unless it be by such an unmistakeable vocation as mine. She said plainly that I was the adviser she required for her sisterhood, and I felt at the moment, as distinctly as possible, that I was bidden to pursue the same self-denying path which she has marked out. I have thought it over since, again and again, and am persuaded that it is a call from God. In short, dear Laura, unless I could be convinced that I am in error, which is, I feel, certainly not the case, I am resolved to follow it."

"Dear Herbert—I don't know what to say! You seem resolved—It appears useless to consult Edward or any one else unless you will listen to their reasons. It is possible you may be right, but my own impression is that you would do wrong to abandon your post here, upon anything so vague as what you tell me."

Herbert remained silent and Laura felt depressed. He had not spoken to her in the tone of one seeking advice, but as if he had made up his mind, and she felt that he had actually done so.

"I suppose, dear Laura, your objections are those which others will also urge. The fact is that now-a-days so few pursue the counsels

of perfection, that men have ceased to acknow-
ledge that if we would be perfect we must give
up all and follow Christ."

She did not reply and they proceeded for
some distance in silence.

" Where is Mr. Winslow?" she said, at
length, as a means of reviving their conver-
sation.

" I left him in London. I almost wish he
had been here yesterday to meet Mr. Montagu,
but he would not come to the *fête*."

" What is he going to do?"

" It is his greatest anxiety to be ordained
deacon."

" Why should not he become chaplain to
Miss Seymour's sisterhood?"

"The very thing she suggested, when she
hinted that she should prefer me."

" He is much better suited in age, to such a
task."

" I am not too young, Laura!" he returned
smiling.

"May I venture to ask you, dear Herbert, whether if any other than Miss Seymour were the superior of this sisterhood, you would have considered such a task to be your vocation?"

This question was the suggestion of that feminine tact which jealousy had heightened to a more acute perception of the truth.

"What nonsense, Laura," he rejoined somewhat hastily, "do you suppose that if this call proceeds from God, it could not, just as well, have came in some other form. For instance might I not have been called to go forth as a missionary, to New Zealand or the Cape?"

She said no more upon the subject, and Herbert changed the discourse to other themes, merely observing, as they entered the house :

"Remember your promise not to disclose what I have told you."

The Lisles of Carrowsby left upon the following day, and Herbert found himself alone in the ancestral mansion. He asked Penrose to dine with him, and received a satisfactory account of his parochial labours. The curate gave him a pleasing impression of the widow Arnstein, whose restored health and sincere penitence promised well for the future.

Herbert found much occupation in looking over the accounts and transacting business relating to the property. This detained him rather longer than he had intended, and delayed his proposed visit to West-Langton. During this time his thoughts were much occupied with his resolve, and he spent many hours in meditating upon it.

One evening he went into the church, and soon found that he was not alone in the building. A female form was kneeling not far off, in whom he recognised the widow Arnstein.

He lingered about the porch until she came out, anxious to ask her when she was going to Munich.

"Good evening, sir," she said, in answer to his salutation.

"When are you going to set off upon your journey?"

She drew a breath as she replied :

"Oh, sir, I have been praying about it. I wish I knew how to act !"

"What do you mean?"

"I dread leaving my old home."

"Remember your children."

"There it is. If it were not for them I should not hesitate."

"I think you ought to go for their sakes."

"So they all tell me, sir. I have had a kind letter to-day from Mr. Montagu, begging me to visit his house in Surrey on my way. I have promised this."

"When shall you start?"

"If I am to go, I ought not to delay."

"To-morrow?"

"Or the day after," she said, with a sigh of which Herbert felt the deep reality. "It is so

sad," she pursued, "to leave dear old Caw-
thorne again. I hoped I was stationed here for
ever."

After he had parted from her, these words
continued to haunt him, and when he looked
at the old gray church and the glorious Tudor
mansion, it came forcibly across his mind that
it would be a terrible trial indeed to leave
Cawthorne, dear old Cawthorne, perhaps for
ever !

As the day of his departure approached,
the terror of his resolve seemed to increase
upon him. The night before he started he was
unable to sleep, and rising, paced up and
down his room and along the corridor, battling
with his feelings. It was a terrible struggle,
as terrible as the legendary conflicts of saints
with the powers of evil, but he contended
valiantly and came off victorious. His head
ached violently as he drove away from
the old court, down the long avenue of elms,

and through the village with its neat cottages.
He concealed his sensations heroically, and
bowed graciously to the villagers, who saluted
him as he passed along the lane.

Mary Baring had been persuaded to accompany her mother to Carrowsby, and had taken
her children with her, so that Edward was
alone at his vicarage.

This was an advantage to Herbert, who was
able freely to open his heart to his cousin.

When he had listened to his story, and
had heard his resolution, Edward said :

" Well, Herbert—I am not surprised at
your feelings. It will take some time for you
to be ordained a priest   Who is to be Miss Seymour's chaplain in the interim ?"

" The very question I wanted to ask you,"
said Herbert, rather surprised at his way of
taking it.

" Is she in immediate want of one ?"

" Yes."

" What is Penrose doing ? Is he very busy ?"

" I should scarcely think he could leave."

- " I have a friend, by-the-bye, whom I will ask to do my duty for a month, if you think I should be equal to undertaking the chaplaincy provisionally, for that time. By then we might find some one better fitted for it."

" Better suited than you, Edward, is quite impossible !"

" Why, you are better suited, I suppose ?"

" Not half so well," replied Lisle.

" Much better. My vocation was never revealed to me by miracle," said Baring, " and, it seems, that yours has been."

" You are joking," rejoined Herbert.

" Not at all ; it is no joking matter. You have either been called by God to be a priest, or you have made some mistake about it. One or the other. There can be no doubt of that. I confess I always thought you had a special vocation to be a squire, for you make a very good landlord, but I conclude that I was mistaken, and that you will be still better as a clergyman and chaplain."

"Well, but tell me honestly, Edward, your opinion, because I want to know it?"

"My opinion, dear Herbert? If God has really called you, my opinion is of no value at all. You would not set up my dictum against the word of the Almighty. On the other hand, if you merely wish to know whether I think God has called you, I have no means whatever of judging, excepting your own doubts, and, from these, I simply conclude that he has not."

"Do you mean to say that the counsels of God are not sometimes addressed to us in ambiguous and doubtful language?"

"Well, perhaps, I concluded too hastily."

Herbert was unable to get much more from his cousin, and left him somewhat dissatisfied with his visit.

CHAPTER III.

RE-ONCILIATION.

CECIL MONTAGU's chambers in the Albany showed symptoms of the same refined taste, for which his country house was conspicuous. His inclination towards the beautiful was manifested in every detail of life, and there was scarcely an article of common use which did not reflect the Athenian sensitiveness of its owner.

Elegance and luxury alone might have imparted the appearance of effeminacy, but here they were combined with much which bespoke the masculine genius of the mind of their possessor. His was not the finikin taste which finds delight in Parisian objects of *vertu*

or in the perfumed elegance of a rococo
boudoir. There was a solidity in the art which
he patronised and a simplicity in the forms
which he admired. He revelled in the luxury
of sterling productions and loved to contem-
plate the *bassi-relievi* of Thorwaldsen and Gib-
son, with which the walls of his library were
enlivened. His bronzes had all been collected
during his sojourn at Naples and, among them,
he possessed a small statue of Meleager which
was considered to rival the Faun in the Museo
Borbonico. He owned likewise some exquisite
specimens of lamps and vases, and had the
marble bust of a statue of Psyche, found in
Sicily, of which the face bore some resemblance
to that of Elsie Seymour.

The decorations and furniture of his room
were almost as thoroughly Pompeian as those
at Thornwood. There is a simplicity in the
outlines of Grecian art which we seek vainly in
the ecclesiastical styles of the middle-ages or
in the gorgeous luxury of Arabian palaces,

and Montagu, who was not one to depreciate
other systems, felt that this harmonised best
with domestic ease and refinement.

A few mornings after his return from Caw-
thorne, he was seated in his library engaged in
a literary task, which had occupied him for
some months, undertaken perhaps to divert
his thoughts from a sorrow, which, notwith-
standing all his philosophy, he had been un-
able entirely to banish.

Upon his return he had hastened once again to
Frank Elliott's chambers, but found that he had
not yet come back, although he was daily ex-
pected. At one moment he had almost deter-
mined to write him a letter, but, upon
reflection, it appeared to him that a personal
interview would, in all respects, be more satis-
factory. Much as he had felt hurt by Katha-
rine's conduct during the previous winter he
had never been able to believe that she had
acted upon her own free impulse and he had
longed for some opportunity for a personal

explanation with her. At the same time it
was obvious that he himself was the party
aggrieved, and that it was her duty to make
the first step towards healing the breach which
she and her friends had effected. The account
which he heard at Cawthorne of her having
warmly taken up his defence, had impressed
him, more than ever, with the conviction that,
however wanting in strength of purpose, she
had not been a consenting party to breaking
off the engagement.

He was frequently interrupted in his com-
position by recollections of Miss Elliott which,
notwithstanding his hard struggles to overcome
them, would occasionally get the better of him.
While he was thus meditating his servant
announced a visitor in whom he was delighted
to recognise Frank Elliott.

Having greeted him warmly Montagu pro-
ceeded to enquire after the health of Lady
Elliott and his sister, determined to show no
coldness which might widen their separation.

VOL. III.   P

"My mother and Kate are much better for the country air," returned Frank very cordially, "Kate has been very ill. But, Mr. Montagu, I must not shrink from telling you how deeply she has grieved over the past. She has written you a letter and it was partly my fault that she did not send it sooner, for I thought it better to see you myself."

"May you shew me the letter? pray show it to me?"

"Here it is," said Frank, "but my reason for persuading her not to send it was that I wished to see you myself, in order to protest against my uncle's conduct in the affair of last winter. I have felt so indignant about the whole thing that I determined to come and tell you how very indiscreet I consider his behaviour to have been."

Montagu opened the note which he read in silence.

"DEAR MR. MONTAGU—

"I feel bound to offer

You this unworthy amends for the past. I am aware that what I have done has made a breach which nothing can ever restore. You must have become convinced, long ere this, that she who could thus trifle with such a noble heart was utterly unworthy of it. I will not attempt to excuse my conduct, nor do I wish you to blame my friends for what has happened. It was not to them, but to *me*, that you once declared that your honour had ever remained unsullied and, painful as it is to be deserving of your censure, I would rather bear it myself than throw the burden upon others. Their misconceptions are no excuse for *my* behaviour in allowing anything to intervene between us. I do not write to justify my outward actions but to vindicate my *feelings*. Whatever may have been blameable in my conduct has been the result of mistaken duty, not of my own conviction, for I have never ceased to trust you *with all my heart and without reserve.* It

P 3

may seem bold in me to venture upon this
step, but I have suffered more than I can tell
from the thought that, even, although we may
probably never meet again, you will recollect
me as having broken my word and ceased to
trust you. It is, I think, and I have thought
very long upon the subject, far better we
should never meet again. If we should en-
counter by accident we may regard each other
as ordinary friends, but it would be safer, if
possible, never to see each other any more in
this world. There are many reasons for this.
Forget me if you like, yes, forget me but first
forgive me, if you can. My prayers shall
follow you through life, and one heart shall
always feel with you in your sorrow and your
joy. I cannot write more.

"But believe me ever yours in trust and
faith,

"KATHARINE B. ELLIOTT."

Montagu read the letter twice.

" Tell me," he said to Frank, " what were Madame Hoffner's insinuations to your uncle ?"

Elliott proceeded to recount all that he had heard upon this subject, from his mother, and from Mr. Reginald Elliott himself. The details were of the grossest description, and much of what Lady Elliott had heard, she had, of course, never repeated to her daughter.

" What can have been the woman's motive in fabricating these lies? I cannot understand."

" No ; I am unable to tell you that," replied Frank, " she is evidently full of spite towards you, for a short time ago, when Herbert Lisle happened to come over to Lockwood, and to tell them the true story about the mad woman—is not her name Arnstein ?——she grew furious and called you by all sorts of names. I am glad to say that my uncle has sent her to the right about since then. It seems that you did not sufficiently consider her exalted rank, she said, and, that she could never overlook the degradation to which one of her high caste had been subjected, by having been made to act duenna to a peasant girl."

"Ah! There must have been something more, I imagine, than that. I will endeavour to find out, from my old German servant, who is now a courier, but is at present, I fear, out of London. Is your sister coming to town?"

"I believe they are to be here next week."

"I shall venture to write to her. There is one point which seems to need explanation, that of my feigned name. Allardyce was a name, in our family, which I had adopted years before, intending to claim a peerage, to which I then considered myself entitled. It was wrong, no doubt, to pass myself off, even in a freak, under this designation, but Arthur Winslow's intimates were generally of a kind to make me timid of associating with them, under my real name."

"Arthur Winslow!"

"Yes—you met him in the East, I hear?"

"Yes. Had he any part in this story?"

Montagu felt a delicacy in betraying Wins-
low's share in a transaction which he was con-
vinced he would now entirely repudiate, and
he regretted having mentioned his name.

"She was acquainted with some friends of
his," returned Montagu, evasively, "but he
has given up all that now, I am told. By-the-
bye, Elliott, I have to congratulate you, I hear,
upon your approaching happiness. Lady
Morden has promised to come to Thornwood
before she leaves London, and I must beg you
will consent to accompany them there next
week. The place is famous for its lovers'
walks. If your sister will condescend to come,
she shall hear my vindication from the lips of
the widow Arnstein herself, who is on her way
to Munich, where she has succeeded to her
husband's property."

"I cannot speak for my sister," rejoined
Frank, who added, with an expression of de-
light, "but as for myself, I shall be most

happy to renew my acquaintance with Thorn-
wood, in such good company."

"Very well! Are you inclined to call with
me in Belgrave Square, that we may fix the
day ?"

After some more conversation, which turned
chiefly upon Frank's travels, they proceeded,
on foot, towards Belgravia. They had not ad-
vanced far along Piccadilly, when Montagu,
who was quick at recognizing acquaintances,
perceived a figure in sombre and not very neat
attire, in whom he discovered the features of
Arthur Winslow.

The convert showed no desire to avoid him,
and, therefore, although he had been prepared
for a shirk, Montagu replied to his addresses
with his usual ease and courtesy of manner.

"Montagu !" he said, "you, perhaps, do not
recognize me ?"

"Oh, yes, I do, Winslow, and I am glad to
see you looking so well."

"I hope you have not forgotten *me?*" said Frank.

And they shook hands and made many mutual enquiries touching their respective fellow travellers.

"You will think it, perhaps, an impertinence in me," pursued Winslow, turning to Montagu, as he was preparing to move forward; "but I should esteem it a great favour if you would let me call upon you."

"Certainly," replied Cecil, "what time would suit you? will you breakfast with me?"

"Very well—I will."

"Our friend has a bad hat," said Montagu, when he was out of hearing.

"The coat is not much better," returned Frank.

"And yet I have been told that the property, which he once possessed, sold much better than was expected, and that, after paying his debts, there remained a certain sum to

P 5

live upon.   What sort of travelling companion,
by-the-bye, did you find Herbert Lisle?"

"Very well!" rejoined Frank, who had,
perhaps, never quite forgiven him, for being a
favourite of Elsie's.

"I cannot help thinking," said Montagu,
"that, whatever may be his peculiarities, he is
a man of very excellent feeling."

The Mordens, pressed both by Frank Elliott
and Montagu, readily agreed to the expedition
to Thornwood, and Cecil, so far successful,
returned home to compose his reply to Katha-
rine.

"MY DEAR MISS ELLIOTT,

"I did not require your note to
persuade me that you were blameless, and I
knew that, whatever your actions might appear,
they could only be the result of the highest
principle and duty.   There is one point in your
letter from which I must entirely differ.   I
implore you, at all events, to grant me one

more meeting before we separate for ever, if you still persist in so terrible a resolution. Your brother has kindly promised to accompany the Mordens to Thornwood next week, and he will also lend his assistance in endeavouring to persuade Lady Elliott and yourself to afford me the highest pleasure which I can enjoy upon earth, namely, that of your society. Pray grant me this favour. I shall fancy that the mad-woman's songs have left an indelible impression if you will not allow me an opportunity of protesting against past misconceptions, and pledging an unblemished future to *her* whom I once ventured to call 'my Katharine.'"

"My dear Miss Elliott,

"I remain, with unchanged feelings,

"Yours devotedly,

"CECIL MONTAGU."

He also wrote to Lady Elliott, but induced

Frank to enclose this latter epistle in a persuasive appeal of his own, urging her to accept the invitation to Thornwood.

On the following morning, Arthur Winslow appeared at breakfast.

"I scarcely fancied you would recognize me," he said to Montagu in the course of conversation, "few of my former friends seem to know me. I suppose I am a good deal changed in appearance—but I have frequently been repulsed when I have addressed myself to men with whom I was once upon intimate terms."

"I am not in the habit of forgetting the faces of old friends," returned Cecil.

"No, I am sure you are not. I should not think they did it purposely. I imagine that my appearance is altered."

"Perhaps it is," replied Montagu, who was careful to avoid all questions of discussion, and who did not even broach the subject of his past life or subsequent change, lest it might pain Winslow and perhaps lead to unpleasant topics. In addressing him, Cecil seemed constantly to assume that he was now what he had always been. Winslow had perhaps hoped to be attacked upon these points, in order that he might, in defending himself, bring forward some of the objects and opinions which he had at heart. In that case he was disappointed, for whenever he led the conversation to any subject involving religion, Montagu dexterously warded off the attack, and turned the discourse to other things.

"My principal object, in desiring to see you," commenced Winslow, at length, "was to speak to you upon the subject of Ann Dolby, or Arnstein, which is, I am told, her present name. You have kindly interested yourself in her fate, and saved her by your noble conduct from the evils into which she would have been irretrievably plunged by mine. I would to God I had it in my power to make any atonement for the past—but oh ! how often I find that the injuries which I have inflicted are irreparable. A few weeks since, when I was in the country, my nephew happened to mention that he had met, at Mr. Elliott's, a German woman named Madame Hoffner, who had formerly been selected by you as duenna to Ann Dolby, and he heard that she is now most bitter against you, and determined to be revenged by disseminating evil reports concerning your character. I think I can inform you of the cause of all this."

" How so? what do you mean, Winslow?" enquired Montagu, courteously.

" Well, I will tell you," he replied: " I was at Wiesbaden in the summer of 18———, and chanced to meet Madame Hoffner at the *Table d'hôte*. I believe that she was, at that time, travelling as governess in a Russian family. Happening to sit next her, I found her very conversational and very pertinacious in her questions respecting my acquaintances in England. I was somewhat taken by surprise when she asked me whether I knew a Mr.

Allardyce, and then proceeded to describe your person and appearance in such a manner that I could not doubt the identity. I was curious to learn what she had to say about you, and confessed to the acquaintance. She then went on to catechise me as to whether I had ever heard of your romantic engagement to Ann Dolby. I listened to this with great interest and drew from her the whole story of her travels with your *protégée*, whom she supposed to be your ward, and also your intended, at least so she declared. She described your conduct in Rome as cruel to the girl and insulting to herself, and spoke with extreme wrath and indignation."

"Well, that is exactly what she appears still to feel towards me," rejoined Montagu; "I cannot account for it, I confess, for, in Rome, although she may have been cold in her manner, she never gave vent to any open abuse of this kind."

"I think I can explain it," pursued Winslow, " as you shall hear.   She sat by me again upon the following day, and soon re-commenced about you, asking me whether I knew your proper direction.   I was careful not to inform her of your name, but she then enquired whether letters directed to C. Allardyce, Esq., Surrey, would be certain to find you.   I forget how I contrived to evade her question, but she was very confidential, and I was amused to find how easily I could draw her out upon these topics.   She told me that you had never answered her letters.   I asked whether they were important, for I felt that, if so, it would be as well to give her your real address, or else to inform you of what she had done.   After a sort of cross-examination, for I questioned her very minutely, 1 discovered that she had been, for a long time, unemployed and in great pecuniary difficulties, and had written to you for money.   I urged that you could not have received the letters, upon which she grew indig-

nant and said that your conduct was infamous.
'Mr. Allardyce!' she exclaimed, 'has not
only broken poor Ann Dolby's heart, and driven
her mad, but has tried to make me an accom-
plice to his wickedness.' I protested against her
conclusions, but she would not hear me, and
went on—'Yes, he has trampled me under his
foot. He has not even the grace to pay me for
keeping his secret. I will not keep it, I can
tell him. I will publish it to all the world.'
When I heard all this, I kept my counsel
about your name. I heard sufficient about her
afterwards, to confirm me in my bad opinion.
During the following winter, I made acquaint-
ance with the Russian Count, in whose family
she had been residing. I met him in the
Cercle, at Paris. He informed me that he
was in difficulties about his governess, who
had brought strangers into his house. One
night there had been a robbery, and the police
had informed him that some inmate of his

establishment must have been in league with
the thieves.   He evidently suspected Madame
Hoffner of some share in the matter, and,
although he had no proofs whatever, he, never-
theless, dismissed her at once.   He told me
that he had long suspected her of mal-practices,
and that at Wiesbaden, he had once found her
in the Kursaal, among the crowd assembled
round the gambling table, at a time when he
imagined her to have retired to rest."

"This is a bad history," answered Montagu.

"Yes," rejoined the other, "and I think
her malice towards you seems to be explained
by this incident.   I suppose you have never
received the letters."

"Never, but what you have told me ac-
counts for everything.   Thank you Winslow,
with all my heart, for taking the trouble of
coming to tell me.   It is of more consequence
than you can imagine, for that woman has
inflicted an injury upon me," he pursued,

with a sigh, " from which I have not yet recovered."

"And I was, alas! the cause of your first meeting her."

"The innocent cause, certainly!" replied Montagu.

"The guilty cause, you mean! I wish I might make some contribution towards Ann Dolby and her children."

"They are well provided for," returned Montagu, "their title to their grandfather's estate, in Bavaria, has been proved, and they have succeeded to their share of the inheritance."

"That is *your* doing, Montagu, I am sure of it. What a noble fellow you are! I only desire one thing for you," he continued, as he arose to leave.

"You flatter me," replied Cecil.

"No, you are chivalry itself. You only require to become a knight and liegeman of the Cross, to be perfect."

"Ah, my dear Winslow, we may, perhaps,

view these things with different eyes, but we are now both of us agreed that honour, truth, and justice are the sterling qualities at which all men should aim."

Winslow seemed distressed, but did not reply.

"Do not let us quarrel about such points," continued Montagu, "I entirely approve of the course you have pursued, in giving up the turf and all such things, for they can only end in utter misery. Depend upon it, you are a much happier man."

"Happier man! Indeed, indeed, I am a happier man. I only wish you were half as happy. Oh! it may seem presumptuous in such an one as myself to venture upon speaking thus to the high-minded, cultivated philosopher, Cecil Montagu, but, oh! if you would only try the selfsame way that I have tried, the humble, lowly pathway of the cross, you too would be so very, very happy. I promise you, you would."

There was a slight curl upon the lip of the handsome Montagu, and a sparkle in his eye, but the convert had not finished his say, and he resigned himself to listen to his story:

"I was never what you were. I was a mere profligate, while you have always been a refined and polished gentleman. My pursuit through life was after excitement and pleasure. But tell me, Cecil Montagu, whether your object, as mine was once, is not earthly happiness? True, you do not seek it in the same gross attractions. You look for it in works of taste and deeds of chivalry, but is it not with the same end in view?"

"Earthly happiness? Well!"

"Yes, it is," pursued the unrelenting convert, "and that is simply worth nothing; just nothing. In a very few years this world will have faded away, and where shall we be? There is no other road and no other name than His, who is *the* way, the truth, and the life.   Oh! *if* I could convince you, Montagu!"

The fascinating man of the world shook his head and Winslow brushed away a tear from his eye, as he departed sorrowfully from the room.

CHAPTER IV.

THE REPULSE.

MR. and Mrs. Seymour were in London and saw a good deal of Elsie. Her letter had produced a salutary effect upon their minds, and had led them to conclusions somewhat different from any which she had anticipated, for it had taught them to sympathise more in her devotion than they had yet attempted to do. Her scheme had already attracted some degree of public attention. A certain class of newspapers and periodicals had taken it up with warmth, and the philanthropic peers and grand ladies were loud and enthusiastic in its praise. It costs nothing either to applaud or to criticise heroism, and people are ready enough to do either as it suits them best. In an age when the combination of genius and courage is so rare, it was strange to find its greatest example in a woman, and, no wonder if the world's attention should, at some moments, have been withdrawn from the failure of statesmen and generals, to contemplate a successful heroine of the cross!

The Seymours were staying at a quiet hotel, and entered very little into society. They never passed a day without seeing Elsie, whose whole time was devoted to the prosecution of her vast enterprise.

They were in their drawing-room after breakfast, Mr. Seymour reading the "Times" and his wife busy about some work for her daughter, when Herbert Lisle was announced. They were both delighted to see him, for whatever his views or singularities, he was a warm friend of Elsie's, besides being a believer in the great undertaking of her life.

"Have you read this article upon Elsie in the paper?" enquired Mrs. Seymour.

"Yes, and two or three more besides," he replied.

"The world begins to do justice to her scheme," returned Mrs. Seymour, "I suppose you have seen her?"

"I saw her when I was last in town," rejoined Herbert, "and I made another attempt yesterday, but she was out nursing. What a cold world it would be if it did not begin to applaud. It would be even worse than I took it for."

"I almost begin to believe that it is her true mission," said her mother. "Tell me, Mr. Lisle, don't you think it would be cruel of us to take her away from her work?"

"Well, I don't know what to say."

"Yes, I know very well that you have been consulted upon the other side."

"Really?"

"Yes, Elsie told us all about it."

"Well, but you know that counsel never give their opinion to both sides."

VOL. III.   Q

"Yes, but tell me whether you do not think we are right in determining not to accept her offer of coming home? Oh! I really feel that it would be quite selfish and wrong in us to deprive the country of her services. Everybody says that she is doing so much good, and that the machinery of her scheme, and especially its extension, requires her own mind to superintend it."

"To say the truth," said Herbert, "the question upon which I was consulted was not as to whether the country required her services, but whether her own duty lay in serving the public or staying at home."

"Yes, as a general principle you were certainly right," said Mrs. Seymour, "but Elsie is not like other girls. There are exceptions to all rules, you know."

"Unquestionably; but could not you make some compromise?" ventured Herbert, who understood from Mrs. Seymour's tone of voice, that she was in a measure doing violence to herself, and arguing against her own secret wishes : "for instance, could not Miss Seymour spend a part of the year at home and the remainder in London ? It might be so arranged that her residence in town should correspond with yours. It is, perhaps, rather bold in me to venture these suggestions ?"

"Oh no, not at all, Mr. Lisle. I am sure I feel extremely indebted to you for the interest you take in it, and I like your plan very much, if it would not be taking Elsie too much from her sisterhood. What do you think ?"

"No. I think her health will require long periods of change. Why should not she establish a sanatorium for invalided sisters near your own place, which would afford her occupation when in the country, and enable the others to enjoy the occasional benefit of fresh air ?"

"What a bright idea ! you must suggest it to her. Promise me you will ?"

"Very well ; as part of the compromise."

Q 3

Both Mr. and Mrs. Seymour were much comforted by Herbert's propositions, as they had felt a difficulty in robbing the institution of her presence altogether. They appeared anxious that he should lose no time in broaching the subject to Elsie, and thus furnished with a plea, he willingly set forth upon a fresh attempt to obtain an interview with her.

His mind was bent upon a single object, and neither Laura's arguments nor Baring's satire had in the least weakened his resolution. He had seen Arthur Winslow on the previous evening, but he had not said a word to him upon a point; which he regretted having mentioned to his cousins. He had accompanied his uncle to the church, where he had first been awakened from the lethargy of sin, and there, Herbert had once more reflected upon the great step which he meditated, and which appeared to him, more than ever, as in obedience to God's call, and as destined to bring him into closer contact with his Saviour.

Weighed in the balances of the sanctuary, the undertaking was not one to terrify. "A few years," he thought, "and none of us will be the better for the riches of this world. One day with Christ will stand us in better stead than a brief period of earthly enjoyment, and how much happier for those who have unreservedly followed their Lord and have laid up the heavenly treasure!"

There were occasional doubts to perplex him but he strove hard to reject them, and to forget the dear old village and the Tudor Court, regarding them as faded memories of the past! On the morning of the day upon which he visited the Seymours, he had, as it were, renewed his resolve, and it seemed to him as if he had already completed the sacrifice of his future existence.

Walking through the crowded streets, he felt that he had accepted a new state of being. The carriages and the noble mansions were no

longer anything more to him, for he had vol-
untarily forsaken his position to become a
brother of the poor. How few in that vast
throng of business or pleasure could have res-
ponded to the feelings of his soul, as he threaded
his way among them !

As he approached the house of the Bloomsbury
sisterhood he perceived that workmen were en-
gaged in making extensive alterations; convert-
ing two or three of the adjoining houses into one.
He made enquiries, and found that it was for
Elsie's institution.

He was presently introduced into the same
parlour where his former interview had taken
place, and there he anxiously awaited her
arrival, for he was told that, although she was
engaged, she had desired that, if he happened
to call, he might not be sent away without see-
ing her.

His heart beat as he considered his singular
errand, and man that he was, he could not

entirely subdue the mingled sensations which he experienced at the prospect of his interview with the beautiful girl.

The door opened. Paler than before, the tall and graceful sister entered the room. Hard worked but not depressed, the lovely woman seemed to have acquired yet more of that saint-like character, which the old painters succeeded in pourtraying. There she stood stately in her humility before Herbert, who felt a thrill of joy at receiving her gracious smile.

"You will wonder at my coming," said Herbert after the usual enquiries: "I have an excuse for my visit as well as an object, and, I will begin by the former. I have just seen Mr. and Mrs. Seymour, and have been conversing with them upon the subject of which we have already spoken."

"You mean my resolution to go home?" returned Elsie in a faltering voice.

"I do. But they have both begged me to

come and propose a compromise. They want
you to spend a certain time with them and the
remainder of the year in London."

" Was that your idea ?"

" In so far that I suggested it to them, for
their sakes. Mrs. Seymour had first said that
she thought it wrong of them to take you away
at all ; so that this is by way of giving them
more of your society than they were willing to
require."

"Remember, Mr. Lisle, that you were the first
to point out the path of duty. Do you wish
me now to shrink from following it ?"

" I do not consider it in that light," replied
Herbert, " they propose to remain in London
for the months you spend here. During the
part of the year passed at your father's place,
you might establish a sanatorium for your
sisters or others who may require it, and thus
you will find constant occupation in the coun-
try. Surely many of the patients require
country air."

" And is this your excuse for calling ?" enquired Elsie.

" This is the excuse, and now I come to the real object of my visit. You asked me to find you a chaplain for your society. My cousin, Edward Baring, has offered to come up immediately, for at least one month, to supply the place until some one else can be found. My proposition is a strange one, but I want Mr. Baring's successor to be also a temporary appointment, until the permanent chaplain can be ordained."

" You mean your uncle, Mr. Winslow ?"

" I mean myself."

" Yourself ?"

" Do you refuse me the post ? I fear I am but ill fitted for it. Yet a word escaped you when we last met, which encouraged me to make the offer. I make it after due deliberation, and will endeavour to qualify myself for the duties of the position."

Q 5

"I spoke hastily," replied Elsie : "I remember my words, for I regretted them."

"Regretted them!" exclaimed Lisle : "I almost feared I should be unworthy of such a trust as this. As it is I am totally unprepared for it, and it were, perhaps, presumptuous in a layman to anticipate the days of his ordination. A thousand circumstances and impediments may intervene. It may not be God's will that I should be spared so long."

Elsie seemed wrapped in meditation while he spoke, and then said :

"You mistake me, Mr. Lisle. There is no one whom I should have preferred for the chaplaincy, no one ;" (Herbert's heart fluttered, and he appeared to hang intently upon her words) "but is it not a very rash determination? What is to become of Cawthorne, and of the place you occupy, or the duties you fulfil in Gloucestershire?"

"I could resign my life-interest to Lord

Lisle, whose father is, next to my uncle, the heir in tail."

"Lord Lisle? Do you know him?"

"Not well. It is some years since I saw him, and he was then quite a boy, but he promised well."

"Lord Portaldowne, you know, is a neighbour of ours," returned Elsie, "and I do not think that if you knew his son, you would resign the influence you possess into such hands as his?"

Herbert remained silent.

"I do not mean to say anything against Lord Lisle," she continued, "but he is quite young and untried and, from what little one can judge of him, not at all likely to keep in view the objects which you regard as those of the highest moment. His pursuits consist in hunting, shooting, and London gaiety. I feel convinced that he is perfectly indifferent to the education and care of the poor, the reform of young criminals, or any religious or philanthropic objects and, to what shall I say? to all, in short, which occupied the thoughts of Herbert Lisle and made him likely to become the most useful magistrate in Gloucestershire.''

"I am not *obliged* to make over the life-interest to Lord Lisle. There are plenty of others.''

"Shall I remind you of your words to me?'' said Elsie. "You asked me whether I had no *' home duties to the tenants, the villagers and the school—duties, obvious, humble and near at hand?'* These were your own words, and they apply with double force to yourself. My father's landed property is very small, and few of the villagers are his tenants. Should anything happen to him, it is probable the house would be sold. Your property, on the contrary, is very large and you are unable to sell it. You are placed upon it by Providence as a steward, to administer it to God's glory. Can you resign your stewardship, at your own will and fancy, and take another, for which, to say the least, you cannot be better fitted, I should think ?"

" No," returned Herbert, gloomily.

" Mr. Lisle, I scarcely dare accept your services," pursued Elsie.

Lisle bent his eyes upon the ground, and strove to conceal his emotion.

" Was it impossible," he thought, " to link his future with hers ?"

And his imagination carried him back to the rock-glen of Hasbeyah with its foaming stream, and he regretted from the depths of his soul, the resolutions of that moonlight walk.

" You refuse me ?" he said, in a voice almost of agony, " oh, Miss Seymour, it would have been such happiness to me."

Their eyes met and a momentary colour tinged her cheek, but she resumed her composure, and, looking down, spoke firmly :

" Our paths in life may run in a parallel direction, although they cannot approximate.

Our great objects are now the same, and as it
would be cowardice in me permanently to aban-
don the work which I have undertaken, so it
would be equally wrong in you to shrink from
the duties of your position."

"I wish it could be otherwise," returned
Herbert, who was balancing in his mind as to
whether he could not reveal to sister Elsie the
secret of his heart. But ere he had time to
determine, she had perhaps perceived the
danger of delay."

"I am afraid I must not remain longer,"
she said, "I have to thank you for many,
many bright and blessed thoughts. I still
wear the agate cross from the wells of Elim.
We must always pray for each other, but I
fear we may but seldom, very seldom, meet on
this side the grave. Good bye, Mr. Lisle."

And she had left the room before he could
do more than return her farewell.

She hurried away, and ascending the stairs,

entered her own chamber and closed the door. She remained long, and when she came forth, an intimate friend might have discovered the mark of recent tears in her eyes, but there were no other symptoms of sorrow. She went out upon her daily task and worked from morn to even. Her heart had not been broken by its earthly grief, it had, perhaps, been softened and qualified for that true and lasting happiness which she had now found in Him to whom she had at length learned to offer up its sadness and its joy.

Herbert left the House of Mercy in a state of utter misery and, after placing his uncle and Edward Baring in communication with Miss Seymour upon the subject of the chaplaincy, he returned to Cawthorne, and endeavoured to devote himself to his old pursuits and duties. He lived almost in complete seclusion, but spent his whole time in philanthropic objects, giving himself up especially to those which Elsie had named to him.

He felt as if he had lost all interest in life
and could gladly welcome the moment when
its brief scenes should be closed to him for ever
in the grave.

CHAPTER V

THE PASTIMES OF THORNWOOD.

THE sun shone brightly o'er the beautiful villa and its terraces were gorgeous with gay flowers. Never were the effects of colour better studied than in Cecil Montagu's lovely retreat. The red and blue sunblinds which shaded the windows gave additional richness to the painted building, while the vases of scarlet geranium, the beds of verbena and other blossoms of equal brilliancy, not to mention the long wreaths of nasturtion clustering between the balustrades, imparted a splendour to the gardens, which required the contrast of the dark green glen and its Italian pines to subdue its too glaring effect. In recalling this enchanting scene we must not omit the addition of the plashing fountains, the marble statues, or the frescoed colonnades and seats. Never was the place seen to greater advantage than in the sunshine of July and when, as upon the present occasion, it was enlivened by the presence of a gay assemblage of guests.

Cecil Montagu had gone beforehand to prepare for the reception of his party, and the deserted peristyle had resumed that air of cheerful elegance which it seemed especially to acquire when tenanted by its refined possessor. He had inspected each corner of his domain, and the whole had reacquired an appearance of order and comfort from the moment of his return.

The first to arrive were the Mordens. They came soon after luncheon and Cecil did them the honours of the place, exhibiting its treasures of art as well as the natural beauties of its position. He learnt from Lady Morden that the Elliotts would probably come down by the next train and he sent the carriage to meet them at the station.

Emmeline was in unusually high spirits, even for her, and Fred was the more amiable in consequence of her having said less than usual to annoy him, although she could not help occasionally giving vent to her satirical humours at his expense.

"Remember, Morden," said Montagu, "you have never yet given me the account of your feats with the crocodiles!"

"Oh! pray spare us now!" rejoined Emmeline: "It is an everlasting history when he once begins. Fred will give you the complete biography of the crocodile he shot, and of all the crocodile tears which it shed up to the time when he ate it, for he ended by having it cooked at Cairo, and served up in the form of crocodile steaks. I wish Mr. Bateson could have tasted it."

"Imagine a *gigêt de crocodile!*" exclaimed Montagu, laughing.

" The *gigót* is the leg, is not it ?" drawled Morden.

" Of course, Fred, why what are you thinking about ?" retorted the merry girl.

" I was thinking," replied Fred, looking very witty, " that I could not possibly have eaten a crocodile's leg without myself turning into *a leg eater*, alligator !"

" Not so bad," said the courteous host.

" You ought to be much obliged to Mr. Montagu," remarked Emmeline, in a malicious voice, " for praising your bad puns, for you certainly do *croak a deal* when you once begin."

" Wretched !" rejoined Fred, " excuse Latin, but it is certainly *vox et præteria Nihil* (Nile, you know !")

" Worse and worse !"

" Latin in the presence of ladies too !" exclaimed Lady Morden, " for shame, Fred !"

" Oh ! mamma," rejoined Emmeline, " Grace and Agnes have learnt some Latin and it is well for Fred to keep up what little he knows so as to be up to them. Is not it?"

The Mordens were very colloquial in their conversation and ideas, and Cecil Montagu found it a considerable effort to draw them out upon other subjects. Lady Morden and her daughter both professed a love for pictures and statues, but when invited to inspect them it became evident that their taste was a simple compliance with the requirements of the world, not a property of their own imaginations. They would scarcely have been the less happy had the thought of Rafaelle or Shakespeare never been immortalised.

Cecil felt relieved when the time approached at which his other guests were expected, and, it is possible that Emmeline was no less delighted at the prospect of their coming. She was sauntering alone with her brother, upon the lower terrace, while Cecil was engaged in conversation with Lady Morden, at some distance in advance.

"Well, Emmeline," said Fred, anxious, if

possible, to return some of the scratches which she had inflicted upon him, "it would have been a jolly go if you could have secured Cecil Montagu and Thornwood."

"I don't see that at all," returned Emmeline, in a tone of pique, "in the first place he would not have suited me in the least. I have no fancy for a man whose whole mind is upon stilts, and who never comes down from the heroics. I hate Athenians, and Romans, and all that kind of thing."

"I thought you were always sighing and dying to go to Italy ?—you used to be."

"Italy! That is very different."

"It is the land of poetry, they say, you know," rejoined Fred.

"Are you so stupid as to think that everybody speaks in poetry, in Italy?" answered Emmeline; "I suppose there are plenty of merry people there as elsewhere, who can laugh and talk about things of every day. I like the world as it is, and I hate people who

want to make it what it should be. Now, Mr.
Montagu has a *little* of that about him."

" He is considered very agreeable."

" Well—so he is."

" But the grapes are sour, Emmie ?"

" Not at all," retorted Emmeline, wrath-
fully.

" Now, I can understand," said Fred, " that
you might not fancy Herbert Lisle. He is
quite in the tragics."

" Dreadful monster ! how he must have
bored you all in the East, with his high and
lofty notions. He is a specimen of high art,
without relief I he would do for a tragic
actor at a fair, for it gives one the blues to
look at him."

" I know it always gave me a stomach-ache
when he came prating upon religion in poor
Elliott's tent," returned Fred, " but then you
know, I never could endure any of those
exalted gentry. The Carrowsby people drive

me wild ; and, to tell you the truth, I am not
half fond of your indigo friend, Miss Elsie."

"Ah ! well, I always will defend her.
You are very hard upon her."

"Well, she has been and done it now with
a vengeance. She has turned black and blue
at last, and may run in pairs with Herbert
Lisle, and do the tragic queen. I say, Emmie,
why would Elsie be the proper person to reform
Arthur Winslow ? (I don't know whether
you know that specimen ; *he* is more like a
murderer at a penny show.) But do you guess
my riddle ?"

"I know who you mean. Let me think ?"

"Give it up ?"

"Yes."

"Because she has taken to restoring *broken
legs.*"

"You are improving, I declare. You are
getting quite a clever boy."

As the hour of Katharine's arrival drew

near, Montagu had contrived to approach the side of the house which faced the carriage-drive. In answer to his and Frank's pressing letters, Lady Elliott had, after some hesitation, accepted the invitation to Thornwood, but, owing to an unavoidable delay in their journey to London, the lovers had not been able to meet before the present occasion.

"We must follow suit," said Fred Morden, to his sister, when he perceived that Montagu and his mother had left the terraces. "It would not be *suitable* not to meet your suitor, would it, *sweet* Emmie? Does your heart palpitate?" he said, as he threw himself into a comic attitude.

"You are very witty, to-day!"

They had scarcely made the circuit of the house when the sound of a slamming gate met their ears, followed by the noise of wheels. Emmeline's heart fluttered as the carriage approached, and Montagu also looked with some anxiety for the appearance of the barouche.

"Well, Emmie, how do you feel now? Does your heart go pit-a-pat, eh?"

"No, it only goes one stroke at a time. It is not like your's, which beats double time, for Grace and Agnes alternately. How happy could I be with either! eh, Fred?"

Cecil Montagu drew near as the carriage stopped. Katharine looked lovely. The confusion which she had felt at the thought of meeting him once more, had slightly flushed her face, but her bright eyes shone with additional lustre and an indescribable happiness seemed to underline her momentary timidity.

Frank shook hands warmly and Lady Elliott spoke most graciously, as Montagu assisted her to alight. It was Katharine's turn next, and when she had placed her small hand in his, he received it with a gentle pressure, which spoke whole volumes to her heart.

"Katharine!" he whispered: "how kind of you to come!"

Her answer was conveyed in a look which could not be mistaken.

Frank had soon disappeared with Emmeline, and, while Montagu was escorting his new guests into the house, Frederick remarked to his mother:

"I think it is awfully slow here! I wonder if there are any trout in yonder stream? I declare I shall hang myself!"

They sauntered into the conservatories, and thence, after a time, back to the terraces where they met Lady Elliott, from whose account it appeared that Montagu was walking with Katharine.

"Well!" said Fred, (not, it is to be hoped, in allusion to walking with these two elderly ladies,) "I can stand this sort of thing no longer. I shall go and see what there is in the stables."

And he left the matrons to pursue their conversation without interruption. It is a pity that Mary Elliott had not accompanied her

R 3

mother instead of remaining behind at Aunt Fortescue's, as she never could possibly have had a better chance, under more promising circumstances! Perhaps some such thought may have crossed the mind of the prudent parent.

But let us follow the lovers.

"Thornwood is more beautiful than ever!" Kate said.

"It should be so, to welcome you upon your farewell visit. Is it to be so, Katharine? You could not mean what you wrote?"

"Yes."

"Let it be a prolonged farewell."

"Very well."

"But you shall not positively decide its duration until you have been through the woods with me. I know a certain nook where the memories of the past will plead for me, Katharine!"

They proceeded onwards, through the same narrow pathways of the glen which they had followed upon the day of his proposal, nearly nine months before. Kate could not divine why he spoke so little upon the subject nearest to their hearts, and why he should reserve his declaration for that one favoured retreat.

As they approached the well-known spot, along the same narrow pathway, now green with moss, they caught the words of a song, and Katharine, startled at recognising the voice, turned enquiringly to her companion as if doubtful whether to proceed.

SONG.

A poet who lived in the days of old
    Fell in love with a princely dame !
His only reward was a dungeon cold,
    Where, in fetters, he rued his fame !

And have I not suffered the self-same fate,
    As I culled of the self-same vine ?
For my love was repaid by a princely hate ;
    Like poor Tasso, the Sorrentine !

And were not Sorrento's bowers *my* home,
　　Where lingers Torquato's spell ?
And was not *my* glory and grief in Rome,
　　Where great Tasso triumphed and fell ?

The air was a singular mixture of mirth and pathos, but there was no mistaking the tones of the voice which Katharine, might have recognised had the associations of the place been even less calculated to recall them.

Montagu seemed anxious to avoid disturbing the singer until she had concluded her effusion.

" Are you afraid of the mad-woman, Katharine ? shall we go forward ?" enquired Cecil, with a voice in which love and courtesy struggled for pre-eminence.

" I am not afraid of accompanying you," she replied, somewhat timidly.

The widow Arnstein was seated upon the very

bench where Katharine had received Montagu's first declaration of love, and the two children stood by her side. Her dress was so altered that Miss Elliott would have found it hard to have recognised her as the same wild creature who had terrified her in days of yore. She arose, as they approached, and made a curtsey.

"Katharine! this is Madame Arnstein,' said Montagu, who also presented Miss Elliott to the widow; he then continued, "have you ever seen Madame Hoffner since you were in Italy?"

"Madame Hoffner? no!"

"What is her spite against me?"

"Against you, Mr. Montagu? I cannot tell."

"She has been circulating all kinds of stories about me. The only cause for her wrath that I can discover is that she sent various begging letters which I have never received. Do you mind doing me a favour, Madame Arnstein?"

"Anything in my power?"

"This lady has been informed, through Madame Hoffner, that my past conduct towards you has not been honourable and true. Do you object to recounting her the story of your life?"

"Not honourable? Oh! Mr. Allardyce—— Mr. Montagu! I wish I had proved more worthy of such pure unselfishness as yours."

"Do not say that. We are all selfish in some way or other. But, while you sit there, Katharine, and listen to her tale, for," he whispered, "I require this of you, my adored one! I will play at hide and seek with these children. What are their names?"

"Ann and William," returned the widow, "the boy is really Wilhelm, but at Cawthorne they were known as Nancy and Bill."

"'Come along, children?" he said, and they followed him through the intricate labyrinth of the wood, while he left Miss Elliott to listen to Ann Dolby's history, at the close of which she did not fail to mention Mr. Montagu's last act of disinterested generosity in vindicating her children's right to their father' inheritance, which she was now setting forth to claim."

"Do you remember, Katharine, how, once before, I addressed you near this very spot," said Montagu, as she rose to meet him on his return, "do you recollect that I then fancied that a cloud of suspicion lingered upon your brow, and that I only forgave it upon condition of your never suspecting me again?"

"Oh, Mr. Montagu! can you forgive me now?"

"Not if you call me Mr. Montagu, my Katharine."

"Cecil! can you forgive me?"

"Will you trust me now?"

"I have ever believed and trusted you at heart—but —"

"But—you shall tell me all now, my be-

R 5

trothed one! Let me first say farewell to Madame Arnstein."

The widow, who had been disentangling some brambles from her children's frocks, now rose and turned towards Montagu.

"Pray, Mr. Montagu," she said, "did Madame Hoffner know you by any name but Allardyce?"

"Not to my knowledge."

"She learnt your true name," interrupted Katharine, "from a German courier you had."

"Ah! that accounts for it. Winslow told me the other day——"

"Mr. Winslow!" exclaimed Ann.

"Yes—he called expressly to inform me of this woman's proceedings. He met her in Germany, and heard from her own lips that she had addressed several letters to me, as Allardyce, demanding money under threat of exposing me—exposing my conduct towards Ann Dolby! The letters, of course, never reached me and this is her revenge! and terrible it has been my Katharine," he added in a whisper.

"Far worse for me," replied Kate : " and yet, when she found that your name was Montagu she must have guessed that her letters could not have reached you. I wonder at her continued hatred."

"She had exposed herself to Winslow," rejoined Cecil, " and may have counted upon his betraying her. But," he continued, when he perceived that the widow's attention was once more drawn to the playful children, " there is one point, my Katharine, which I endeavoured to explain to your brother and which seems to tinge with suspicion the whole story of my life. It is this name of Allardyce which I assumed. My mother was the heiress of the Allardyces and it had been the ambition of my boyhood to adcpt that ancient family appellation as my own, and at some future time, if possible, to claim an old Scottish peerage belonging to my maternal ancestors which, to avoid its being merged in a higher title, would have gone to the second son. When at Oxford, I had so entirely determined to adopt it that, in a boyish freak, I caused a set of cards to be engraved with the name of " Cecil Allardyce." When Mr. Winslow first invited me to visit this lady I confess that, knowing his reputation, I hesitated to bring forward my real designation among the associates whom he frequented and, happening to stumble upon these cards, availed myself of them for the purpose of concealment, strictly warning my servant to preserve an incognito, from which I was unwilling afterwards to depart. I cannot help thinking that Madame Hoffner's dignity must have been rather offended by finding that I never trusted her with my real name. Can you forgive all this ? I think I did not say too much when I declared that my honour has been untarnished."

" Oh ! Cecil, I am unworthy of you."

" No ! appearances were against me I allow, but I once again venture to pledge you

an unblemished future if you will accept it !"
And before she could reply he had turned to
the widow Arnstein.

"When do you leave for Munich?" he en-
quired.

"To-morrow morning."

"Pray accept *this* ; and farewell !" rejoined
Montagu, as he gave her a handsome memo-
randum-book with a rich lining of bank notes,
of which she was not aware when she re-
ceived it.

Katharine took her lover's arm and they
sauntered through the glen, not returning
to the house until the other guests had retired
to prepare for dinner.

It was a happy evening in the Pompeian
villa. The music room resounded once more to
Cecil's exquisite tones, as well as to Emmeline's
merry songs. Frank was in high spirits, for
fortune seemed to smile upon him now.

"Lady Morden !" he said, after having con-
sulted his mother and Katharine, "I have a

great favour to ask of you.   I am most anxious
that my sister's wedding should take place upon
the same day as mine."

"By all means! then it must be at Alfre-
ton.   Do you think Lady Elliott would con-
sent? it would be delightful if she would."

And so the matter was arranged.

Early upon the following day the guests
prepared to return to London.   Katharine
could not resist a walk through the beautiful
grounds with Montagu.

"Are you going so soon, Katharine?"

"My farewell you know!"

"That is to be postponed."

"Until my return?"

"Yes, and then it is to last for ever!"

"Yes, for ever, in this world."

"My beloved!"

Were there no misgivings now in Katha-
rine's heart?   If so, it was too late to heed
them.   Their fates were bound for life, but life

is not eternal and her woman's spirit some-
times strove to soar to the world beyond the
grave.

Yet withal, there was joy in the face of
Katharine when the eyes of Montagu, resting
upon hers, seemed to read the secrets of her
soul.

CHAPTER VI.

THALIA.

OUR tale reverts to the stately four-turretted mansion on the borders of the Trent, where it first opened.   Autumn was again tinting the woods of Alfreton, and the morning dews freshened the rank fern beneath the sturdy oaks in the Park.

We have preserved a kind of unity of time in detailing the events of this history, which have barely occupied a year from their first commencement until their approaching close.

It was the wedding-day and Katharine had risen early to look forth from her window upon the same forest scene which she had enjoyed nearly a year before.   The deer were reclining beneath the oak trees or browsing among the gorse and fern, and the broad river beyond was backed by the wooded hills. She felt happy, very happy, but there was a melancholy mingled with her joy. She was about to leave her mother, and embark upon a fresh existence, but the future looked bright and promising. There was only that one little drawback which she sometimes felt without acknowledging. Oh! banish the thought Katharine, or seek relief in prayer, for it seems too late to change thy destiny! At all events she did not change it, and the doubt had, perhaps, passed away when, a few hours later, she gave her troth to remain his own until death.

In the interval between the return from the church and the *déjeuner* many of the guests—for this double wedding was one of the gayest events which the county had witnessed for many a day, and the provincial press devoted two columns and a half to the affair—wandered through the open windows of the drawing-room, upon the terrace and the grass-plots beneath.

Emmeline seemed in tolerable spirits. She alone, of the two brides, made her appearance out of doors. There may have been a slight shade of melancholy even in *her* merry face, but not caused by the events of the day. She felt that her loss would be fully appreciated by her parents and that she could, therefore, afford to be happy. She was standing upon the terrace, talking to Lady Elliott and Sir Edward when Frank came up.

"Look at Fred flirting with your bridesmaids," said Sir Edward laughing. "I suppose we must get him to return thanks for them when their health is drunk?"

"O yes, there he is, with Grace and Agnes. I only hope, papa, that you will never give your consent to his marrying one of those girls."

"Here comes Edmund!" rejoined her father.

"And Mr. Bateson. What a bore !"

"Emmie dearest, you looked so sad in church !" whispered Frank.

"Enough to make me !"

"Leaving home, dearest ?"

"No, a letter mamma had this morning from Mrs. Seymour about poor Elsie. She is very ill !"

"From what ?" enquired her husband eagerly.

"Ah Frank, I don't like your over anxiety ! I shall be as jealous as a Turk I give you warning and I don't care a bit for your authority for I mumbled 'command' instead of 'obey' in the service," this last remark attracted the attention of the others, who laughed.

"Ha ! ha ! you see what you have got to expect. Caught a tartar. You should have kept to the *tartares* like me !" said Mr. Bateson.

"Been and done it !" ventured Edmund

Spencer, in a facetious tone which greatly displeased Mrs. Francis Elliott.

"Yes," she returned, "he has been and done it. Can you forgive him?"

Edmund appeared somewhat disconcerted at the unexpected question and, after fumbling about for a reply, stuttered out:

"Congratulate you both, most heartily."

"I think Frank has behaved rather ill to you, nevertheless, Mr. Spencer!" pursued the bride, in her most satirical tone, "it is very good and charitable in you to forgive him."

Elliott felt a little uneasy, but he did not see any method of checking his wife's unruly tongue. The eyes of all around were fixed upon her, and if he had not already resigned himself to allowing free vent to her humour, it was high time that he should accustom himself to this necessity of his future life.

"Don't know what you mean Miss—Mrs. Elliott, I mean," replied Edmund timidly, after pausing confusedly and discovering no way of escape," don't suppose Mr. Elliott ever did—anything—not anything to—in short wish him every happiness I'm sure—both of you." These sentences were jerked out in a low voice and, in such a manner, as to allow the hearers to imagine the interstices filled up by something still more inaudible.

"No, it really is too kind of you, Mr Spencer, to forgive and forget as you seem inclined to do," pursued the unrelenting beauty, "it was shameful, after making him a confidant of your feelings, for him to betray you as he has?"

"Hasn't betrayed me—no, no!" returned poor Edmund, endeavouring to reasume his off hand manner, "good friends, I hope, always."

"Glad of it!" rejoined Emmeline, mimicking the omission of pronouns: "great friends, you know, formerly very thick together, eh Mr. Spencer?"

Poor Edmund had, perhaps, already smelt a rat, but he now turned perfectly crimson, and looked as if he would willingly have burrowed into the earth like one of his own ferrets. Frank was not much happier, and rather wished his pretty bride at Jericho just at that moment.

"Now, I'll appeal to you, Mr. Bateson," continued the bride, "don't you think it rather a shame of my husband, after being the confidant to his friend's attachment to go and marry the beloved object?"

"Oh shame! shame!" answered Bateson enjoying the joke.

"Jolly girl, Miss Emmie, eh?" she went on taunting the unfortunate youth."

"Hard upon me!" ventured the martyr making a great effort, "stories out of school— not fair."

"It is hard," said Frank, "I confess! do leave him alone, Emmie!"

"Hard! it is harder upon me I think," retorted the inexorable tormentor, "why, papa!" she exclaimed turning to Sir Edward, who looked displeased, but resigned, "Mr. Edmund Spencer says that he and I were very thick together. I fancied one of us might be thick, but I did flatter myself we were not both thick, together!"

There was a roar of laughter and Frank entreated his bride to cease from her persecutions. Edmund found an opportunity to slink away. He afterwards met Fred Morden with his sisters and heartily agreed with his friend's remark that: "these weddings are awfully slow concerns."

At length the breakfast was announced. The champagne flowed, the cake was cut, and, after a lugubrious oration from Sir Edward, Cecil Montagu and Frank rose, successively, to return thanks. Next came the health of the parents, and lastly that of the bridesmaids.

"Ladies and gentlemen," said Fred, rising

and looking facetiously at the Miss Spencers, who sat on either side of him, " I thank you in the name of the young ladies whose health you have been drinking. They wish they could speak for themselves and tell you how pleased they are. It is the proudest and happiest day, but one, in their lives, and that one will be when they drop the maids and become nothing but brides. They all look forward with anxiety to that moment, and I can only tell the two, between whom I have the honour to be standing, how happy I should be with either."

Cheers and blushes succeeded this very strange but brief oration.

" Why Fred is making a public proposal !" exclaimed Emmeline to Frank, " I do believe he turned Mahommetan in the East and intends to marry both."

" And then his brother-in-law may call you, Emmie !"

" Not for some time, I think ! Have you spoken to those Carrowsby people. I see Miss

Pinsant there, munching away, at something better than her own dry cake."

Old Mr. Lisle, who was seated near to Katharine told her that they had hoped to have brought Herbert, but that they could not induce him to leave Gloucestershire.

"He will be sorry to hear that Mr. and Mrs. Seymour are in great affliction, owing to the state of their daughter's health. Lady Morden heard to-day."

Laura who sat only a short distance off, caught the words :

"Is Miss Seymour very ill ?" she said to Lady Morden.

"I am afraid so—"

In the detailed account of the wedding which was despatched to Cawthorne, this fact was not omitted.

"Katharine !" said Montagu, "may I leave the room with you ?"

"Yes," she replied, and the two happy couples went to prepare for their departure.

CHAPTER VII.

MELPOMENE.

On the same day the house of mercy in Bloomsbury was silent and dreary.

Upon the appointment of the chaplain, a room had been set apart for a chapel and fitted up with propriety and taste. There, in solitude, knelt Edward Baring, when a sister, approaching him gently from behind, whispered : " will you come now, sir ? she has asked for you."

The clergyman followed his guide and entered the small and scantily furnished chamber where Elsie lay. The fever which she had caught in her attendance upon the sick, had so altered her appearance, that it was hard to recognize in that pale exhausted frame, any traces of the beautiful creature she had been a month before.

"Do you feel better?" he enquired.

"Oh, no!" she replied.

"Can you resign yourself to God?"

"Almost entirely now. I feel so much happier since I have thrown all my cares upon Him. I have sometimes been perplexed with doubts, but, upon the whole, I have felt my Saviour very near to me ever since my communion. Tell me of Him—of the Lord Jesus Christ, whom I so long spurned and rejected!"

Edward Baring spoke and read to her.

"Remember me to Mr. Lisle!" she said, feebly, "give him this agate cross and tell him I wore it until the last, and that it ended by triumphing over all that I had formerly opposed to it. Tell him of my baptism, and how I learnt the truth that we must become as little children, babes in Christ."

" I will—I will tell him—do not talk too much."

" Oh, let me tell you—I may never talk again.   Oh ! Mr. Baring, how I wish my own dear mother and my father could see the truth. Promise you will speak to them in my name, and pray for them."

" You may recover and be able to lead them to the truth."

" I shall not—I am sure I shall not recover ! —promise me."

" I promise it—and your sisterhood ?"

" I have left written directions about it, which I wish you to read and act upon, if you see fit.   Pray with me now—I feel so faint."

Mr. and Mrs. Seymour were in the house, and returned to their daughter's room before the chaplain had left her side.

" Father !" said Elsie, " will you promise me something ?"

" Anything, my own darling child ! what is it ?"

" When I am gone, will you remember that some of my last prayers were that you might be led to see as I do now—to believe in Jesus Christ as the very Son of God, and to accept the doctrine of the Holy Trinity ?"

" My child ! my darling ! I will remember all you say. But you are not going to leave us—no, no."

"My father ! do not forget my words."

" No, my dearest Elsie—and I will protect your sisterhood. I promise you I will always befriend it, and subscribe as I have done."

Mr. Seymour said this with considerable effort, for he did not know how else to escape the one point to which she clung, and for which his convictions were unprepared.

The conversation seemed to fatigue her, and she fell once more into a dozing state, from which, after some hours, she awoke with worse symptoms. From that time she scarcely spoke,

and, early on the following morning, breathed
her last.

*   *   *   *   *

Herbert Lisle called during the day. He
had received a letter from Baring and had hur-
ried up to town.

"Is she better ?" he asked.

"It is all over. She died this morning."

Edward Baring related her last words, and
gave him the agate cross.

"May I see her ?"

"Come ! I will ask."

The mother sat by the open shell in which
the body was laid out, and there, in her white
robes, with a face as white as the muslin, lay
the beautiful Elsie Seymour, still lovely in
death.

She had left directions concerning her
funeral. The coffin was placed in the chapel
where, upon the morning of the burial, the
holiest service of the church was celebrated.

The sisters accompanied their foundress to her grave, in one of the cemeteries in the neighbourhood of the metropolis.

"Let us not sorrow as those without hope," said Edward Baring, "her body sleeps here until the resurrection, but her soul is in Paradise with Jesus!"

CONCLUSION.

IT is usual to wind up a tale after some such fashion as the following :

Cecil Montagu and his bride enjoyed their honeymoon tour upon the Wye, and their felicity might have been perfect, but for a newspaper which they opened at Ross, containing the announcement of Elsie's death. This tinged their joy with a shade of sadness. A few months later and the malady which had so long threatened the life of Lord Alcester, proved fatal, and Katharine became a countess.

Frank Elliott and his merry wife were yet more deeply pained by the intelligence, which reached them at Lyons, through the columns of *Galignani*. They were on their road to

Italy, which Emmeline had so long desired to visit, but which she ever connected with memories of Elsie.

It has been reported to us that, during her next visit to Lockwood, Mary Elliott met Mr. Grant, the widower of whom her aunt had spoken so favourably, and that the impression he made was such, that she was induced to overlook the single encumbrance, and to adopt the designation of Mrs. Grant.

It is not certain up to this hour whether Frederick Morden has made up his mind to which of the Miss Spencers he will propose, but it is rumoured that he has never yet made an offer to either, and, what gives additional probability to the story is, that neither has accepted him.

A short time ago, Mr. Bateson was seen enjoying a dinner at the Café Philippe, which he declared was not equal to the old Rocher de Cancale.

Lord Portaldowne was furious when he

heard the particulars of Alfred Johnson's history, but the latter had obtained what he required, and throve as rogues often do in this world. It is to be regretted in this instance (as in so many others) that truth and poetical justice do not coincide, or we might, perchance, have been able to announce a marriage between Alfred Johnson and Madame Hoffner, the two black sheep of the story, who should have concluded tragically, by so wearying each other of life, as severally to commit suicide. The fact is that Madame Hoffner returned to Germany with her savings, and lived much respected by all who did not know her.

Madame Arnstein considered that she owed it to her children to remain at Munich, where they were educated in a manner befitting their new position. She looked forward to a future return to Cawthorne, but, upon learning the death of her parents, postponed it indefinitely. The latter days of the old people were cheered by the society of their favourite son, who had enlisted many years before, and came who back, laden with honours won at Alma and at Inkermann.

The Perdons devoted themselves to their task, but we have never heard whether Herbert succeeded in prevailing upon the bishop to ordain William to the office of deacon. He and Penrose were always upon the most cordial terms.

The people of Winfield continue to obey the rule of Matthew Beakham, notwithstanding sundry democratic threatenings at a rebellion.

Old Mr. and Mrs. Lisle of Carrowsby lived for some years, but were more than ever tied to the society of Miss Pinsant by an event which, whatever may be thought of it, afforded much domestic happiness to the parties concerned, namely, the marriage of Herbert Lisle to his cousin Laura. They have a son, who will, if he lives, deprive the earl of all hopes of Cawthorne. Among the occasional visitors at the court are Mr. and Mrs. Seymour, who often open their hearts about Elsie. When last there, they met Edward Baring, who informed them of the progress of the sisterhood. Upon the death of Arthur Winslow, which occurred before he had been ordained, Baring had undertaken the permanent superintendence of the whole society, Mr. Seymour having appropriated a sufficient sum for his maintenance.

Whether her prayers were ever granted we cannot tell, but, as among the sisters over whom she had presided, so also in the circle of her dearest friends, a halo of light seemed to enshrine and consecrate the memory of Elsie Seymour !

THE END.

F. C. Newby   Printer, 30, Welbeck Street, Cavendish Sq.

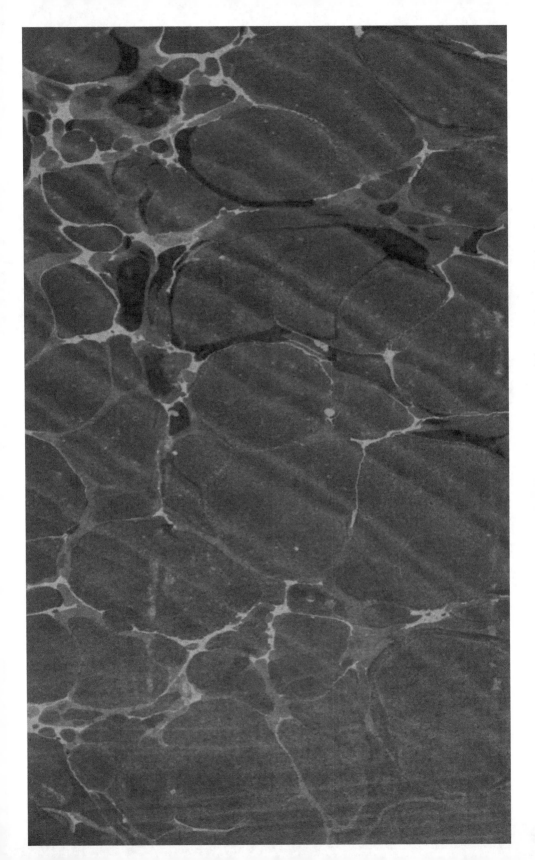

FRANK MERRYWEATHER.

A NOVEL.

BY HENRY G. AINSLIE YOUNG ESQ.

IN TWO VOLUMES.

VOL. I.

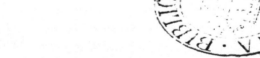

LONDON:

THOMAS CAUTLEY NEWBY, PUBLISHER,
30, WELBECK ST., CAVENDISH SQ.

1853.

FRANK MERRYWEATHER.

CHAPTER I.

He hath an Argosy bound to Tripolis,
another to the Indies ; I understand moreover
upon the Rialto, he hath a third at Mexico,
a fourth for England,—and other ventures he
hath.

Merchant of Venice.

FEW events can be more galling to
man's pride, or more calculated to wound
his self-love, than the discovery that he

has formed a false estimate of his own abilities. The associations by which he has been surrounded may have led him to suppose that the position he enjoys is due exclusively to his own energy and talents, or is the result of his superiority in some particular attribute over those amongst whom he has been thrown. From the success of his plans in one instance, he may have drawn the erroneous conclusion that his capacity is of an order to qualify him for the accomplishment of any task, however difficult, that will conduce to his interest, or gratify his ambition. In prosperity the not unwilling ear drinks in the flattering assurances of parasites who, while they excite the contempt of their dupe, insensibly acquire by their importunity an ascendency over his better judgment, and in despite of his original doubt and mistrust, eventually succeed in instilling their poison into his mind.

But from whatever cause may have sprung the exaggerated notions of his own perfections, when some rough lesson of the world convinces him that his level is amongst those whom he had lately despised, and looked upon as creatures of an inferior mould,—when he is taught that he is not what he fondly supposed himself to be, and that all the projects he had formed for his own personal aggrandisement are chimerical, the disappointment, the most bitter that can occur, the disappointment of himself *by himself*, is susceptible of no alleviation. He would bear with less chagrin the loss of fortune than so deadly a blow to his vanity.

Mr. Munroe had been for years in India, where by steady perseverance and the exercise of talents, which though not resplendent were considerably above mediocrity, he had raised himself to a high position in the mercantile world. His firm, which had been considered one of the best and richest in the East, acquired its celebrity solely through his good management, and how entirely dependent it was upon him for the proper conduct of its affairs, was manifested by his being instantly recalled to resume the reins, when, upon one occasion, he had resigned them for the purpose of spending a short time in the hills.   On his return he found the house had suffered an immense loss, through the failure of a speculation rashly entered into during his absence, and that his partners were on the brink of ruin. His first step towards stopping the mischief that had occurred was to allay the panic occasioned by a report of the loss that had been sustained, and which, large as it was, had, as usual in such cases, been greatly exaggerated.   This he accomplished with the most consummate skill, and his judicious arrangements and indefatigable exertions, in a short time restored the affairs of the house to their former prosperous state.

Two or three years had elapsed since this event when, his wealth having greatly increased, he found himself enabled to retire from business with a princely fortune, and after a residence of thirty years in India, he determined to seek in England a wider field for the exercise of his talents. A seat in the House of Commons, and even his ultimate elevation to the peerage, as the result of a successful parliamentary career, loomed indistinctly in the distance amongst the visions of future ambition which his past success conjured up. Nor did the experience which he had gained in India, nor his undoubted natural talents, suggest to him all that was unreal in these expectations.

An able historian truly tells us that the man, who, having left England when a boy, returns to it after thirty or forty years spent in India, will find, be his talents what they may, that he has much both to learn and unlearn before he can take his place amongst English states-

men.   Of the truth of this remark, even
when applied to those civil servants, who,
with so much ability, govern our vast
empire in the East, Mr. Munroe was
profoundly ignorant, and the idea of
being personally disqualified to discharge
the ordinary duties of the new position
to which he aspired, never entered
his imagination.   When, however, he
changed the scene from the limited
society of India, with its contracted
views, to strive in England amongst
the thronged avenues to distinction, he
was destined quickly to discover the
egregious folly of these expectations.
There was a field here, doubtless, but a
field in which he had as much chance of
success as Gulliver would have had in a
trial of physical strength against a host of
Brobdignags ; and, indeed, could Mr.
Munroe have been transported, after a
long residence in Lilliput, into the
country where this fabulous race was
supposed to dwell, his surprise at the

relative proportions of the inhabitants, could not have been greater, than that which he was about to feel at his own manifest inferiority to the men he had supposed it would prove an easy task to influence and direct.

Happily for the security of our empire and the welfare of the millions whom we govern in India; the modern adventurer can no longer hope to follow in the foot-steps of a Clive or a Warren Hastings. A regular gradation in the civil and military services of the company, and a despotic, but in general a mild and just administration of the government, have long since succeeded the disregard of individual rights, and the anarchy which marked our first establishment on that continent. A faint, perhaps a caricature resemblance, might however be traced between the class of English residents in India to which Mr. Munroe belonged, and the earlier and successful wanderers in the East. Mr. Munroe had never like

Warren Hastings triumphed over a Nun-
comar, or made a chief justice his tool.
He had never, like Clive, after the battle
of Plassey, walked between heaps of
gold, crowned with rubies and diamonds,
and helped himself to two or three
hundred thousand pounds; nor did he
belong either to the civil or military
service of the East India Company. His
experience had been gained in the count-
ing house. His authority had been
exercised over submissive junior partners
and obedient clerks. He daily walked
between the ledgers displayed in his
ample establishment, and his eye rested
upon the rich deposit accounts which
his name and credit attracted to his firm,
with as complacent a glance as Clive
could have bestowed on the spoil of
Surajah Dowlah's treasury: but an un-
usual display of firmness was required
from him, only when a doubtful specula-
tion in indigo or opium, or the inex-
perience or rashness of those with whom

he was associated called for an unwonted
exercise of these qualities. The result
was nevertheless, in one respect, practi-
cally the same, for he returned to Europe
with a fortune, which, even in the days
of Clive and Warren Hastings, would
have been considered not unworthy of a
nabob.

Mr. Munroe was of humble origin,
and his parents had with difficulty
secured him the benefit of such an
education as a day school in a remote
English village could supply. As his
wealth increased, he frequently came
in contact with those in whose minds
the seeds of early instruction had been
carefully sown, and on these occasions
he became transiently and vaguely sen-
sible of some undefined disadvantage
under which he laboured. His busy
life as a merchant did not, however,
afford him sufficient leisure to analyse
this feeling with the accuracy which his
natural activity would otherwise have

prompted him to bestow upon it, and his daily pursuits, crowned with the success which his mercantile skill and experience had rendered familiar to him, banished any permanent sense of inferiority.

The prevailing characteristic of his appearance was rigidity. A rigidity not confined to a countenance most strikingly expressive of this quality, but displayed in every movement of his inflexible person. His speech was slow and measured, every word being solemnly articulated, and his manner patronizing, though reserved and impressive. We say impressive, because he always impressed those with whom he conversed with the feeling, that could his manner have been changed into words, their purport would have been, "I am Mr. Munroe, the great merchant."

One trait in his character, however, stood forth in strong relief amid the harsh and even repulsive qualities of which it was composed, like a struggling beam of sunshine over a stormy sea. He evinced a sincere affection for his wife, which although savouring of his peculiar disposition, nevertheless showed that naturally he was susceptible of other feelings than those which the daily strife for wealth engendered. He had married, some ten or twelve years before leaving India, the daughter of the commander in chief, then a graceful and accomplished girl of seventeen, who contrary to her own inclinations was persuaded into the marriage by her father, a man of good family but of limited means.

The connubial knot having been tied, however, Mrs. Munroe resolved, unpromising as the materials were, to make her home as cheerful as lay in her power. By womanly tact and a happy way she possessed of adapting herself to the diametrically opposite nature of her husband, she maintained

an influence over him, which, while
it added to his happiness, preserved
herself from sinking in his consideration
to a secondary object in comparison
with his pursuits, a result which would
infallibly have taken place had she not
possessed other attractions than her
good looks and youthful figure.   But
the influence thus acquired was after-
wards preserved by a more durable
cement, for there gradually sprang up
in this gentle nature a feeling of love,
and under the influence of this feeling
what excuses could she not make for
his defects, what favourable construc-
tions could she not put upon all his
actions, when she knew herself to
be the only object of any kindlier
feelings that he possessed.   It would
be difficult to trace exactly the course
by which she arrived at this result.
It may have been from a sense of
gratification in the first instance, that
her husband, who was habitually so

reserved and distant, should relax to her alone—it may have been in admiration of that determined self reliance, which, while refusing all extrinsic aid, depended upon himself alone for the furtherance of his plans, or, she may have felt herself bound, from a sense of generosity, to return the insolated affection of a man so cut off from all the sympathies which render life worth preserving.

A year after their marriage Mrs. Munroe gave birth to a daughter, the only child they ever possessed, which became a source of great disappointment to him, as he had anxiously looked forward to having a son, who might inherit the means and position he had already acquired, and the still greater honours he hoped to obtain. It was a circumstance that would naturally rankle deep in the breast of a man whose prospects in the world had as yet met with an uninterrupted tide of success. His daughter consequently found little favour in his eyes, and though perhaps he felt no positive dislike to her, yet there was a total absence of paternal feeling in his breast.

Such then were the feelings and views of Mr. Munroe, when he embarked for England. The wealthy merchant on his departure was not greeted with a salute. No show of military parade indicated that an officer high in the civil or military service of the company, was about to leave the presidency, but with the exception of this official display, few Governors General, on quitting our Eastern possessions, have received more numerous or well deserved marks of respect and attention, than those which attended his embarkation. The stately Indiaman anchored at several miles from the shore, awaited his arrival with her anchor "A peak," that as short a space of time as possible might elapse, between the arrival of the most important

passenger she was about to bear to
Europe, and the moment of her
departure. The side ropes were manned
by the officers of the ship, and the
Captain stood uncovered on the deck to
welcome his distinguished guest. A
suite of cabins had been previously
engaged for Mrs. Munroe and his
daughter, and the care with which they
had been fitted up, and the obsequious
bearing of the Ayahs who had been
engaged to attend upon them, and of
the Portuguese servants whose services
had been secured for himself, all tended
to keep alive the associations he had
formed in India, and were in strict
keeping with this, the last passage of
Oriental life.

As soon as Mr. Munroe had been
ushered into his cabin, the preparations
for departure were rapidly completed.
The Massulah boatmen returned to their
own unwieldy machines, and the owners
of the various Catamarans which

swarmed around the ship, reluctantly abandoned its good cheer to resume their amphibious existence. The anchor was then secured. The huge sails which had hung in folds from the spars, were sheeted home, and the salute which etiquette forbade on shore, boomed from the sides of the gallant vessel, as yielding to the land breeze she gracefully sped upon her homeward voyage, under the influence of a cloud of canvas.

CHAPTER II.

Hark, they whisper ; angels say,
Sister spirit, come away !
What is this absorbs me quite ?
Steals my senses, shuts my sight,
Drowns my spirit, draws my breath ?
Tell me, my soul, can this be death ?

Pope.

IT was a bright day in the month of
March, when the welcome sound of
"land" was heard from the mast head,
as the Indiaman with a favourable
westerly wind proceeded up the English

Channel. Off the Isle of Wight the
services of a pilot boat were easily
secured, to convey Mr. Munroe and his
family to Portsmouth, and the wealthy
Indian merchant landed at the very
place which thirty years before he had
quitted to seek his fortune in the
East.

His first care upon arriving in London
was to secure a house at the West End
of the Town, in which he might at once
assume that position in society, which
he conceived to be open to him without
an effort.   The house was soon obtained
and an unlimited order, accompanied by
a reference to his bankers, quickly
adorned it with all the skill and taste
of London upholstery.   Mr. Munroe
also found himself warmly greeted by
many of his former friends in India, and
particularly by the London correspon-
dents of his house, who acted as his
agents, and who were well informed as
to the extent of his wealth.   Nor did the

aspirants for seats in the direction of the East India Company, fail to present themselves at his door, naturally supposing that his name would figure in the list of Proprietors of East India stock, with a full complement of stars appended to it. To this class of visitors must be added the more cautious approaches of relations, who had not emerged from the humble position in society which he himself occupied previously to his migration to the East, and who timidly sought their wealthy kinsman, in the hope that through his assistance and influence the path to wealth might also be opened to them. These and the few stray acquaintances whom good dinners and a large establishment will always attract in London, Mr. Munroe soon found, however, constituted the whole circle of his associates. In the mean time the great stream of fashionable and political life passed him unnoticed, like one of those eddies which seem chained to a particular spot, while the mighty current of which they form a part flows steadily on.

It has been said,—whether truly or not we cannot affirm, for we seek only to snatch the manners and customs which float on the surface of society, and our modest history does not aspire to the dignity of a Philosophical or Political essay,—but it *has* been said, that the barriers which the policy of our Monarchical and Aristocratical system erects between the various ranks of society, can only be effectually surmounted, and that political power can only be obtained by wealth, sufficient in amount to open the avenues to distinction, combined with abilities capable of making those avenues subservient to the purposes of their possessor. Mere vulgar uneducated wealth, will only attract an amount of ridicule, proportionate to the extent of notoriety

which its owner insists upon acquiring.
Science, genius, learning, unassisted by
wealth, will make its possessor a member
of many a learned society, and the
Mecænas to whom his last work is dedi-
cated, will probably not fail to bid him
welcome to his festive board, where he
will be considered as ornamental and as
much in his proper place, as the last
picture purchased to adorn his ban-
queting room, or the new service of plate
which blazes on his sideboard. If there
have been a few brilliant exceptions to
this rule, they serve but to prove its
general correctness, and it is the rare
union of the two great advantages we
have referred to, that can alone secure
the influence and position to which Mr.
Munroe's ignorance of English society
led him to aspire.

Amongst the acquaintances attracted
by Mr. Munroe's principal establishment
in —— square, was the Honorable
Captain Saville Blakeney, a gentleman

ments, too, though exceedingly superficial, were versatile. Amongst other pursuits, he sometimes dabbled a little in politics, and had once written an article in one of the daily journals,— but only once, for no persuasion could induce the editor to incur a similar risk a second time. He was so incensed at this gross piece of presumption on the part of a mere "quill driver," as he contemptuously styled those who hold almost despotic sway over the public mind, that he never again offered to wield his pen in their service. It remains to say of Captain Blakeney, that he never neglected the duty he owed to himself— a duty which with him involved a total disregard of the rights and feelings of others: that in his vocabulary, principle meant expediency : the world the class to which he belonged ; the welfare of society, the interest of that class, and his own in particular, as its most important entity.

But no one, not even Captain Blakeney, could remain insensible to Mrs. Munroe's charming and fascinating manner; and such was her influence, that he occasionally endeavoured, when in her company, to divest himself of that offensive egotism, which formed so essential a part of his nature. She did not share in the delusion of her husband; and when, with the quick perception of woman, she saw that he was endeavouring to tread a path unsuited to his talents, she advised and implored him to forbear; but finding her opinion disregarded, with equal good feeling she now seconded his views to the utmost of her power, and the attractions of her drawing room were frequently found greater than any to be met with in the fashionable circles, where the *élite* of London society assembled. Her thoughts and energies had always been devoted to him. She had ever entered with an *entente cordiale* into all his busy schemes.

Throughout a life devoid of felicitous associations, she had invariably displayed a willingness to sacrifice her own wishes, when they in any way interfered with his plans, and had preserved unimpaired the serenity of disposition which had characterized her in youth. Notwithstanding her amiable character, however, she could not at first repress a feeling of antipathy to Captain Blakeney, but conceiving it unjust to entertain an unfavourable impression of any one without a cause, she strove to master it. Her efforts in this respect were attended with success, and Captain Blakeney now frequently alluded in his easy manner to the inauspicious commencement of their acquaintance ; and how much his star was in the ascendant, when the mists and clouds had cleared away which so enviously kept the bright sunbeams she scattered around from ever alighting upon him.

" Positively," said Captain Blakeney, as he seated himself at Mr. Munroe's dinner table, towards the close of the London season, "I have been apprehensive, till within the last ten minutes, of my liberty. I have been assailed with remonstrance, entreaties, and even, I assure you, Mrs. Munroe, threats, to induce me to break my promise of dining with you to day. As if any consideration whatever could make me give up such a pleasure! My assailants fortunately left me for a few minutes. I instantly took advantage of the respite, and here I am, once more a happy man."

"I am sure," said Mrs. Munroe, "the exertions you have made to give us the pleasure of your society are worthy of our warmest acknowledgments. From what may have arisen this wish to detain you?"

"This is the anniversary of one of the actions in which our regiment was engaged in India, and though, as you are aware, I have left the army; yet they wished me to be present at a dinner that is to be given in commemoration of

the event.   By the way, I think Mr.
Munroe   knew   Colonel   Merryweather
who commanded us at the commence-
ment of the action?"

"Well," replied Mr. Munroe, "and if
anything could have mitigated the sor-
row I felt at his death, it would have
been the gallant manner in which he fell
—fighting at the head of his regiment."

"Ah," replied Captain Blakeney, "It
was a monstrous thing to send one of
Her Majesty's crack hussar regiments
out to India.   The order would have
done credit to the Goths and Vandals,
but was wholly unworthy of the Horse
Guards in the middle of the nineteenth
century.   The fact is, that the country
cannot spare such men."

"Did you see Colonel Merryweather
fall?" asked Mr. Munroe.

"No, I had been sent with a small
detachment in pursuit of about five
hundred of the enemy that had fled
early in the action."

" And by the help of providence, how many of the infidels did you smite?" asked Mrs. Mackintosh, an elderly widow, who, having been on friendly terms with Mr. Munroe in India, had renewed his acquaintance in England, and had subsequently introduced Captain Blakeney, between whom and herself some mysterious bond of connexion apparently existed.

" How many?" repeated Captain Blakeney. "Oh," he resumed, after a pause, "we rode and they ran till a river stopped their further flight, when they made some show of resistance. They were immediately driven into the river, and the greater part perished within sight of thousands of their countrymen who had come to their rescue on the opposite bank."

" Unconverted of course?" said Mrs. Mackintosh.

" Most probably," replied Captain Blakeney, "for the river, as is frequently the case with such as are fed by mountain streams, was, at that moment, a foaming torrent. I could not, however, allow this consideration to weigh with me.   There was an enemy in front, and I gave the order to charge!   And such was the dauntless resolution of the men and their high state of discipline, that they swam across in line, and landed on the opposite side as if on parade; with the exception of one man, who, having allowed the tail of his horse to become entangled with his accoutrements, so impeded the animal's exertions, that he fell two or three lengths behind his comrades.   Before the evening, however, he had been tried by a drum head Court Martial."

"Ah!" exclaimed Mrs. Mackintosh, in a tone of mingled sorrow and reproof.

"Of course the enemy could offer but little opposition to men so trained," said Mr. Munroe, with a smile.

"Not eventually," replied Captain

Blakeney, "though at first I grant you there was some desperate fighting; but men properly disciplined are equal to anything. Mine were, in the present instance, completely victorious, and such was the number of prisoners we took, that when I ordered all their beards to be cut off—a great indignity to a Mussulman, and therefore a fitting punishment for their presumption in opposing Her Majesty's troops—the whole regiment was supplied with hair mattresses. In the evening we swam across the river again, in line, and returned to camp, but our exultation was immediately checked by hearing of the death of our Colonel. By the way, did he not leave a son called—a—Frank, I think?"

"Yes, yes," said Mr. Munroe impatiently.

"Where is he now?"

"In England."

"In England?" repeated Captain Blakeney.

"Yes, at school, I am his guardian," said Mr. Munroe, abruptly.

Captain Blakeney looked surprised, and evidently wished to pursue his enquiries further, but hesitated to do so in defiance of these manifestations of impatience on the part of his entertainer, and he therefore let the subject drop for the present, but not without glancing significantly at Mrs. Mackintosh, who instantly cast her eyes to the ground. When the ladies had left the room, however, and the jovial god had opened the hearts and loosened the tongues of his votaries, Captain Blakeney again led this part of the conversation up to the point at which it had terminated. He then quickly ascertained that the object of his enquiry was at school in Cornwall, and that Mr. Munroe defrayed the expenses of his education from a fund of about twenty thousand pounds, the accumulation of some prize money, and of surplus income which Colonel Merryweather had most unaccountably left in his hands without any instructions.

Captain Blakeney listened to this latter piece of information with such evident interest, and manifested so much surprise that Mr. Munroe laughingly exclaimed, "Why, you would almost lead one to suppose that you were able to throw some light upon the matter!"

"I?" exclaimed Captain Blakeney, with some embarrassment, "how—by what—what do you mean?"

"I merely spoke in jest," replied Mr. Munroe. "All chance of clearing up that mystery has long ceased. The Colonel's will, however, was altogether an extraordinary document."

"You mean the specific bequest of so large a portion of his property to Mrs. Mackintosh, and the absence of all direction as to the residue?"

Mr. Munroe nodded assent.

"It does not," continued Captain

Blakeney, "argue much in her favour. There must have been reasons——peculiar reasons, one would think, for such a proceeding. As to his son, perhaps he adopted this mode of providing for him, knowing that the law would give him what his will left undisposed of."

"It may be so as to Frank," said Mr. Munroe, resuming his usually reserved manner, "though such a course was inconsistent with the known character and habits of my friend. But," he continued, with increased coldness and reserve, "your suggestion with reference to Mrs. Mackintosh, if I understand it rightly, is still less consistent with his character, to say nothing of the injustice you do the lady."

Captain Blakeney felt that he had pushed the subject as far as discretion would permit; and unwilling to appear to take an interest in arrangements with which he was supposed to have no concern, he drew his chair nearer the

end of the table, and commenced a topic
to which he was aware his host would
not fail to lend a willing ear.

"Of course, Munroe," he com-
menced in a confidential tone, "you
have by this time quite made up your
mind to obtain a seat in parliament
next election ?"

"Nearly," replied Mr. Munroe, "very
nearly. Indeed, I think I may venture
to say I have."

"Venture to say!" repeated Captain
Blakeney almost indignantly, "why your
success in the house does not admit of a
doubt! Not—a—single—doubt! It is
your proper sphere. Your great practical
knowledge, your experience, and your
habits of business, will, to say nothing of
what may happen hereafter, at once
make you a friend of incalculable worth
to the party you espouse, and a
formidable opponent of the adverse side.
I would not insult a person of your
calibre of understanding by asking

which party you would support.   The
suppression of the mob, and the
preservation of the power and influence
of the legitimate rulers of the land, are
of course views which everyone who is
only guided by a sense of justice would
embrace."

"Quite so," returned Mr. Munroe,
"I should decidedly support the landed
interest; and I dare say you would find
that my dislike of the mob is as great as
your own."

"Then it is inveterate! And as for
those demagogues of the present day,
who talk of parliamentary reform and
other similar absurdities, why they
ought, — they ought to be hanged!
What has raised this country to its
present elevation but—"

"And what," interposed Mr. Munroe,
who perceived that wine and politics were
rapidly driving his guest into a high
state of excitement, "what, now, is
your candid opinion of the best means

to be employed to secure the return of a member to parliament; myself, for instance?"

"You must be entirely guided by circumstances," replied Captain Blakeney, with an immediate change of manner. "I have had some experience in these matters, and I should recommend you, as you have never yet been in parliament, to stand for some small borough, and not spend a farthing more than the legitimate expenses; for in these days, if you indulge in ancient English hospitality, you are as likely as not to be unseated for bribery. Promise anything, and everything—more than the whole House of Commons, or any other house, could perform. Ask them to sit down and think of what they would like to have done, and whatever it may be, prove— *prove* to them, that it is not only to their interest, but to the interest of the country, to the interest of every individual in the country—your own

private interest included—to have their
wishes carried out to the letter, and
that they cannot fail to be complied
with.   Should these measures prove
inadequate, you might then pay a sum
of money into the provincial bank for
the purpose, as you would of course
give your supporters to understand, of
distributing amongst them when the
period of petitioning against your
return has passed."

" But the electors may not be willing
to record their votes for one who only
holds out to them an expectation of
future benefit, particularly if some
former candidate has ever adopted the
means you suggest to beguile them
with false hopes, and my opponents
should adopt a more practical mode of
securing their support.   Besides, I
cannot say that I feel quite satisfied as
to the propriety of your manœuvres."

" Not satisfied as to the propriety,
my dear sir ! You really surprise me.

Why everything that secures success is proper under such circumstances. The *end* sanctions the means. You help to preserve the constitution by securing your own return. It must be borne in mind, moreover, that these rascals are really not fit to have a voice in the affairs of the nation. It is a right wrested from us by the demagogues and agitators whom they support, and our only resource is—

" To spoil the spoiler as we may,
  And from the robber rend the prey !"

" The candidate is certainly not exclusively responsible for the necessity of having recourse to artifice," said Mr. Munroe, " for if the electoral body were incorruptible, corruption could scarcely be practised ; but I should leave such minor details to the agents I employed."

" Ah, in your case, again, such a course would be quite right. You

cannot be expected to enter into these
details, any more than a commander
in chief could be expected to lead a
squadron to the charge on the field of
battle. I can only say, be careful in
the selection of your agents, for if
through treachery or want of ability
they should fail to secure your return,
your defeat, I have no hesitation in
saying, would be a public loss."

"Mr. Munroe was in ordinary cases
perfectly aware when Captain Blake-
ney was giving free scope to his
imagination. Yet, wonderful to say,
he listened to these bold assertions
as if they were the candid confession
of his guest's convictions; and as the
same extravagant ideas had frequently
floated before his own vision, it seemed
to him that so unsought and spontaneous
a declaration in another, was the very
strongest testimony in favour of the
soundness of his own views. The
performance of some street musicians,

who commenced playing in front of the open windows, put a stop for the present to further conversation, and Mr. Munroe sat alternately revolving in his mind the ambitious thoughts which he seemed more and more warranted in entertaining, and the comparative obscurity of his present position. Impatient under the restraints which his ambitious temper taught him to believe were unfairly thrown around him, and discontented with the respectable position in which his character and means placed him, he resolved, while thus pondering, to purchase an estate in the country, and to await in retirement with his family the opportunity for action which the next general election would afford. He was partly led to the latter determination by the precarious state of Mrs. Munroe's health, which had become greatly impaired by her long residence in a tropical climate, and the urgent advice of the

family physician, that she should repair
immediately to the sea side.   With
characteristic energy Mr. Munroe pro-
ceeded on the next day to carry these
plans into effect.   Nor was he long
in discovering, with the assistance of
his   solicitor,   that   Ulvacombe,   in
Devonshire, a seat of Lord Carlbrook's,
was for sale.   That nobleman's embar-
rassments had rendered it necessary to
part with this portion of the family
property, and Mr. Munroe deeming it
expedient to act with great liberality,
the transfer was speedily made, and an
acquaintance thus commenced which,
from an unforeseen circumstance, sub-
sequently ripened into great intimacy.

Ulvacombe was a large picturesque
mansion, close to the sea side, and
surrounded by grounds, which, from their
elevated position, commanded an exten-
sive view.   The wings of the building
had evidently been an addition of recent
date,   but   the   turrets,   ornamented

devices, and quaint appearance of the remaining portion showed that it was one of those beautiful relics of the Elizabethan age, of which a few are still preserved to us. A short distance from the house, and visible from all the front windows, was a miniature lake, whose waters were unrivalled for clearness by any spring in the neighbourhood. On all sides but that by which it was approached from the house its edges were fringed with overhanging bushes, conspicuous amongst which were the honeysuckle and wild rose. The side that had been shorn of these natural ornaments, was traversed by a lawn that in colour would have surpassed the most favoured spots in the emerald isle, and extended from the rippling margin of the lake to the garden, a distance of nearly a quarter of a mile. Beyond, again, a long thicket of trees formed a complete screen, and effectually established the privacy of the inmates. Nor

were they less favoured on the side of
the sea, for the grounds comprised a
large bay, which could only be ap-
proached by the shore, when the tide
had receded to its utmost limits.

Such was Ulvacombe, the new abode
of Mr. Munroe, and doubtless the
novelty of finding himself the proprietor
of so magnificent an estate, the plea-
sure he anticipated from managing
it, and the gratification he also ex-
pected to derive from being considered
a person of consequence in the neigh-
bourhood, tended much to alleviate the
disappointment and mortification he had
experienced in London, and constituted
the best balm for his offended pride.

It was soon however his lot to discover,
that a man who has been engaged in a
constant routine of occupation, unless he
is possessed of resources within himself,
instantly finds the inactivity to which he
is compelled to submit in a rural life,
most dispiriting and irksome. At first

the better cultivation of a piece of
ground, the improvement of a hothouse,
the erection of lodges, and other pursuits
of the same trivial character, supplied
the food that was necessary to his
restless disposition, but gradually these
failed to interest him, his mind craved
for more exciting aliment, and in its
absence he grew peevish and discon-
tented. Business through life had at
once been his occupation and his
amusement, and so completely are we
the creatures of habit that he pined for
it as a child pines for a toy, a lover for
his mistress, or the miser for his gold.

But the imaginary evils with which he
allowed his peace of mind to be
disturbed, were soon superseded by a
more legitimate cause for the depression
of spirits with which he was haunted.
The health of Mrs. Munroe now began
to show unequivocal symptoms of
decline. Her strength ebbed day by day,
the colour completely forsook her fair

cheek, her voice became more and more subdued, and it was painfully evident that the last sad scene on the stage of life was fast approaching.

One evening in the early part of the autumn, Mrs. Munroe, accompanied by her daughter who was now in her sixteenth year, was being wheeled in a chair about the beautiful grounds of Ulvacombe, when on attaining a position that commanded a view of the surrounding country, she dismissed her attendants. The sun was setting on the landscape, and in its soft and refulgent rays, the varying hues of autumn were promiscuously blended on the wooded hills that intervened. So beautiful was the scene that both mother and daughter remained for some minutes contemplating it in silent admiration. There was a striking resemblance between the two, the same soft blue eyes, the same fair and delicate complexion belonged to both. Constance had also inherited in all its essential points her mother's character. Perhaps in trifles she was in the least degree wayward, but this fault lay entirely on the surface, and might be attributed to the readiness with which all her childish whims had been acceded to, and the absence of all reproach for those juvenile peccadillos, which are common to all the children of Adam, for she had been the idol of Mrs. Munroe, and her father's interest in her had been too slight to induce him to take any share in the formation of her character.

"How beautiful this landscape is," said Mrs. Munroe, at length breaking silence; "and yet I was thinking of how close a resemblance the departing year bears to those whose end is not far distant. Soon the few ornaments that nature still wears will be strewn by the winds, and then the aspect will be as cold and cheerless as the goal to which we are all hastening; and, Constance, I feel that I shall soon be there."

"Oh! mamma," said her daughter, "pray, pray do not say such things. Your spirits are low this evening. There are many, many happy years for you in prospect."

"Not in this world," replied Mrs. Munroe; "but I have not brought up a subject which I know to be painful to you without a cause. It is to impress upon you, dear child, the necessity to seek the aid of Him, by whose assistance alone you can be safe amidst the perils and dangers of the world you will shortly enter. Remember, that though you may have no watchful mother to protect you, there is one who bears more love to all his creatures than we are able to conceive, and never fails to hear those who call upon him. But above all things, remember how uncertain life is, and that at any moment we may be called hence. None of us can ever count upon a single day; not one can even take up an hour glass and say, 'thy course shall be run before mine.' Therefore, Constance, I entreat you to live in the remembrance that the eye of that Judge, before whom you may be summoned to appear without one moment's warning, is ever upon you."

Constance threw her arms round her mother's neck, and in tears promised compliance.

"And now," said Mrs. Munroe, smiling, "I will tell you of a wish that I have formed. It is that at certain times, on every Sabbath evening, for instance, you should, in the solitude of your own chamber, think over those truths which I have frequently endeavoured to impress upon your mind, and recal some of the happy hours we have spent together. Who knows," continued Mrs. Munroe, a slight tinge transfusing itself over her cheek, while her eye kindled with enthusiasm, "but what I, unknown to you, may be present, reading your thoughts, and

blessing you.   All is mystery beyond
the grave, but, that our spirits are
allowed sometimes to visit the scenes
where they dwelt while inhabiting the
body, does not, I confess, appear to
me improbable.   It will indeed be a
severe trial parting with my darling,
but it would greatly relieve the pain
of separation, could I be assured that
she would grant me this request; or
is it too great a boon to ask?"

"Oh, no, no," replied Constance.
"But why, mamma, why do you
continue to speak in this way? Your
indisposition is only temporary."

"I would that it were so for your
sake, dear Constance," said Mrs.
Munroe.

As she spoke a slight shiver passed
through her frame, which did not escape
the eye of her daughter, who instantly
implored her to return home. "This
wind is so very searching, mamma;
pray do not remain out in it any longer.

I will call the servants." And so saying, Constance ran across the lawn and beckoned to the men, who were only waiting at a little distance till their services should be required. They soon came, and Mrs. Munroe was conveyed back to the house, which she never again quitted alive.

Indeed, her prognostications were but too quickly verified. She had caught cold, which in her delicate state was of itself sufficient cause for apprehension; but the next day, when it settled upon her chest, the medical man who always attended her intimated that the result would be fatal; and in a short time not a hope could be entertained by the most sanguine. Towards evening, on the day when her recovery was finally despaired of, she had been half unconscious for some time, when, as if awakening from a dream, she looked around for a minute, and then, giving one of her hands to her husband and the other to her daughter, with a smile of ineffable sweetness, addressed a parting word to each.   Even the hard nature of Mr. Munroe was so affected, that for the first time since he was a child, tears flowed from his eyes, and he sobbed aloud.   The sorrow of Constance was too deep for any outward manifestation. She glanced from the physician, in whose look was written, as legibly as words could have made it, that there was no hope, and then upon the resigned countenance of her who was passing to another world ; but not a word, not a sound escaped her.   The apathy of grief had benumbed her faculties, and she remained crushed by the immensity of her misfortune.

In a few minutes Mrs. Munroe again evinced a desire to speak, but was unable to articulate aloud.   Constance, seeing that the glance was directed towards herself, leant over and placed her ear close to the pillow, and heard her mother faintly whisper, " Remember your promise." She could only signify acquiescence by a look. A smile now hovered over the lips of Mrs. Munroe. She endeavoured to press the hands that held her own, but the power had ebbed away, and in a few minutes she expired.

Few things after this remained impressed upon the mind of Constance. She only remembered being forced from the room where that dear form lay, and then all recollection ceased. But let us hasten from a scene so mournful ; for although it may be matter for deep reflection why we should look with unalloyed pain on such an event, yet it is beyond a doubt that the greater the virtues, the more kind and bene-volent the disposition, and the more beloved the person who has just left a troubled existence for one of unchangeable bliss, the greater is the grief which falls upon those who have witnessed the effect or reaped the benefit of these qualities.

The arrangements for the funeral having been completed, the fifth day after the decease of Mrs. Munroe was the one appointed for her interment. All the conventional forms which custom has established as proofs of our respect for the dead distinguished the procession which accompanied her remains to the grave. A long line of mourning coaches was followed by one of private carriages equal in extent. Plumes and scarfs nodded and waved in profusion, as if the pomps and vanities of this world could attend us beyond the grave !

When the pageant reached the village church the minister was seen issuing from the porch. The character of the deceased was not unknown to him, and deeply affected by the recollection of the virtues he had so often witnessed, and by the general sympathy evinced by those around him, he unconsciously performed in a more impressive manner, and with deeper pathos than usual, the sublime and affecting service for the burial of the dead. When these last rites had been performed, and Constance quitted the grave of the only person who had ever evinced any sincere affection for her, and to whom her young heart had clung with such devoted fondness, she felt more acutely than she had hitherto done her desolate position, and for the first time began to comprehend the full extent of the loss she had sustained.

In the evening, as her father and herself sat together in the drawing room, which had always been rendered so cheerful by her whom they had that day followed to the tomb, they remained silently engaged with their own thoughts till the clock on the mantel piece pointed out the hour of midnight.

Constance rose, paused for a minute as if in doubt, and then, with one of those impulses not unfrequently displayed by the gentler sex, went up to her father and threw her arms round his neck, but he frigidly disengaged himself from her embrace, and the scarcely audible good night seemed to freeze upon his lips. She ran to her own room and buried her sorrows in her pillow.

Good night! How universal the salutation, but under what different circumstances is it uttered by thousands! With what love does the mother bend over her first-born; and while uttering with her lips, good night, silently offer up a prayer for the protection of her infant. With what seeming mockery, again, does the jailor bid the condemned felon, good night, who the next morning is to expiate his crimes upon the scaffold; and yet they are the same words, and have the same meaning ; are used in palaces and in roofless huts ; by the rich man in his luxurious abode, and by wayfarers in desert places, whose only canopy is the sky, while they rely upon Him who slumbers not for protection.

CHAPTER III.

The civil law has wisely determined, that a master who strikes at a scholar's eye shall be considered as criminal.—*Doctor Johnson.*

THERE is an exuberance of spirits in youth which is impatient of sorrow. At that happy period of life, if the feelings can be diverted from the subject which has painfully engrossed them, they rush with impetuosity into their natural channels, and the burden, which bears down those of maturer age, is so lightly and unconsciously cast aside,——the reaction from a state of deep despondency to one of comparative happiness and enjoyment is apparently so sudden and complete,——as to lead the superficial observer to suppose that the change, which can be traced almost entirely to physical causes, is the result of heartless or selfish indifference.

Constance's grief, which had been infinitely deeper and more acute than that of Mr. Munroe, was the first to subside. Gradually the woe, which she at first thought would prove unconquerable, began to yield to that melancholy consolation, which the bereaved derive from recalling the virtues and personal attributes of those for whom they grieve, and from dwelling with a mournful and almost religious pleasure on the various acts of kindness and affection they have experienced. Not so Mr. Munroe. He continued for months in the morbid state into which he had at first been plunged. His grief was far less disinterested than that of his daughter, and his regret for himself far more poignant than for the death of the person for whom he seemed to mourn. The only being on whom he had ever bestowed the least affection was lost to him for ever, and the feeling paramount in his mind was, that an irremediable injury had been unjustly inflicted upon himself.

After several months thus spent, he became vaguely sensible of the futility of persevering in such a line of conduct, and prepared sullenly to submit to his fate. The first thing that occurred to him, on this change taking place, was the necessity of placing some person at the head of his household; but upon considering which of his relations would prove most eligible for this office, each appeared deficient in so many necessary qualifications, that he was unable at first to determine upon the least objectionable. After a careful review, his choice was at length divided between two of his sisters. One of these ladies was an inveterate enemy to the king's English, and the other, who had taken a studious turn, had rushed into the opposite extreme, and put forward lofty, though very questionable claims to scientific acquirements. The ultimate conclusion he arrived at, however, was that the objections to the learned Dorothy were light when compared with the coarseness and ignorance of her sister. To her, therefore, he eventually sent an invitation to make Ulvacombe her home — an invitation she readily accepted; but as it is now quite time to introduce to the reader one who is destined to occupy an important position in this history, we must leave Miss Dorothy Munroe to make her *entré* at Ulvacombe, and proceed to a description of Mr. Frank Merryweather.

Colonel Merryweather, as already stated, had met his death in action; but before entering on the campaign in which he fell, he had appointed his half brother, Mr. Ponsonby, a civil servant of the East India Company, and Mr. Munroe, his brother-in-law, joint guardians of his only child, Frank, then a boy of eight years of age. His wife had been dead some years previously to this period, and to superintend his house, as well as to take care of his son, he had availed himself of the services of Mrs. Mackintosh, the widow of an officer who had been in his own regiment, and whose death had left her in reduced circumstances. Thus matters remained for some time, but at last rumour, upon whose tongue " continual slanders ride," hesitated not to assert that the protracted stay of Mrs. Mackintosh in Colonel Merryweather's house, was attributable to other motives than a matronly affection for Frank, or any particular *penchant* for the office of housekeeper.

These insinuations had no sooner reached her ears than she immediately sought a private interview with Colonel Merryweather, and during a passionate flood of tears, painted in glowing terms the calumnies with which she was assailed. Colonel Merryweather was not proof against this appeal, and, whether from an exaggerated sense of the personal obligation he had incurred to protect from injury, one so entirely dependent upon him, or whether he had really formed an attachment to her :——certain it is that the result of the interview, was an agreement to have recourse to a marriage as the most effectual way of silencing a censorious world. It was also agreed at the suggestion of Mrs. Mackintosh, that they should separate for a few months before the ceremony took place, lest it should appear that they were driven to this step by the censures of their neighbours, rather than urged to adopt it by their own free will. Mrs. Mackintosh therefore left the province in which Colonel Merryweather's regiment was stationed, and proceeded to Bombay whither she had not arrived many days before there appeared among the *on dits* of one of the newspapers of that renowned presidency, a paragraph, informing the inhabitants that the amiable, accomplished, and talented Mrs. M——k——h, who had just arrived from one of the upper provincies, would, it was confidently expected, in a few months, bestow her hand upon the no less distinguished Colonel M——r. Harlequin's wand could not have wrought a more immediate change than did this announcement in Mrs. Mackintosh's position. All her former detractors now vied with one another in paying her attention, and no one thought of giving an entertainment without eagerly soliciting the pleasure of her presence. But at the very zenith of her popularity, a war suddenly broke out. Colonel Merryweather's regiment was one of the first ordered to the scene of action, and with the exception of a hurried letter he wrote to her on the eve of marching, his death was the only intelligence she received of him. There were not wanting those who professed to condole with her. There were not perhaps wanting those who did so with sincerity; but all alike were wonder struck when it appeared that Colonel Merryweather had left her the great bulk of his property, and that his own son Frank, who, on the first commencement of the war, had been despatched to Bombay and placed under the care of his uncle, Mr. Ponsonby, was not mentioned in his father's will.

The lawyers, however, could discover no flaw in the document, and Mrs. Mackintosh returned to England the possessor of some thousands a-year. She set up a large establishment in Eton Place, and having surrounded herself with every comfort she could devise, prepared to devote the remainder of her life to the practice of evangelical principles.

In the mean time Mr. Ponsonby and Mr. Munroe, who had been requested by Colonel Merryweather to become the guardians of his child, in case of any accident happening to himself, having conferred together, deemed it expedient to send Frank to England, that he might commence his pilgrimage in that path in which the chief land marks are an Ainsworth's Dictionary and a Greek Lexicon on the one side, and a rod on the other. On his arrival he was forthwith consigned to the care of his aunt, Miss Dorothy Munroe, under whose auspices with the assistance of a private tutor, he proceeded to take the first sip at the fountain of knowledge. This arrangement, however, lasted but a short time. Miss Dorothy Munroe's temper was not of the serenest kind nor that of her charge the most complying and personal encounters became of such frequent occurrence, that she was fain to send him to school, where he had been suffered to remain without even the intermission of holidays up to the present time.

He was now seventeen years of age, of an average height, and with no reason to complain of his personal appearance, unless indeed it were on account of its being so favourable, for as yet that circumstance had been rather a drawback than an advantage to him. Dr. Puzzle, the learned Theban at the head of the establishment where he was placed, used frequently to say, that it was entirely owing to his outward appearance that he was such an idle, self-willed fellow, and after an oration, which Frank Merryweather had long known off by heart, invariably wound up by telling him, that he was "a goodly looking apple but rotten at the core ;"—a saying which his pupils were made to believe was original.

Frank Merryweather, upon first making his appearance at Dr. Puzzle's establishment, had, as a preliminary measure, been well browbeaten, assured that he was a dunce, that it was quite impossible to make anything of him, and that he was sent to school because he must be sent somewhere, with various other remarks of a like encouraging nature. Whereupon, he very naturally imbibed a dislike for that which he was compelled to drudge at, without as he supposed a chance of ever being able to acquire. This feeling having once become implanted in his mind, was not likely soon to be eradicated, and the consequence was, that as he advanced in years, he turned his attention to things which presented greater attractions to him.

It cannot be denied, therefore, that frequently when he ought to have been engaged in translating a Greek play, or an ode of Horace, he was deep in the mysteries of Madame de Stael's " Corinne," Scott's " Marmion," Byron's " Corsair," or Shakspeare's plays, all of which had been surreptitiously introduced amongst a heap of dictionaries and Latin and Greek authors, into the desk at which he sat.

During the latter portion of his sojourn at Doctor Puzzle's seminary, that worthy pedagogue had also taken an extreme dislike to him. This dislike was occasioned partly by Frank having never in the Doctor's opinion, thrown a lustre on his establishment, by prodigies of learning, but it was chiefly due to a conviction in the Doctor's mind, that Frank Merryweather was the principal party in a practical joke that had been played upon himself, and which he

never thought of without a deep feeling
of resentment.

Doctor Puzzle was particularly sleek
in person, and neither his appearance
nor his immense powers of deglutition,
would, *a priori*, lead to the supposition
that his occupation as a schoolmaster
was unfavourable to his health.   As he
dined with the boys, it was at dinner that
his gastronomic powers were chiefly dis-
played, and there also it was that these
attributes chiefly attracted the remarks
and criticisms of those by whom he was
surrounded.   Indeed we have it on the
authenticity of several of the junior boys,
that the Doctor had frequently been
known to help himself five times to
mutton, although he had refused them
a second slice.   It was also Doctor
Puzzle's practice during school hours, to
write long letters to his friends, bemoan-
ing the unhappy fate, which had con-
signed his talents and acquirements to
the drudgery of a school, and it was

moreover his wont, to draw alarming but
fanciful pictures of the effects he antici-
pated to his health, from the severity
and monotony of his daily pursuits. On
one of these occasions he was engaged
in the construction of a well rounded
period, into which he had infused a
greater degree of pathos than usual,
from his recent ineffectual efforts to
make a particularly dull lad construe
Dido's lament for Æneas, when he was
suddenly called out, and left his unfinish-
ed effusion open on his desk. During
his absence he had not ceased to think
of the glowing description of his suffer-
ings which he was about to convey to his
friend, and in his own mind had settled
the touching appeal by which he intend-
ed to stir his feelings to their inmost
depths. His mingled astonishment and
indignation may therefore be imagined,
when he found, upon his return, his task
already performed, and that in addition
to "The cares of this school make me

weary of life," with which he had com-
menced the laboured and classical par-
agraph which occupied his thoughts, he
found carefully introduced in a hand-
writing which imitated his own, the
words, "And if it were not for the
mutton I should die." The doctor
stormed, fumed, and threatened, but to
no purpose. No one was found suffi-
ciently treacherous to betray the perpe-
trators of this gross act of insubordina-
tion, and finding that his efforts were of
no avail, he swallowed his indignation
with his next dinner, though he ever
afterwards entertained a firm belief that
Frank Merryweather was the culprit.

The only permanent friendship that
Frank Merryweather formed at Doctor
Puzzle's school was with a lad about his
own age, whose name was Somerville.
Both had good natural abilities, though
entirely different in character. Merry-
weather seldom mastered the details of
any subject accurately and perhaps from

impatience, or a mistaken notion that it was not necessary, had almost disqualified himself from doing so. This defect however was in some measure redeemed by the ability and power with which he arrived at a sound conclusion, even from imperfect premises. With him the great and immediate object was always the result, and with Somerville on the other hand, this was totally disregarded till the details had been carefully analysed.

In their scholastic attainments, therefore, they were not unequally matched, though each was astonished at the performances of the other. Merryweather, at the accuracy with which Somerville could make a quotation, remember a date, or explain the most trivial matter connected with the subject upon which they were engaged, while the latter would wonder equally how his school-fellow could possibly have formed a sound opinion, without examining step by step the grounds on which it was based.

Differing from each other in these respects, they had nevertheless many noble traits of character in common, and the frequent instances in which the natural generosity of their dispositions had prompted them to act in concert, had perhaps served to cement their friendship more closely than would have been the case had their talents been more similar in character.

Merryweather and Somerville had now arrived at the age looked forward to by the school boy with so much eagerness, when jackets are finally discarded for tail coats, and the discipline of school is exchanged for the temptations, the dangers, and severer discipline of the world. Somerville was to leave that half year, but had it not been for an unforeseen occurrence it is probable, under the circumstances, that Merryweather would have been allowed to continue his studies for a much longer time at our worthy pedagogue's.

One day a little boy, while playing near the Doctor's study, happened to kick a football through one of the panes of glass. It unfortunately alighted on his head, and caused his long nose to come into violent contact with the book he was reading. It would require one of the similes of Homer adequately to illustrate the fury with which the indignant pedagogue rushed out, cane in hand, and demanded the name of the culprit. The little urchin was just about to beg piteously for mercy, when Merryweather, glancing first at his feeble frame and diminutive size, and then at the symptoms of ungovernable passion evinced by Dr. Puzzle, stepped up to the irate school master, and with unparalleled coolness said, " It was my doing."

" Then," said the Doctor grasping more firmly his cane, " you have merited and shall receive exemplary punishment notwithstanding your years." But glancing first at the instrument

which was to carry his threat into
execution, and from thence to the broad
shoulders of Merryweather, and the
determined expression of his eye, he
added in a voice almost choked by
passion " I'll expel you, sir. That's what
I'll do, and then you will be disgraced
for life, and cast out from all society."

" I would suggest to you," replied
Merryweather, " that you slightly over-
rate your powers, if you think that any
act of your's can ever have an effect
upon my movements hereafter."

" We shall see. Go and pack up your
things, and be off. Get away with you.
Go along."

" *If it were not for the mutton I should
die*," said Merryweather as he still kept
the same position.

The Doctor could no longer restrain
himself. With his cheeks puffed out,
and his face the colour of vermillion, he
rushed at his pupil. Merryweather on
the other hand excited by the threat

and insulting language which had been addressed to him, defended himself with all the skill and strength he could command. The Doctor's good living had entirely unfitted him for the encounter he was now engaged in, and although he maintained the contest with great perseverance, it soon became evident that he was incapable of supporting the unusual exertions he was compelled to make, while his starting eyes, and red and puffed out cheeks, gave his face an appearance as if it was about to explode with his efforts to draw breath. In the mean time the play-ground echoed with cries of " go it Merryweather, at him again, he'll soon be done," which were vociferated with all the glee which a recollection of canes and rods engendered when their favourite had the advantage, and were uttered in tones of encouragement when he was temporarily worsted.

" There," said Merryweather, finally seating his opponent on a quickset hedge, which bounded one side of the playground, and extricating himself from his grasp, " perhaps that will be a lesson to you for the future that you have no right to gratify your temper by ill treating your pupils."

" Get away out of my house," said the Doctor rising with evident pain from the seat he had been accommodated with, and making the best of his way into the house.

There was now a general clustering round Merryweather, and three cheers were given him in honour of his victory, but these manifestations of delight quickly subsided, for it immediately occurred to those who were thus testifying their joy, that their schoolfellow was about to leave them, and as he was a great favourite, this was looked forward to with general regret.

" Will you be obliged to go Merryweather?" said the little fellow whom he had saved from an unjust chastisement.

"There can be little doubt about that," said Merryweather, laying his hand kindly upon the shoulder of his young *protegé*. "For the future you must take care not to let footballs alight on the Doctor's head."

"Dont go till he makes you," was the unsophisticated entreaty of the boy.

"Aye, dont go till he makes you," was now re-echoed by the bystanders.

But he was saved the trouble of making any answer to this appeal, for a servant who now made his appearance informed Merryweather that he had his master's orders to have the gig ready in half an hour, to convey him and his luggage to the place where the coach passed, which would take him almost to the gates of Ulvacombe, his guardian's residence.

The preparations for departure were soon completed, and the hardest part of all came — parting with his school-fellows—and with Merryweather this was

a much greater trial than it would have
proved for those amongst their number,
who had always been kindly received
every holidays by relations and friends.
At last the moment came, when the
farewell word could no longer be de-
layed. Every one came eagerly forward
to give him a cordial shake of the hand.
Promises to write, which however were
never kept, were reiterated with the most
solemn assurances by every individual.
One hearty cheer was given him when
he entered the gig, and as Merryweather
waved his hat in acknowledgement, the
horse started forward at a brisk pace,
and soon he had left behind him the
house that for so many years had been
his only home.

CHAPTER IV.

Let the proud sex possess their vaunted powers ;
Be other triumphs, other glories ours !
The gentler charms which wait on female life,
Which grace the daughter and adorn the wife,
Be these our boast ;—
Hannah More.

IT was late in the evening before the coach in which Merryweather had obtained a place, arrived opposite the

E 5

lodge of Mr. Munroe's house, but as the spring was far advanced, there still lingered a remnant of light. Descending from his place beside the coachman, who on receiving a larger fee than usual, was considerate enough to express a hope that he should have the pleasure of taking him up again some day, he presented himself and his portmanteau at the gate and just as the " All right" of the guard, followed by an application of the coachman's whip, was heard, Merryweather pulled the lodge bell. It was a rich deep toned bell, well calculated to impress the mind of the candidate for admission with a due sense of the extent and importance of the mansion he was about to enter, as well as of the affluence and dignity of the proprietor. Scarcely had its reverbaratory sounds ceased, when the gate was opened by a prim looking matron, much to whose astonishment, for his arrival was of course unexpected, Merryweather, after leaving directions respecting his portmanteau, walked past on his way to the house. Although not one to attach much importance to wealth or rank for their own intrinsic worth, yet he could not help feeling his disinclination for the approaching interview with his uncle, which under any circumstances could not fail of being disagreeable, considerably increased, as he observed the manifold signs of the former which on every side met his gaze as he advanced. There were no means of escaping it however. It was to be gone through and the sooner therefore the better. I really see no reason, he thought, why I should attach so much importance to this guardian of mine. I suppose it is that the impressions of childhood are not easily effaced, for he is a perfect stranger to me and nepotism not being one of his characteristics, he has never but once thought it worth while to see me. If I were only independent——" but *laissez aller*," he said aloud, as he lifted the knocker of the door and gave a sharp rat-tat-tat.

"Mr. Munroe is at home I presume?" said Merryweather entering the hall as soon as the door opened.

"I'll go and see sir," said the servant.

"You may spare yourself that trouble," said Merrywaether, taking off his upper coat, "and show me in at once because I must see him."

"Oh, very well, sir, if it's important," replied the servant, "this way if you please,—Name—sir?"

"It's of no consequence—I will announce myself." As he said this he entered a spacious library, where a globe lamp with a shade around it, cast a flood of light upon the table, but left the remainder of the room in comparative obscurity.

Mr. Munroe who had heard the knock at the door, rose as Merryweather entered, and lifted the shade from the lamp. Seeing how young a man his visitor was, he said in a testy tone, while the slight inclination of his head could scarcely be called an acknowledgment of Merryweather's bow. " May I ask to what particular circumstance I am indebted for the honour of a visit at this unusual hour?"

"I am your nephew," said Merryweather.

" Nephew? nephew?" said Mr. Munroe, " I have no such relation."

" There is no tie of consanguinity between us, I am perfectly aware," said Merryweather rather pointedly, " but I am your nephew by marriage, and what is perhaps more to the purpose, I am your ward, and my name, Frank Merryweather, is doubtless more familiar to you than my appearance. In your hands have been placed means for my support, and there is now no other house than yours to which I can go, or I should not have troubled you with my presence."

"And pray, what is the reason" said
Mr. Munroe, his wrath rapidly rising,
"that you have left the school at which
you were placed ?"

"Circumstances occurred which pre-
vented my remaining any longer there."

"Circumstances occurred indeed !
What do you mean by 'circumstances
occurred' ? I suppose the real fact is that
you have been misbehaving yourself and
have been expelled ?"

"If it is not your intention, sir," said
Merryweather, "to receive the explana-
tions I am ready to give in a more tem-
perate mood, I must decline giving them
altogether."

"Oh ! indeed, young gentleman. Well
proceed. Let us hear," said Mr. Mun-
roe, throwing himself back in a chair.

"The facts are soon told," said Merry-
weather seating himself. "I took upon
myself the blame of an accident that
happened. Doctor Puzzle made use of
most abusive language, which drew a re-

tort from me, and in a very short time we were engaged in a harmless, though well contested struggle, which lasted upwards of a quarter of an hour."

"So you call this an explanation, young gentleman, do you?" said Mr. Munroe. "I should rather look upon it as a confession of your guilt; which you know it would be of no use endeavouring to conceal.

"Call it what you will," said Merryweather, the natural impetuosity of his disposition obtaining a complete mastery of his feelings. "I am indifferent. But though my conduct may be censurable, surely I may with some justice complain of yours. To whom, sir, I would ask are you indebted for your present position? Friendless you were on your first arrival in India, and had it not been for my father, who took you by the hand, introduced you, aye, and from his own means helped you to set up in business; it is not perhaps too much to say that your present position would be that of a subordinate in some house of agency. In what manner you have repaid the kindness of your benefactor towards his only child, I leave you to answer."

"I—I sent you to school," said Mr. Munroe. "I could not have done more if you had been my own son. But how have you learnt so much concerning affairs connected with—with the family?"

"My Uncle Ponsonby has written to me by every mail for two or three years past," said Merryweather, unable to repress a smile at the change which his words had effected; "and amongst other kind things has kept my purse well supplied, which otherwise 1 think would have gone pretty empty. What I valued far more than this, however, was the kindness of his letters."

"Well," said Mr. Munroe, after some consideration, "I suppose you have learnt from the same source that I am one of your father's executors? Now, you have only to enter some profession, and I shall be able to place in your own hands the property you are entitled to; and then, of course, you will be able to choose an abode for yourself. Have you ever considered this question?"

"Yes," said Merryweather, "I should wish to enter the army."

"Yes, yes, it was your father's profession," said Mr. Munroe, pensively, whilst a ray of good feeling struggled for pre-eminence in his breast; "and a braver officer or a worthier man never existed. I cannot wish you better than to follow in his footsteps. However," he continued, resuming his former manner, "you are of course aware that some delay must take place before you can obtain a commission?"

Merryweather instantly perceived the course of ideas which had suggested the latter part of Mr. Munroe's remark, and it effectually checked the expression of gratitude which had risen to his lips on bearing the eulogium paid to the memory of his father.

"And in the meantime," he said, "may I ask what plan you think of adopting with regard to me?"

"The only course that I can see open," said Mr. Munroe, "is for you to remain here. I will write to Lord Carlbrook about you to-morrow, who, I have no doubt, will be willing to serve me in this matter; but at the soonest a commission will not be procurable for three or four months. You will find," he resumed, after a pause, "my sister in the drawing room. I suppose you recollect her?"

Merryweather, on whose mind existed an indelible impression of Miss Dorothy Munroe's appearance, answered in the affirmative, and, after thanking Mr. Munroe for the trouble he was about to take on his behalf, he made his way to the drawing

On opening the door, he was surprised to see, not the countenance of his former instructress, of which he entertained so lively a recollection, but that of a young and beautiful girl. He was so bewildered at what seemed to be a strange and wonderful metamorphosis, that he remained with the door in his hand, without either advancing or retreating. On the table was an urn, hissing and bubbling away in a most lively manner, aud sending up a little column of steam from its troubled depths towards the ceiling. The remainder of the "tea equipage" was also there, and seated before it was the young lady with a book in her lap.

Just as it had occurred to Merryweather that this could be no other than his cousin, mention of whom he now recollected had been made in one of his letters from India, though the circumstance had entirely escaped him in the excitement of the day; the young lady herself, without lifting her eyes from her book, broke the silence by saying, "you may tell your master that tea is ready, John."

There was something that struck Merryweather as being so particularly ludicrous in his position at that moment, that in spite of his efforts, he broke into an immoderate fit of laughter, which caused Constance to look up with astonishment at so unexpected a departure from decorum on the part, as she thought, of one of the domestics.

"Oh, I beg your pardon," she said, hastily closing the book she had been so intent upon and rising with some confusion.

"The apology is due from me," said Merryweather advancing to the table, "though really I must be sufficiently ungallant make your mistake the conduct. I think was any kind person present to introduce us, we should hear that we were cousins."

"Cousins?" said Constance, with animation, "then you are Frank Merryweather?"

"Ah I see," said Merryweather, taking the hand that was held out to him, "that you are well versed in the family history."

"My Mother," replied Constance, as a shade passed over her handsome features, "used frequently to talk about you and therefore I have long known you by name. She used often to say when we first arrived here, that as soon as she recovered sufficient strength she should pay you a visit, but—but, alas! that time never came."

As Constance said this, she had turned her face away from the light, and Merryweather perceiving that she with difficulty controlled the emotion which the subject had caused her, remained silent for some moments. At last he observed, "Why Cousin, it is surely not advisable to allow our thoughts to dwell so much upon the past."

"True, true," she said, replacing a handkerchief by her side and endeavouring to look cheerful. "I do not intend the first moment we have become acquainted to weary you with my sorrows. That would be a poor welcome and make you speedily regret your arrival among us. I would not on any account that you should do so, for indeed I am very glad that you have come."

"And I am equally glad of it now," replied Merryweather, "though half an hour ago I confess I entertained very different feelings on the subject. But fortune is frequently most bountiful to us when we least expect any of her favours, and this day, which has made us acquainted I shall ever esteem the happiest of my life."

Merryweather had not yet learnt to conceal his thoughts, and he uttered these words with a sincerity and warmth, that made the colour rise to his cousin's cheek. There is, however, a freemasonry in youth, dificult to define, and unintelligible perhaps to themselves, which by a far quicker process than speech, transmits the favourable impression they make upon each other,—a mysterious but intuitive feeling, which refuses utterance to ought that can either wound or offend. Constance, therefore, evinced no symptoms of annoyance, but looking up archly, she said, " Have you ever—ever formed such sudden friendship *before*, cousin ?"

" No, indeed," replied Merryweather, " nor, I am bound to say, such sincere ones, for though I do not mean to underrate my attachment for my late companions, still they were not—not in any way related to me. Indeed, for years past I have not seen any one even remotely connected with my family."

"You do not return into Cornwall, cousin, I hope?" said Constance, after a pause. "It would be so very tiresome if you were to run away again, now that you have at last come to see us.

"No; I shall never go back there. But the profession I have just told my uncle I should wish to enter, will probably oblige me to travel much further than the spot I have just quitted."

"You mean the army, of course," said Constance, taking down a screen with apparent unconcern from the mantelshelf; "but why do you choose such a profession? There are surely plenty of others to go abroad and fight our battles for us?"

"Why, yes, I suppose there are," replied Merryweather, laughing, "but they probably all have friends wishing them to stay at home, who would

consider it a great hardship that *their*
relatives should be selected to incur
danger and privation for the public
good. Seriously, however, cousin, I
must make a choice of a profession,
you know, and I think the army is the
one for which I am best adapted. Not
that I am at all sure that I do not
begin to repent my decision; but my
uncle has promised to write to Lord
Carlbrook for a commission for me,
and he would think me a vacillating
sort of person if I were to tell him
that I had changed my mind. I must
say, though, that were it possible I
should be very glad to remain here,—
I will not say *for ever*, because I am
superstitious enough to consider that
a term of ill omen,—but for a period
to which I will assign no limit. What-
ever were to be the lapse of time, I
should be unjustly diffident, were I
to doubt of happiness with a cousin for
my companion, whose bright looks and

VOL. I. F

kind words have already revolutionised most of my thoughts and feelings."

What reply Constance would have made to this gallant speech must ever remain unknown, for at this moment the door opened, and Miss Dorothy Munroe, whom Merryweather instantly recognised, made her appearance.

She was now a lady of a " certain age," a saying which, however, we know from very high authority, has a signification very different from that which the words taken literally would imply; for of all things a lady's age is, *par excellence,* most uncertain when defined by such a term. To be more accurate, then, Dorothy Munroe was beyond being called *passée,* and had certain undeniable marks of age about her, which were rendered perhaps more conspicuous by the pertinacous manner in which she kept her eyes closed to the fact.—her own opinion being that she was quite as yo

she was twenty years of age. A dis-
position on the part of her hair to fall
off might certainly have been considered
characteristic of the longevity of its
capillary existence; but this difficulty
was got over by giving the name
of "incipient baldness" to such patches
as were denuded of this natural orna-
ment. At such moments she would
express much regret that caps were not
worn by young people, quickly adding,
however, "It is quite impossible to
begin wearing them at my time of life."
A low dress was certainly not the most
becoming attire that Dorothy Munroe
could have assumed, her attenuated
figure showing to a considerable disad-
vantage in such a costume. But of
course the objection to her wearing caps,
applied equally to her going otherwise
than *decolté* of an evening. If Dorothy
Munroe, however, was eccentric in her
dress, infinitely more eccentric was she
in her form of speech,—in the choice

of words it was her pleasure to make,
and in her manner of delivering them.
It having always been her ambition to
be considered a person of great literary
attainments, she had read to some
extent, if that could be called reading
which enabled her to extract just enough
from the works which engaged her
attention, to confound the ignorant with
words of—

"Learned length and thund'ring sound,"

and to convince the well informed of
the emptiness of her pretensions. The
acquirement on which she most prided
herself, therefore, was her command of
language, and however trivial the
conversation or whoever the person
she was addressing, she never lost an
opportunity of evolving some word
interminably long and unusually sono-
rous. While giving utterance to this
singular phraseology she would gradually

bend forward in her chair, protruding her long and now sharpened chin in the same progressive manner, till the chosen word was fairly jerked over this acute and intervening promontory. Her exertions, too, on these occasions always appeared to afford her considerable constitutional relief, and every such achievement was invariably followed by a look of mingled placidity and triumph, which spread itself in smiles over her satisfied countenance,—the *tout ensemble*, as she recovered her former position, forcibly recalling to the military man the one, two, *three* of the drill sergeant.

"How do you do, aunt?" said Merryweather, when she had advanced a little way into the room.

"Ah!" replied Dorothy Munroe, "and is it really so, or am I under some infatuated delusion?"

" Delightful coincidence ! But what happy combination of circumstances has produced your arrival here ?"

Merryweather now recapitulated the whole of the day's adventures, at which Dorothy Munroe was of course proportionably shocked, and said,—"Subordination to proper authority was never one of your characteristics, Frank. But how did you like Cornwall; did you find the air salubrious ?"

" The *first* time," said Merryweather with some emphasis, "that such questions have ever been put to me. I can answer them both, however, in the affirmative. The part of the country in which I lived was beautiful, and the air extremely healthy."

" I have heard that the soil is not so feracious as in this county ?"

" I believe not," replied Merryweather, drawing a deep breath, and leaning back in his chair, with the look of one who was about to be made a martyr.

Miss Dorothy paused, eyed him in this quiescent state for a moment, a little distrustfully, but unable to repress what was at that moment surging in her mind, she hurriedly asked, "Does not the indigency of the lower classes upon that part of the coast compel them to become exclusively icthyophagists?"

"Not that I am aware of," said Merryweather, after some hesitation. "But may I ask why you should seek out so unusual a term? I confess I should not have known your meaning, had I not been so recently engaged on my Greek Lexicon, and thought of the derivation of the word."

"My dear Frank, your surprise is really most flattering," said Dorothy, with the most affable of smiles. "There are those, I know, who maintain that to excel in scholastic acquirements is not the province of our sex, and indeed such are the anfractuosities of the human mind that though there is much divarication upon the subject, yet with some it has undoubtedly become established as a fact. I need not say that I am one who entertains totally different views, and you must therefore really excuse me if the indelible effect of my interesting studies, should occasionally make my conversation burst through those conventional shackles which imprison the ordinary speech of social intercourse, and induce me to soar upwards in a purer strain."

"Oh certainly," said Merryweather, "but I think you overlook one thing, aunt, that on such occasions you may sometimes fail to be quite intelligible to those whom you address."

The effect of this equivocal remark on Dorothy Munroe's countenance, was to make it crimson with anger, and throwing herself back in her chair, she commenced speaking in a key which, compared with her former one, was as the whistling of a steam engine to the warbling of a wren.

"And the first thing you do, sir, on your arrival in my brother's habitation, is to cut me with the keen edge of your satire! But I would have you know, sir, that however inopinate your conduct may be, a mind strengthened by the study of philosophy and by general research, is at any moment ready to cope, in a calm collected manner, with the most covert and subtle invectives, or the most terrible abuse."

"But my dear aunt," said Merryweather, really distressed at the effect produced by his observation. "I did not intend to use words that by any ingenuity could be construed into meaning either one or the other."

"Think not" said Dorothy Munroe, in the same excited manner, "that I am unable to tear aside the veil which would hide your meaning from a less penetrating eye."——

Here the current of her ideas apparently became checked by her feelings, and she allowed a profusion of tears to flow, which seemed to mock all her efforts to stop them with a pocket handkerchief; but upon finding that this useful article of dress had become impregnated with *rouge*, she hastily left the room to calm her agitation in her own apartment.

"I see" said Merryweather to his cousin as soon as she had closed the door, "that years have not effected any change in my aunt."

"Oh! I assure you that aunt Dorothy is extremely partial to me," replied Constance. "This is partly owing I believe to the great attention I pay to her long dissertations, which you would allow to be very creditable, if you only knew how very tedious I find them. However," she continued, laughing, "you shall do penance for me sometimes now."

Merryweather not only promised compliance but declared that he would do everything in his power to shield his cousin, and when Dorothy Munroe re-appeared he made so many apologies, paid her so much attention, and listened to her with an air of such profound respect, that she very soon favoured him with a desultory lecture on Botany, Chemistry, Moral Philosophy, and many other things which it would require more space than we can allow to enumerate. How long she would have continued, it is impossible to say, had not Mr. Munroe and his daughter happened to leave the room when tea was removed, and had not Merryweather not only fallen fast asleep, but given audible proof of the fact just as Dorothy Munroe had come to the termination of a most lucid dissertation on the difference between testaceous and crustaceous shells. Fortunately for Merryweather, Mr. Munroe, of whom his sister stood rather in awe, entered the room at this moment, and signified that it was time to retire for the night. She contented herself, therefore, with an angry glance, and retired apparently in great indignation, a circumstance Merry-weather never became acquainted with, as Dorothy Munroe, however liable to a sudden ebullition of temper, was not in the habit of allowing the sun to go down upon her wrath, and by the converse of the same rule, that luminary upon rising the next morning, found her in as peaceful a frame of mind as if nothing had occurred on the previous evening, to disturb her serenity. Thus matters stood at Ulvacombe,—Dorothy Munroe favouring her nephew and niece alternately with her opinions, researches and observations, and occasionally diversifying the whole with one of those lively displays of temper, which she gave

Merryweather to understand, were at once a proof of delicacy of temperament and strength of mind.

CHAPTER V.

They lov'd : But such their guileless passion was,
As in the dawn of time inform'd the heart
Of innocence, and undissembling truth.
'Twas friendship heightened by the mutual wish,
Th' enchanting hope, and sympathetic glow,
Beam'd from the mutual eye.   Devoting all
To love, each was to each a dearer self ;
Supremely happy in th' awakened power
Of giving joy.

Thomson's Seasons.

THE profound peace in which nature is
clothed on a fine summer's morning in
the country, the deep silence broken only

by the song of birds, the repose in which every object appears hushed before man is abroad and the busy hum of life is heard, impart to us the calm and hallowed feelings, which inspired the poet to exclaim—

" God made the country, man the town."

Both Merryweather and his cousin were sensitively alive to the beauties of nature, and after his establishment at Ulvacombe on many such a morning, so soon as Aurora had flung open her gates, he and his cousin might have been seen, had not that dull god Morpheus weighed down the eyes of those who should have been wakeful, quaffing the fresh air in company as they either strolled on the verdant lawn, or skimmed over the surface of the lake, in a boat whose glistening sail caught the rays of the rising sun.

This, however, was not the only time that they were thrown together, for Mr. Munroe seldom made his appearance in

the drawing room, and the pursuits of
their aunt Dorothy left her but little un-
occupied time in the morning, a portion
of the day which she generally spent in
her own room. Merryweather and his
cousin thus left to themselves, soon
found that their tastes were similar in
many respects, that poetry, music, and
painting, were the delight of both, and it
is not surprising, therefore, that as their
intimacy increased, a deeper feeling than
the friendship of connexions should have
sprung up in their breasts, yet it stole
upon them unconsciously, and it was not
till an event occurred by which their
lives were placed in imminent peril, that
they became aware of the extent to
which their affections were engaged.

One day when they were seated as
usual in the drawing room, deeply im-
mersed in their favourite Dante, Miss
Dorothy Munroe made her appearance
with a basket full of weeds and rubbish,
and placing it on the table before her

nephew and niece, who were regarding it
with looks of considerable alarm, not
unmixed perhaps with disappointment at
their studies being thus interrupted, said,
" Here is something indeed precious.
What can be more beautiful than that spe-
cimen of the *Hippuris Vulgaris!* I observe,
however," she continued, " that you have
not yet, Frank, turned your attention to
this most interesting study, a circum-
stance more particularly to be regretted,
as its captivating allurements would be
an inexhaustible resource to you in many
countries, which, from the nature of your
profession, you will be obliged to visit.
It is really a matter of amazement to me
that you are not struck with this view
of the question proleptically !"

" The only way in which it strikes me
at present," said Merryweather, consider-
ably out of temper, " is, that if the
pursuit involves the necessity of diving
into every dirty pool I may happen to
pass, and of placing whatever I may

collect by such a process upon a table at which other people are seated to their great annoyance, it is one I should recommend everybody to avoid."

"No, no, aunt," said Constance, rising, and casting a reproachful glance at her cousin, "you do not annoy me, and I should like to hear about that specimen which you prize so much."

"It is of the class Monandria," said Dorothy Munroe, contenting herself with casting a look of triumphant disdain at her nephew. "On examination you will find that it has only one pistil. It is the first specimen of the kind that I have been able to procure, and will be a valuable addition to my collection."

"I must confess," said Merryweather, regretting his hastiness, "that my denunciations of botany were just then caused by a piece of that 'mares tail,'—for really," he continued, with a very affable smile, "I must leave the more classical and refined term for those who are so much more learned on the subject than myself;——falling over the leaf of the book which I am reading, and, as you may see, aunt, causing divers marks, which to a certain extent obliterate the type and spoil the appearance of the leaf. I propose, therefore, as we both have subjects for complaint, that we compromise the matter by a mutual forgiveness, which you shall testify by accompanying me in the boat to the rock on which that curious sea weed grows, when we will bring home as many baskets full of specimens as you like."

" It will, indeed," said Dorothy, elated at the idea, for she had frequently expressed a desire to visit this rock, but had never before met with any encouragement from her nephew— " It will indeed be productive of the most interesting results to me, as I shall be able to obtain several specimens of the class Cryptogamia, which as yet do not adorn my collection, and since I perceive a

newly awakened sympathy in you, my
dear niece, for this beautiful science, I
think you had better accompany us."

Constance having expressed her wil-
lingness to do so, they were quickly *en
route* to the beach, where a boat, which
Merryweather had purchased a day or
two previously, at a neighbouring town,
was in readiness for them.

To reach the sea shore, they had to
descend a long flight of steps cut into
the face of the perpendicular cliff, and
flanked on the outside by a rude balus-
trade to protect the passenger.   As they
descended, the massive grandeur of the
barren but stately cliff bounded their
view on one side, while before them the
broad expanse of ocean stretched far
away to the distant horizon, its heaving
and restless bosom, when viewed from
that dizzy height, appearing almost calm,
or as the surface of a lake just ruffled
by a gentle breeze.   The boat in which
they were about to embark also, seemed

such a very cockle shell, as it rested upon the beach, that the idea of going to sea in anything so frail and diminutive would have struck those of the party who had not yet given it a closer inspection as preposterous, had not the figure of the man who stood close beside it, also appeared reduced to such a pigmy size, as to convince them of the deception which distance lent to the scene. Winding over the face of the cliff, they reached the white shingle which bestrewed the beach beneath, and the boat being speedily launched, and the wind favourable, they were soon bounding over the green waves towards the rock on which flourished the sea-weed so much prized by Dorothy Munroe.

The fineness of the day, however, induced the fairer portion of the party to propose a further trip, and Merryweather who had become an accomplished boatman while in Cornwall, instantly acceding to their request, stood out to sea, till they had attained a distance of seven or eight miles from the shore, when the wind died away and left them completely becalmed. The heat now became excessive, and Merryweather in order to protect his freight from its effects, quickly rigged up a sort of temporary awning with a spare sail. Fishing lines were then produced, and while Dorothy Munroe busily employed herself in arranging her newly acquired treasures, and Constance read aloud a new publication which had been recently received from Town, Merryweather employed himself in ensnaring a few members of the finny tribe. Two or three hours thus passed rapidly away, when a low rumbling sound attracted their attention, Merryweather sprung up, pulled aside the awning and beheld with undisguised consternation the scene which presented itself. The heavens had assumed a most threatening appearance. A violent storm was evidently near at hand, and a dark mass of clouds, which was rapidly rising in the opposite direction to that from which they had come, even while he gazed, gave forth another peal of thunder.

His first thought was to employ the best means at his disposal in encountering the danger, for he saw immediately that to avoid it was impossible. When, however, he looked upon his cousin, and upon the unfortunate Dorothy Munroe, who had already been seized with a panic, and had commenced bemoaning her unhappy fate in language which it passes our ingenuity to record, his heart sunk within him. But he was not one long to give way to feelings of a desponding character, and knowing that their safety depended entirely upon his exertions, he set about making preparations for the approaching struggle. Having stowed away the awning and made fast the ballast and everything

that could " fetch way, " he stepped the
smaller of the two masts forward, and
secured it with backstays to enable it the
better to sustain the great pressure to
which it would be subjected when run-
ning before the wind.   After reefing the
small lug sail which belonged to this
mast, he made fast the sheets, and
pulling the head of the boat round, he
went himself to the helm, first however
depositing Dorothy Munroe at the foot
of the mast, a position she was the more
readily induced to occupy, by being
informed that it was the safest place.
His cousin he placed close to him, and
all his arrangements having been com-
pleted, the whole party awaited with
intense anxiety the approach of the
tempest.

Not a breath of wind could yet be
felt, and the boat was riding lazily over
the gently heaving sea, as if partaking
of the languid feeling which the heat
of the day had produced on its occupants.

This inaction made them feel more acutely their critical position, and few perhaps could be more trying. They were out at sea in an open boat, with the certainty that a storm of no ordinary violence was about to assail them, from which even Merryweather was obliged inwardly to confess that their chance of escape was but small. Finding under these circumstances that his efforts to inspire a hope which he did not feel himself were of no avail, he gave up the attempt, and awaited in silence the fortune that was in store for them.

Darker and darker grew the heavens. The thunder at every successive peal became louder, and the massive clouds gradually encircled the whole expanse of the horizon. Immediately over them, the scud had the appearance of being the sport of tumultuous eddies, now driven with impetuous force in one direction, and then suddenly dispersed as some opposing gust stopped its onward progress. The agitated appearance of the sea in the direction which from the first had appeared so threatening, now gave Merryweather notice that the time for action had arrived, a sign which he had not long observed, when a gust of tremendous force drove down upon their frail bark with winged speed. The boat staggered under the pressure, but the next moment as if endowed with life bounded forward at a rate which almost rivalled the sea gulls that hovered around. The rain poured down in almost unbroken streams, and a flash of lightning, so vivid as to leave behind it for some moments an appearance of complete obscurity, shot from a cloud immediately over them. This was followed by an oppressively loud peal of thunder, which rolling along the surface of the water was echoed back by the distant cliffs. The first burst of the storm over the wind continued blowing steadily though with un diminished violence from the same quarter, which proved to Merryweather that there was now little chance of a sudden shift of wind, a danger which he had at first apprehended. The sea, however, was becoming more and more turbulent under the goading influence of its powerful agitator, and every wave that buoyed up the stern of their light boat, as with greater fleetness it passed them on its destined course, assumed a more threatening aspect than its predecessor. Thus in doubt and uncertainty they flew before the gale for about an hour, when Merryweather began anxiously to look out for the land, which he knew could not be far distant, though the torrents of hail and rain, as well as the general obscurity, concealed it from his view. Gradually the atmosphere before them assumed a denser appearance, and the cause of this change was soon apparent by the outline of the cliffs, at first becoming dimly traceable and then standing forth in strong relief, as an invincible barrier to their further progress. To what part, however, of the coast the storm had driven them, or whether a landing could be effected, Merryweather was of course ignorant, and it could not but suggest itself to his mind, that perhaps after all his efforts, they were about to be cast against the face of the inhospitable cliff which rose before them.

" I would to heaven, Constance," said Merryweather, as this possibility occured to him, " that you were seated in your own home at this moment. I could then look lightly upon the danger. — But Constance,——dear Constance, even if the worst should happen, this arm shall support you as long as its owner lives."

" I know," said Constance, looking with womanly confidence into his face, " that you would do everything in your power for my safety, but you must not forget, dear Frank, that there is another here equally entitled to your protection."

" God bless you, Constance," said Merryweather, deeply touched by her disinterestedness at a moment so full of danger, " and if other days are in store for us, I will ever sacredly treasure up your noble words. I wish though, more than I can express that you were safe at the present moment."

" And I," said Constance, who had watched with unbounded admiration the presence of mind and undaunted aspect of her cousin during the perilous events of the last hour, " wish to be nowhere but by your side."

" Constance," said Merryweather hurriedly, " this is no time to conceal our thoughts from each other. Whatever fate may be in store for us," he continued, as a peal of thunder made every plank in their boat quiver, " and though each moment threaten our lives, yet will I avow that it has been love, and love only that I have felt for you, and not the cold friendship of distant connexions. And this love, unextinguishable by death, if death we must now meet, will rise, I trust, with the soul itself, superior to all corruption."

He seized her hand as he spoke, and glanced fondly into her face, and when she lifted her eyes to his, he was at no loss to understand their look of deep rooted affection.

As they approached nearer the cliff, Merryweather's worst surmises appeared about to be realized. A long line of breakers immediately before them became plainly visible, while the height to which the clouds of spray were driven into the air, as plainly showed, that some more formidable obstruction than a sandy shore opposed the encroaching power of the sea.

" I know where we are," said Merryweather, starting up and peering forward with intense eagerness. "There is an opening there in the rocks, which I went through the other day in calm weather, but it is a desperate thing to attempt now. However, it is the only chance left."

Again he seated himself at the helm, and placing one-arm round his cousin, steered directly for the narrow channel.

There was but little hope that anything of so fragile a nature as a boat could survive the tumult which raged within its narrow limits. As the huge billows fruitlessly expended their vast force upon the natural barriers around, they rushed through the apertures and chasms formed by their continued action with a power which nothing of a nature less impervious than the solid rocks could have withstood. The largest of these apertures was the one to which Merryweather steered, and once penetrated, their position would be one of safety, for although the rocks in most places lay wedged in close connection from their seaward extremity to the very foot of the cliffs that skirted the shore, yet here a ledge served as a breakwater and within its boundary the water was comparatively smooth. There was little time for reflection, for, lifted on the summit of a gigantic wave, they were swept through the opening, but only to be hurled back again by the retreating waters. The stern of their boat was stove in and began rapidly to fill with water, when another wave, similar to the first, hurried them to the furthermost end of the channel; and this time the undertow was not sufficiently strong to carry them back through its whole extent. The boat, in consequence, though nearly filled with water, once more became manageable, and they glided into the smooth basin, and touched the shore at the very moment when they were about to sink.

As soon as they found themselves safely landed, they spontaneously faltered their thanks to Heaven with sincere and deep-felt gratitude, when, after they had stood for some minutes gazing upon the raging ocean, Merryweather said—

"We must make haste and reach the end of this bay before the tide advances and shuts us in, for we shall appeal in vain to these merciless cliffs for protection."

So saying, he gave one arm to Dorothy Munroe and the other to his cousin, and after casting a parting look of regret upon the gallant little craft which had borne them through so much peril, he led them swiftly towards the nearest of the two promontories that formed the bay, the rising tide already throwing a briny spray over the spot they had to pass.

They now readily found a path which led from the shore, and after pursuing it for some distance, they came to a farm house and were received by the inmates, at first, with frank hospitality and unaffected commiseration, and afterwards with a greater degree of respect, but less cordiality, when it became known that they were the Ulvacombe party, for Mr. Munroe was far from being popular in the neighbourhood.

Their rough but honest host, however, did everything in his power to assist them. He belonged to that substantial class of farmers so frequently found in Devonshire, and being, amongst other chattels, the owner of a neat though rustic conveyance, which carried the good wife and her grown up daughters to church on Sundays,it was instantly placed at their disposal, and after thanking their entertainer they set off for Ulvacombe, which was about five miles distant.

On their arrival they found Mr. Munroe ignorant even of their absence from the house, but happening to pass through the hall as they entered, he did not omit to ask with surprise the cause of the unusual condition in which they appeared.

" My dear brother," said Dorothy, now recovered from her fright, and delighted at so favourable an opportunity for display, " we have been surrounded by the perils which attend those whose business is on great waters. My indefatigable exertions to master every detail connected with that interesting science, botany, led me to accept the proffered escort of this our courageous deliverer, to a rock where some particular specimens of the class " Cryptogamia " can alone be procured in this neighbourhood. Tempted by the fineness of the weather, we proceeded further. The storm which has just past overtook us. Unable to cope with its violence we ran after it,"—

" Scudded before it," suggested Merryweather.

" Yes, such I suppose is the idiomatic phraseology of mariners, in which you must now, of course, be considered an adept, my dear Frank. We scudded before it. The thunder, the sea, and the boat rolled fearfully. All at once, as if by magic, we were amongst rocks. Hail, rain, foam, spray, lightning, and wind raged around us, and the next minute I was unexpectedly standing upon the shore, repeating, I hope fervently, the form of prayer to be used at sea."

" Which was scarcely applicable under the circumstances, Dorothy," said Mr. Munroe, without relaxing a muscle of his countenance, " and perhaps it would have been as well," he continued, without offering the slightest congratulation to any of the party on their escape, " if with this statement you had coupled some expression of regret at having exposed my daughter to such danger."

" I am quite as much in fault as aunt Dorothy," said Constance, speaking with that diffidence which resulted from the general harshness of her sire. " We both wished to prolong our trip, and we owe our escape from the storm that overtook us to my cousin."

" Humph !" ejaculated Mr. Munroe, a look of extreme displeasure crossing his countenance. " At present," he continued, speaking generally, "my advice is, that you change your apparel before any evil consequences ensue."

"Abracadabra!" exclaimed Dorothy, placing herself in the van and leading the way upstairs. "A saying which you are doubtless aware, my dear nephew, was first promulgated in the dark ages as a charm against ague, and although at our time of life it might be deemed unnecessary,—even if the enlightened era in which we live had not removed all belief in its efficacy,—yet the word itself being easy of pronunciation, and taxing neither our time nor patience in its acquirement, we may as well give ourselves the benefit of any doubt that may exist on the subject, and if there should be any virtue in the expression reap the advantage that will accrue from its use."

So saying she opened the door of her apartment, and retired within its precincts to perform her mysterious toilet.

That evening when Merryweather joined the ladies in the drawing room after dinner, he found his cousin seated at her piano, which was near an open French window, and he placed himself quickly by her side. She sang his favourite melodies, and if occasionally she slightly trembled on the upper notes, yet as the exciting events of the day with all their dangers and associations crowded on her mind, her voice breathed a deeper feeling into the song.

The wind which had now subsided into a gentle breeze, rustled amongst the leaves, while it wafted towards them many a reminiscence of the rose, which clustered round the mansion. It is not surprising, under these circumstances, when Merryweather proposed a walk in the garden, that Constance should have acquiesced. Dangerous moments! How could they remain silent on the subject which so engrossed their thoughts, when everything in the scene around invited them to throw off all reserve. The only sound that met their ear was the low murmur of the surf as it beat incessantly on the distant beach. High in the blue vault of Heaven rode the serene but haughty Empress of the night, her silvery rays infusing a brilliant light into the drops of rain that still hung upon the boughs, and casting upon the troubled surface of the distant ocean that broad bright track, which, to our imagination, seems best adapted for the transit from fairy land, of those elfin forms with which the graceful mythology of the northern nations has peopled their shores.

"Constance," said Merryweather, as he pressed the hand that leant upon his arm, "you recollect what I said to-day when we were in the midst of such dangers?"

Constance thought she did, but was not sure. She was so frightened, she remembered that better than anything else.

"Then without recapitulating it," said Merryweather, smiling as he recalled the somewhat melodramatic speech he made under the excitement of the moment. "Tell me,—do tell me, Constance, if I may hope at some future time to call you by a dearer,—a far dearer name than that of cousin?"

Constance paused for a moment to still the beatings of her heart, and then answered with forced calmness, "You know I cannot, I must not promise, Frank. Be generous and do not ask me at present. Papa's anger would be greater than you can conceive, if he knew that we even thought of such a thing."

"I will not then, Constance," said Merryweather, "ask you to enter into any engagement, but listen to me for one minute. Wherever I may go, whatever may be my pursuits, neither time, nor distance, nor change of scene, nor the temptations, nor the trials of the world, shall ever impair my love,—my deep love for you. It shall be my guide,— the goal to which all my plans, all my efforts shall tend. I will nourish it,— I will dwell upon it, and when we meet again, though my views on every other subject may have altered, though contact with the world may have dulled some of the early feelings of youth, yet this predominant one shall remain as bright and pure as at this moment. Surely then, dear Constance, I may ask if you will entirely cease to think of one, who will always love you so truly ? "

"Never !—never ! " said Constance, in a low tone.

For the first time he pressed the lips that uttered these words with his own, and from that moment, both felt that they had been irrevocably swept into the vortex of that passion which confers so much happiness, and yet such misery upon its votaries. They thought not, however, of the future, and the happiest moments of their lives were perhaps the present.

Remorseless time hastens not, nor delays the measured moments that fall from his hand for insignificant mortals. With the same stoical indifference and inexorable steadiness he looks upon the sufferings of the tortured wretch upon the rack and the lover's stolen interview, nor quickens his movements to assuage the sufferings of the one, or to prolong the fleeting happiness of the other. It is not therefore matter of wonder, that when the clock in the drawing room had twice sent forth its shrill notes into the night air as a warning to return, Constance and Frank should have thought the time had passed with incredible swiftness.

There is, too, a fatality in true love, and its course we know seldom runs clear, nor do the events we are bound to record in this truthful narrative form an exception to this general rule. The following morning Mr. Munroe came down to the breakfast room with a large packet in his hand, endorsed "On Her Majesty's Service," in which was intimated Her Majesty's pleasure, that Frank Merryweather, gentleman, should obey and be obeyed as an ensign in her military service.

"I mentioned to Lord Carlbrook," said Mr. Munroe, after he had presented the ' despatch ' to his nephew, "that you had a near relation at Bombay, and I perceive that this circumstance has induced him, with his usual kindness, to get you gazetted to the —— th regiment, which, by the last ' Indian News,' was at Poona. They have only been in India a short time, therefore you must make up your mind to pass a few years in a foreign country. It is all in the way of service you know, and a soldier must not shrink from that. Although not in the army, I was out there thirty years."

"That 'indeed," said Merryweather, glancing at his cousin, and inwardly resolving, *coute qui coute*, that not a tenth part of that time should elapse before his return. " That indeed was a long banishment. But then, sir, you must remember that it will be in my power to exchange into another regiment, and therefore it does not necessarily follow that I shall be in India more than a year or two."

The latter part of this sentence Merry-weather said as pointedly as he could, for he saw that his cousin had turned deadly pale, and was in violent agitation. Unable indeed longer to conceal it, she rose and left the room, when Mr. Munroe, who had not noticed his daughter's emotion, said,—

"A year or two! sir, a year or two! If you intend running about the world just as every whim strikes you, it is much to be regretted that my interest was employed in getting you a commission.   Do   you   know that   this changing about from one regiment to another will do you more injury at the Horse Guards than aught else, and may eventually oblige you to resign? It is the fact," continued Mr. Munroe, perceiving an incredulous smile upon his nephew's countenance, " and I could tell you instances of it."

" Well sir, " said Merryweather, changing his manner, " when I have had more experience, I have no doubt, I shall see these things in the same point of view as yourself. But there is now another subject which I wish to say a few words to you upon."

" Oh ! about your money affairs. That shall be all arranged in as short a time as possible, and before you leave England."

" It is of more importance far than that."

" More importance !" exclaimed Mr. Munroe, inwardly drawing the conclusion that his nephew was partially demented.

"Yes, of infinitely more importance; and if in making the matter known to you I should not be quite coherent, you must attribute it to the excitement under which I speak. You must be aware, sir, that we, that is to say, your daughter (Mr. Munroe started) and myself have been left very much to each other's society since my arrival here?"

"Indeed, I know nothing of the sort," said Mr. Munroe, sharply.

"It is the fact, nevertheless," said Merryweather, "and I have resolved, before leaving Ulvacombe, to inform you of the consequences — we are engaged."

"Engaged!" said Mr. Munroe, aghast.

"I do not mean to say," continued Merryweather, "that any actual compact in words exists between us, on the contrary, sir, your daughter refused, without the consent of her parent, to make any such promise. But our engagement is based upon far more durable grounds. It rests on the state of our own affections."

"What your reason may be," said Mr. Munroe, after looking with extreme dislike for some moments upon his nephew, "for favouring me with a confession of this very disinterested attachment, upon your part, I confess myself unable to discover. If, however, you imagine that my sanction will ever be given to anything so preposterous, you are vastly in error."

"Then I suppose," said Merryweather dejectedly, for this decisive reply had somewhat staggered him, "we have no resource but in hope."

"Hope," replied Mr. Munroe, rising and standing with his back to the fireplace, "when enlisted in a legitimate object, cannot be too carefully fostered, but when it is manifestly absurd to entertain it, any one who is not prepared to forfeit all claim to common

sense, will crush it in the bud.   There-
fore," he continued, assuming a patron-
izing manner, "I recommend you for
your own peace of mind, instantly to
banish all thoughts of, what I will call,
this boyish fancy."

"But you would not," said Merry-
weather dubiously as he glanced at
Mr. Munroe, "force the inclinations
of your daughter?"

"I am more inclined," said Mr.
Munroe in the same patronizing manner,
"to endeavour to convince you of your
folly, than disposed to find fault with
what you say, however unbecoming it
may be, and as I think that to produce
this result the most efficacious way
will be to convince you that the hand
of my daughter is far beyond what you
can ever hope to aspire to, I will enter
into explanations, which my interest
for your welfare alone induces me to
My daughter, sir, will inherit a
fortune. My daughter, sir, pos-

sesses the same personal attractions which placed her mother at the head of this house, and therefore it is confidently expected by her family that she will some day enter the very highest ranks of society."

"In other words," said Merryweather, "it is confidently expected by her family, that she will sacrifice all her own inclinations, in order to secure the possession of that which can never afford her one moment's happiness. However, sir, I can assure you, that though Miss Munroe will never enter into any matrimonial engagement without your sanction, yet it is equally certain that she will never give her hand where she cannot bestow her affections, and these are already engaged. The confidence with which I speak may in some measure open your eyes to the real state of the case ; and in dropping the subject, let me assure you that my own feelings, will ever remain unaltered."

"The meaning of which assertion," said Mr. Munroe, his lip quivering with anger, "is, that you have resolved, if it be in your power, to maintain the influence that you have secretly acquired, by the most despicable means, over the mind of a mere child. But you will find that young gentlemen are not always so clever as they imagine themselves to be. And now, sir, since your presence is no longer desired in this house, you will be pleased to leave it immediately. Here," he continued, drawing a card from his pocket as he was leaving the room, "is the direction of some lodgings which I have engaged for you in town. I will moreover give you a letter of introduction to Captain Blakeney, an officer who has been in India, and who will, I have no doubt, give you the benefit of his advice in procuring whatever is necessary before your departure from England. Whether to call upon Mrs.

Mackintosh or not, is a matter on which you can exercise your own judgment; but since you have already evinced so much confidence in it, my advice would of course be superfluous, and I shall not therefore offer any. I have merely to add that my carriage will be ready in an hour."

So saying he quitted the room, and Merryweather was left to his meditations.

These soon brought him to the conclusion that he had just done a very indiscreet thing, and that the mischief being irreparable, all that remained was to get ready for his departure. This was soon accomplished, and his luggage having been taken down to the lodge, and a correspondence arranged between his guardian and himself, he had no excuse for tarrying longer. Still, however, he lingered with the hope of being able to say adieu to his cousin, but in this he was destined to be disappointed, for Mr. Munroe was on the alert and his precautions were too well taken. On leaving the house, however, he saw a handkerchief waved from the window of his cousin's boudoir. He kissed his hand in return, and not daring to trust himself with another look, he strode onwards to the lodge, under a sense of the deepest depression.

CHAPTER VI.

They take religion in their mouth ;
They talk o' mercy, grace, an' truth,
For what ? to gie their malice skouth
      On some puir wight ;
An' hunt him down, o'er right an' ruth,
      To ruin streight.
All hail religion ! maid divine !
Pardon a muse sae mean as mine,
Who, in her rough imperfect line,
      Thus daurs to name thee ;
To stigmatize false friends of thine,
      Can ne'er defame thee.
              Burns's Poems.

THE day after Merryweather's arrival in
town, he proceeded to Captain Blakeney's
residence, but not finding him at home,

left his card and the letter of introduction
he had received from Mr. Munroe, with
the servant. Towards the latter end of the
day a note was delivered to him from
that gentleman, expressing his regret at
having been away from home when Merry-
weather called, and containing a request
that he might have the pleasure of meet-
ing him at the house of Mrs. Mackintosh
in Eton Place, in the course of the
evening. Merryweather accordingly at
about nine o'clock drove up to the door,
and was forthwith shown into a drawing
room, furnished in the most costly man-
ner. As there was no one in the room,
he had ample time to make his
observations, and amongst other things
to look into some of the handsomely
bound books arranged round the table.
They were of an exceedingly serious turn,
and he read successively the titles. " The
rod gently administered;" " The rod
sharply administered;"   " Comforting
food for the sick sinner;" " A barbed

fork to stir up a lazy conscience;" "Fastenings for a Backslider;" and several others of the same remarkable tenor.

Just as he had arrived at the conclusion that they were not the kind of books he should much care to peruse, Captain Blakeney and Mrs. Mackintosh, entered, and the former stepping up to Merryweather with rather a studied politeness of manner, expressed the pleasure it gave him to make the acquaintance of one whose father, he, in common with his other friends, had estimated so highly. "Let me" continued Captain Blakeney "introduce— but I mistake,—you must surely remember Mrs. Mackintosh?"

Merryweather explained that so many years had intervened since he was under her maternal control, that he was obliged to confess that Mrs. Mackintosh, in all but in name, had faded from his recollection.

"Ah, I suppose so," replied Captain Blakeney, "but you are most fortunate in having the opportunity of again making her acquaintance. I speak from experience,—her worth is inappreciable!"

"You should not, Captain Blakeney, raise expectations which can never be realised," said Mrs. Mackintosh, after shaking hands with Merryweather. "I am but a weak vessel, little able to do any good thing, and though I am never weary of trying, yet it is seldom that I accomplish all that my desire for the welfare of others bids me attempt."

"But if you attempt much, madam, and perform but a tithe," said Merryweather, seating himself in obedience to a motion from Mrs. Mackintosh, "that tithe may be considerable."

"Oh no, Mr. Merryweather, I will not call it considerable, because it falls so far short of what I would wish it to be,—falls short of what I have seen others perform. It is true that my humble efforts have sometimes been attended with success, but it is not for me to speak of them; they are recorded I trust elsewhere. Have you ever turned your thoughts to serious subjects ?"

" Very frequently, madam," replied Merryweather.

" How refreshing to hear the young say this with sincerity. Let one who has gone through much trial and affliction, entreat you, for your own sake, to keep in this frame of mind, and never to allow the merry and the gay to allure you to seek for happiness anywhere but in secret meditation. Nights of weeping and days of mourning are such healthful preparations for the duties and avocations of life, and so subdue to meekness and resignation the proud heart of man, that those who avail themselves of these privileges, experience, it is not perhaps presumptuous to say, a foretaste of paradise."

"You never I suppose read any books but such as I see upon your table?" asked Merryweather.

"They principally employ my leisure hours," was the reply.

"Then you are unacquainted with the works of Mr. ——— and Mr. ———?"

"I have read the latter's 'Travels in the Holy Land," replied Mrs. Mackintosh, "but I have since heard that he has published other works of a light, not to say immoral tendency. Such productions I would not look at for all that this world can offer, and I hope and trust they are equally far from ever engaging your attention."

"On the contrary," replied Merryweather, "I am bound to confess that I have read most of the works they have written with delight, frequently with instruction, and I must say that I have never found anything approaching to immorality in any of them. Those works are immoral in which it is sought so to clothe vice that it may please the eye and corrupt the heart. No such attempt is made by the authors I have mentioned. They paint men as they find them. They hold up a looking glass to crime, in which it may see its own hideous visage, and so completely rend the veil of hypocrisy from the impostor as to make him a laughing stock to the world; or, on the other hand, they draw pictures on the brighter side of human nature, which, if sometimes too highly coloured, are nevertheless in most cases beautiful creations, such as soften the feelings and make us more charitable in our dealings with others. No one surely would accuse Hogarth of immorality for producing those inimitable Pictures, in which licentiousness is so represented as to make even the vitiated recoil from its false charms; and yet much the same spirit, I think, prevails in the works you condemn. They are drawn with the pen it is true, instead of

to detract from the sublimity of the gospel they profess to teach. If they are so anxious to become authors, there are many subjects which claim their attention. But no. Here is one that they know will secure a certain amount of circulation, and thus every impostor who can turn up his eyes, and in a sepulchral tone of voice talk of 'the world' as of something with which he has no connection whatever, pesters society with the trash, pardon the expression, you recommend me. In all of them it is sought to terrify the reader by the punishments that are stated to be waiting for him, or he is favoured with a sickly and mawkish sentimentality which is absolutely loathsome, and a cruel mockery of the high authority which it pretends to vindicate."

"Oh! my young friend, you are on the brink of ruin!" exclaimed Mrs. Mackintosh. "The very strongest remedies are necessary for your case. Pray let me entreat you to read this tract."

Merryweather glanced at the title of the pamphlet that was handed to him across the table, and his eye encountered in letters an inch high, the rather startling query, 'Young man, do you know you are close to hell?"   Refraining from any further observation, and subduing the disgust that arose in his mind, he placed it on the top of the other books which he had rejected, and said, "I see plainly that we should never understand each other;" and then turning to Captain Blakeney in order to end the discussion, he continued—"My uncle tells me that you have been in India, and you will not, perhaps, refuse me the benefit of your experience and advice in procuring whatever is requisite for so long a voyage."

"Certainly, I shall be most happy," replied Captain Blakeney, "but do you not go over-land?"

"I was thinking of going round the Cape," said Merryweather, "for I am very partial to the sea."

"In that case I should recommend you to trust yourself to the tender mercies of an outfitter. They are gifted with the most retentive memories, which certainly do not fail them when they are making out their accounts, but they are a set of fellows whose services are invaluable on such an occasion. I well remember that during a voyage, which, from having the wind without a moment's intermission dead in our teeth, except when it blew from some other quarter, extended over six months; I never once fancied I should like anything, but it was discovered in some unknown recess. I often thought that the whole of London must have been squeezed into those six bullock trunks."

"Captain Blakeney!" exclaimed Mrs. Mackintosh, holding up her finger warningly.

"Well, such was frequently my impression, I assure you, but our amiable friend, if she will allow us to call her so," continued Captain Blakeney, addressing Merryweather, " has such exquisitively sensitive feelings and is gifted with such a high sense of morality, that she dislikes the slightest appearance of exaggeration, even when it is only used figuratively by way of illustration.   I have frequently seen her very uneasy when people have casually mentioned such fabulous animals as unicorns and dragons, because as there never were such creatures, she considers it a violation of the truth to speak of them as if they had ever existed.   Such is her sensitiveness!"

" Prodigious !"   exclaimed   Merryweather, laughing at what he conceived a joke of Captain Blakeney's.

"Yes! let the world laugh !" said Mrs. Mackintosh, with every appearance of enthusiasm.   " Let the World scoff! The World has always done so and will, it is to be feared, continue to do so. But there are those who know what the World is,—who shrink from its contaminating touch, and are proud when they have merited its jeers. Such people are enveloped in a case of such impenetrable sanctity, that the World's assaults move them no more than the wind moves the solid rock, and if they ever think of the worldly, it is with sorrow and compassion."

"There, I told you so," said Captain Blakeney, fixing his eyes on the ceiling. "It is quite a pleasure to hear her," he added, while be fanned himself with, "The Barbed Fork."

"Is it so?" said Mrs. Mackintosh, with a dubious sigh. "I wish I could benefit as well as please, those who hear me. Our young friend, I fear, is not prepared to afford me this delight. But yet I will endeavour to sow good seed in his mind, and I trust that though it may now lay dormant, it will nevertheless in the time to come shoot up, and in spite of the weeds that at present usurp the soil, yield an abundant crop. Then oh! my beloved young brother, let me arouse

you !   Pray shake off dull sleep and
slothful indifference.   Open your eyes,
look around you and start !   Is it not
better that you ˙should awake of your
own accord than wait till some heavy
calamity, which may be close upon you,
and will overtake you unless you repent
in time, dispels with fearful suddenness
your quiet slumbers ?   Oh ! I remember
to have seen an infant tossing its inno-
cent limbs from side to side in all the
luxuriance of repose, a smile dimpling
its cheek whilst its cherub lips ever and
anon unconsciously called for its proud
and happy mother, and Oh ! I had not
long looked on this bright and pleasing
vision when the side of the cot gave way,
and the child rolled with deafening
screams to the ground.   No longer was
its countenance radiant with smiles, but
from its mouth, now opened far and wide,
nature called loudly for assistance.   And
Oh ! for words to express my delight,
when I found that it had not been

injured! No, it had only been aroused. And such, my dear young friend, may be your case, but do you hope like the blessed infant to escape unhurt? Ah, no. Believe me you will not. Therefore be aroused at once. Oh Arouse! Arouse!!

"Well, Madam," said Merryweather, rising to depart, "I thank you very much for the interest you take in my spiritual welfare, but I will not encroach any longer upon your time, particularly after the useful manner in which you tell me it is employed. I will now wish you good evening."

"One request you must grant me," said Mrs. Mackintosh with fervour.

"I will endeavour to comply with it," said Merryweather hesitatingly, as a variety of absurd propositions flashed across his mind.

"Then it is to take these books for your own private perusal, and this bundle of tracts to distribute amongst the natives in India."

"I have already declined those books,
Madam," replied Merryweather. "I beg
you will not force me to appear discour-
teous; and as for the tracts, I think it
will appear to you on consideration, that
being written in English, they would
scarcely be understood by Hindoos. I
wish you good evening," and so saying
Merryweather beat a precipitate retreat,
muttering as he descended the stairs, "I
always thought my poor aunt was the
greatest   fool   in   the   world,   but
this woman is ten thousand times
worse."

No sooner did the closing of the street
door announce to Captain Blakeney that
Merryweather had left the house, than
he threw himself upon one of the sofas
and with a burst of laughter, in which,
however, there was little real merriment,
exclaimed, "Well, that was not so bad,
but he has taken none of those pretty
little books away with him, has he Mrs.
Mackintosh?"

"Of course," was the reply, "you will now commence turning everything that is serious into ridicule. That I expect. I should indeed be astonished if *you* could admire anything of the kind."

"Oh, dear yes, I do!" said Captain Blakeney, with a sarcastic smile. "I admire exceedingly your manner of dealing with such subjects—the astonishing facility with which you contrive to cultivate spiritual thoughts without ever neglecting your worldly interests, which, to say the least, are in your case of such a nature as to impose upon you the necessity of not being very scrupulous. Not admire! Believe me, a mind so formed becomes a most interesting study, and shows that the most contradictory feelings can be cherished and even enjoyed at one and the same time. People who had not witnessed the phenomenon might be afraid of their clashing, but so cleverly do you contrive to adjust matters, that, upon my word, their harmonious action is truly wonderful. Not admire! I assure you that my admiration is unbounded."

Mrs. Mackintosh listened to these remarks without making any reply, although she well understood their meaning. But the cloak that is first put on to deceive others, eventually hides from the wearer the defects around which it is thrown. The impostor, who carries his hand in a sling whilst imploring alms, and carefully guards the uninjured member from coming in contact with the passer by, finds that at night, even in the midst of low and riotous scenes, he is unable to free himself from the impression that it requires his care. Infinitely stronger are such impressions when the fraud has to be sustained by continual exertions of the mind, which, growing weary of supporting an assumed character, at last yields obedience to outward observances, and fashions itself to the deceit it is perpetually called upon to practise. Mrs. Mackintosh had arrived at this happy state of self-delusion. She was an impostor in every sense of the word. She knew that she had neither right nor show of right to the property she was at present enjoying, and that she had acquired it entirely by means of a forged document. Yet, she had contrived so completely to palliate this transaction in her own eyes, and had moreover so habituated herself to an outward observance of what she termed her religious duties,——though at first they were performed for the purpose of warding off the suspicion which attached to her,——that even Captain Blakeney himself, found it difficult sometimes to recognise in her his accomplice in fraud. It was in some such state of bewilderment, that after a few minutes silence he observed,——"That young Merryweather is a shrewd sort of fellow, and should he by any chance ever get a clue to the manner in which he was relieved of his property, I venture to say he will never rest till he unravels the whole matter.   I do not say that this is likely, or even possible to happen ; but supposing such a case, I am very much afraid, my dear Mrs. Mackintosh—I really am very much afraid, that he would scarcely give you credit for sincerity in reading him that delightful little lecture this evening."

"Then he would wrong me," said Mrs. Mackintosh, solemnly.

"You would have some difficulty, I fear, in convincing him of that ; for he would naturally think, that however well inclined you might be to set him right in the next world, you were certainly wronging him in this."

"I ?" exclaimed Mrs. Mackintosh. It is not my doing.   I was led into it and found afterwards that the step was irrevocable. Besides it was so ordained, or it could not have happened, and I rejoice to think that I have been made the instrument of doing good to others, for I contribute largely, as you are aware, to the missionary funds, which would not be aided by the young man we have just seen."

"I have no doubt," said Captain Blakeney, "that you apply his funds for him in a most conscientious manner, and really, so long as no diminution in my income takes place, I am far from having any objection to this disinterested expenditure. I can only hope that our arrangements may continue to be made in the same amicable manner as hitherto, and that this young stripling will not hear anything in India prejudicial to our interests. But faugh! There was not a scrap of writing to be found, and it is almost impossible that anything can come to light after so many years. You need be under no apprehension."

"Whatever were to happen I should feel quite resigned to the will of Providence," said Mrs. Mackintosh meekly. "My only fault has been want of sufficient firmness,—a fault which I cannot repent, since it has been productive of such beneficial results to the Heathen in foreign lands. The part you have played, Captain Blakeney cannot, I fear, be looked upon with equal indulgence. I do not however wish to judge between us. Society will do that in case of anything transpiring."

"Why, you see," returned Captain Blakeney, settling himself more comfortably on the sofa, "there would be a slight difficulty in proving that I was in any way concerned in the matter. I do not put this forward as a menace, but merely state it as a fact. However, there is no use," he continued after a pause, "in imagining what we should do under circumstances that can never occur. There are many ways in which our time can be more profitably employed, so I will leave you to the quiet enjoyment of the pursuits in which you delight, whilst I adjourn to the dining room to finish the glass of claret which young Merryweather's arrival compelled me to leave."

Mrs. Mackintosh sighed and said something about keeping our appetites under subjection, but with apparently not much effect, for Captain Blakeney quitted the room without further remark, and she was left to ruminate alone over the duties of the morrow.

CHAPTER VII.

But where to find that happiest spot below,
Who can direct when all pretend to know?
The shuddering tenant of the frigid zone
Boldly proclaims that happiest spot his own;
Extols the treasures of the stormy seas,
And his long nights of revelry and ease:
The naked negro, panting at the line,
Boasts of his golden sands and palmy wine,
Basks in the glare, or stems the tepid wave,
And thanks his gods for all the good they gave.
Such is the patriot's boast where'er we roam,
His first, best country ever is at home.
                    Goldsmith's Traveller.

MERRYWEATHER had in accordance with Captain Blakeney's advice, given his instructions to one of those accomodating people, whose intimate acquaintance with the wants of their fellow men, enable them to supply the traveller with an outfit, comprising everything that can possibly be required during a long voyage, and was debating how he could best employ the few weeks that remained to him before leaving England, when one day, happening to pass through Leadenhall street, he saw his old school-fellow, Somerville, coming out of the India House. Their meeting was cordial in the extreme, and after the first demonstrations of pleasure had a little subsided, they began to discuss their future prospects. Although they had occasionally corresponded, Merryweather now heard for the first time that his friend was going out to India, an opportunity of obtaining a cadetship having unexpectedly occurred, of which his family had taken advantage. The choice of the two presidencies, Bombay or Madras, having been offered to him, he was, at Merryweather's earnest solicitation, induced to choose the former, and they thereupon agreed so to time their departure as to enable them to sail for their destination in the same ship.   This arrangement having been made, Merryweather readily accepted an invitation to pass the remainder of the time before leaving England with Somerville, and they accordingly went together to the latter's residence in the country.   As usual with those who are about to make a long pilgrimage into a distant land they were kindly and hospitably received by all whom they visited.   Every one moreover had an advice to give them.   A gentleman, whose experience in nautical matters, had been acquired between Dover and Calais, strongly recommended his panacea for sea sickness.   Another, who had just risen from a perusal of Mills' History of British India, thought they could not do better than take His Grace the Duke of Wellington as their model, and endeavour, on the first convenient opportunity, to rival the military renown acquired by that far-famed chief at the battle of Assaye. A third had convinced himself by a long and painful process of deductive reasoning, that Mulligatauny soup, curry powder, Chutney sauce, and iced champagne are the true enemies of the British constitution in India, and that the plain dictates of common sense manifestly required that the European who visited the country of the Hindoo, should conform to the habits of the latter, and adopt a rice diet. We are bound in candour to admit that although this varied advice was listened to with patience and submission by our Hero and Somerville, it made little impression upon them, for independently of its intrinsic value, their minds were engrossed with one paramount idea,—their approaching banishment from their native land.

Time flies! If this be the impression of its fleetness made by the absorbing interest of the ordinary events of life, some infinitely more expressive term must be invented to convey an idea of its movements, when home, surrounded by all the bright hopes which the imagination of youth loves to paint, is about to be exchanged for a long exile in a foreign land. Somerville was more sensitively alive to these feelings than Merryweather, for the latter, as already mentioned, had determined not to remain in India longer than three years. But three years! or even two! He looked back upon the last two years he had passed at school, and they appeared to him an age. He had yet to learn that every succeeding year in a man's life passes more quickly than the one preceding it. The occurrences of each day in the mean time appeared to flit as quickly before them as the ever varying phases of a Kaleidoscope, and it was almost with a feeling of wonder, that at the expiration of a couple of months, they found themselves standing upon the deck of the Indiaman which was to convey them to Bombay.

Merryweather had completely under-rated the trial of leaving home. The excitement created by the preparations for his departure, the novelty of his situation, and the intuitive feeling which urges us to shrink from the contemplation of approaching pain, by forcing the mind to take an interest in passing occurrences, had tended much to distract his thoughts and divert his attention from an event which had become inevitable. But when the shores of England grew dim in the distance, and he pictured to himself the many unforeseen accidents which time and absence might produce, a morbid feeling of despondency took possession of his mind, and his actual position seemed the hallucination of some hideous dream converted into a reality. Every person, that he could recall to mind in the loved land now quickly fading from his view, became for the

moment an object of envy, for he
enjoyed what seemed the greatest of
earthly blessings,——a residence in his own
country, open to all the aspirations
which give social happiness and vitality
to man, and surrounded by all the asso-
ciations, without which, life is a dreary
blank, a hollow artificial state of existence.

Such were the thoughts of our Hero,
as he gazed out of one of the stern
windows of the Indiaman, but from this
train of ideas he was suddenly roused by
a violent noise in his cabin, and he gra-
dually became aware that a large sea
chest, which the foresight of his outfitter
had provided for his use during the voy-
age, was skipping about in a lively man-
ner, and threatening destruction to itself
and to all who approached it.   To
secure this waif became an immediate
necessity, and his attention being directed
to the fact that his personal comfort
would be much promoted by checking
the propensity which his moveables had

acquired to change their position with the unceasing motion of the ship, he summoned the necessary assistance, and soon gave his quarters such an air of comfort, as to induce him internally to acknowledge, that there might be more objectionable places in the world than one of the principal cabins of an India-man of twelve hundred tons.

The incidents of an Indian voyage in general vary but little. On this occasion there was the average amount of storms in the atmosphere, and amongst the pas-sengers; these occurrences forming the standing phenomena of a passage round the cape, and the latter in particular being apparently as necessary as spreading the canvass to the wind, or letting the anchor drop on arrival in port. Without, therefore attempting to record that to which we should probably fail to do justice, let us at once transport our hero to Bombay harbour.

Almost the first person who then came on board was Mr. Ponsonby, the uncle of Merryweather, for whom he instantly made enquiries. This gentleman was attired in very loose trousers, and an enormous shooting coat, both made of jean and as white as snow. A piece of black ribbon round his shirt collar served as an apology for a cravat. He encumbered himself with no vest, wore shoes, and a wide-awake hat, over which was a quilted white cover, thick enough to protect him from the rays of the sun. His age was about fifty, though a long residence in a tropical climate gave him a much older appearance. His complexion partook strongly of the colour of saffron, but there was a goodnatured expression in his countenance, and a great deal of shrewdness in the twinkle of his little grey eye.

" Very glad indeed to see you, nephew," said Mr. Ponsonby, holding out his hand to Merryweather.

"And I have long looked forward," said Merryweather, cordially grasping his uncle's hand, "to the pleasure of becoming acquainted with one who has been so kind to me."

"Never mind that now," said the old gentleman, evidently much delighted, "Make haste and get your kit over the side, and come ashore. You have been cooped up in a ship long enough. Who was that, by the way, to whom you were talking when I first saw you ?"

"An old schoolfellow of mine whom I think I have mentioned in my letters. His name is Somerville, and he is a cadet in the Company's service."

"Oh, ho! Arcades ambo ! Griffins both; eh ?" said Mr. Ponsonby. "Bring him along with you. I daresay I can manage to give him a 'shake down' as we old Indians call it."

Somerville having been introduced to Mr. Ponsonby, readily accepted the offer of a "shake down," and the whole party were therefore quickly seated with a countless number of packages, in a boat which soon deposited them at the custom house. A few silver coins administered to the itching palms of the officials, procured the transmission of their baggage without the annoyance of a search, and three palanquins forthwith conveyed the whole party to the bungalow of Mr. Ponsonby, which was situated on the Esplanade, facing the sea.

"You'll find it cooler here than in those palanquins," said Mr. Ponsonby, throwing himself into a seat in the verandah, behind a large screen made of Cuscus grass, and inviting his guests to do the same.

"You certainly have little to complain of here, Uncle," said Merryweather, glancing round the well furnished rooms, in which there was a profusion of every luxurious appliance that ingenuity could devise to minister to ease and promote comfort, "and as to heat, why all the cool breezes in the country are I should think imprisoned here; and what a delicious perfume is imparted by those screens!"

"Well they *are* a great comfort," said Mr. Ponsonby, "and do their work well enough. You see they are hung up all round the verandah, and effectually keep off the glare of the sun. Then I have a couple of Bearers watering them, so as to keep the grass well saturated and the breeze passing through them when in this state, not only imparts the pleasant fragrance you noticed just now to the atmosphere, but keeps every room in the Bungalow cool. People say, you know, that the separation between India and his Satanic Majesty's dominions, is as transparent as a Benares turban! Now granting this to be the case, I own that I prefer interposing something less pervious to heat between them and my person, and long experience has taught me that a little wet grass damps the ardour of that august

personage more than anything else. But
I had nearly forgotten,—Qui Hai!"

"Sahib!" replied a turbaned black
servant with great gravity, suddenly ap-
pearing from some recess where he would
have remained perfectly quiet for hours
had not his services been required.

"*Beer lao!*"

"*Sahib baraf hona?*" said this function-
ary with still greater gravity, a slight
movement of his lips, and the sound of
a voice proceeding from the direction
where he stood, being the only indica-
tions that he was speaking.

"Albatta," said Mr. Ponsonby.

"Achha sahib'" again replied the
automaton with increased gravity, and
disappearing in the same noiseless man-
ner with which he had made himself
visible.

"May I ask," said Merryweather,
laughing, "if the mission you have just
despatched that solemn personage upon
involves the fate of our Eastern Empire,

because his manner is that of a man burdened with mighty secrets?"

"You will have an opportunity of judging for yourself," replied Mr. Ponsonby, and at this moment the black servant re-appeared, bearing a silver salver, on which were a couple of bottles of pale ale, a crystal vase full of ice, and three tumblers.

"This is the important business he had to transact," continued Mr. Ponsonby, "but notwithstanding his stoical appearance, I would venture to say that he is listening attentively to every word that falls from us, and although I have never heard him utter an English word, yet I would hazard long odds that he understands our language just as well as I do Hindustani. Ah, you need not try to read his countenance, these fellows have a great deal too much face to betray what is passing in their minds. *Nani ka pani tayar karo, dono sahib ke waste!*" continued Mr. Ponsonby to the native attendant, who instantly withdrew. "I have ordered some baths to be got ready for both of you, for I well remember what a luxury it is to have a plentiful supply of fresh water after a long voyage. But come,—try some beer, you will find this the favourite beverage in India, and taken in moderation a very wholesome one, though not so if two dozen bottles be drunk in one day; a feat I once heard a person boast of having performed."

"That certainly is delicious," said Merryweather, setting down a glass in which the transparent lumps of ice which had recently floated on the surface of the chilled beverage now formed a cool mass at the bottom of the tumbler, "but I do not think my partiality for it would ever induce me to put myself to the inconvenience the person you speak of must have suffered."

"No. That was a feat highly disgusting in itself and quite worthy, I am sorry to say, of the person who accomplished it. But I was only waiting, Frank, for that black fellow to leave us, to tell you that he was once your father's servant, and that this is the sole reason why I have allowed him to remain with me, for I believe him to be as arrant a thief as there is in the world."

"My father's servant!" exclaimed Merryweather.

"Yes. He was with him in his last campaign, and from all accounts served him well, and according to their notions, faithfully, for it appears that he was much attached to him. This is not at all unfrequent with these natives, though at the same time the difference between *meum* and *tuum* being very apt to escape their memories, they frequently appropriate what does not belong to them. The first mentioned trait however, is certainly a very redeeming point, and considering the universal disregard of principle in the East, it would not perhaps be

fair to judge individuals by too high a
standard of morality."

" Do the natives like our rule ?" asked
Somerville.

" Well, the great mass of the popula-
tion have, it appears to me, ceased to
think about it. New generations have
sprung up since we began to govern the
country, who are accustomed to our
presence amongst them, and since we
never interfere with any of their religious
prejudices, they are as contented to let us
govern them as any one else. I have no
doubt however, that amongst the higher
order of Hindoos, there is an *arrière
pensée*, that after all we are but Pariahs—
clever Pariahs it may be,—but neverthe-
less a very degraded set of people when
compared with themselves. I have also
frequently heard some of the Mussul-
mans express a regret that their rulers
are not of the 'faithful;' but these
trivial discontents are wholly unimportant
under the circumstances, for the difference

of caste entirely prohibits any combination for political purposes, unless indeed some such misgovernment as that which has commonly prevailed in our other colonies, were to force the people to lay aside their prejudices and compel them to act in concert. But so long as the Company is suffered to retain its present power, I hold this to be almost impossible, for the Direction is composed of men who have passed the greater part of their lives in India, and they are fully aware of the effect their measures will produce. It would be but bad policy I think to curtail their privileges, for there would probably be wanting, in an English parliament, that practical knowledge of the country which is so essential to the proper administration of its affairs ; and I moreover very much doubt if any government of her Majesty's could spare enough time, or any section of her government sufficiently abstract its ideas from the numerous important questions that daily come

under discussion, to prevent the affairs
of India falling into confusion. I
do not however mean to give the
company more than their due. They
are much blamed, and to a certain
extent with justice, for not developing the
resources of the country, and improving
the condition of the people. Their sys-
tem of taxation moreover is, I conceive
susceptible of much improvement. At
present it presses so heavily upon the
Agriculturist, or ' Ryots,' as we call them,
that not only are they entirely without
capital, but in many districts it is with
the greatest difficulty that they can
obtain a livelihood by their daily toil.
Then again the various appliances of the
labourers and the means of transition for
articles of native growth are much in the
same primitive state as in the days of
Aurungzebe. As you proceed up the
country, you will see the cotton coming
down from the districts in which it is
grown, packed on the backs of jaded and

foot-sore animals, that travel at the average rate of a mile and a half an hour, along,—I was about to say, the road,—but rather along tracks that are frequently intersected by nullahs several feet deep, and which in wet weather are perfectly impassable."

" And what success," said Merryweather, " attends the efforts of the missionaries ? You will be surprised to hear that I was requested by Mrs. Mackintosh to take out some . tracts, and distribute them amongst the natives !"

" None whatever. That they do occasionally make converts is unquestionable, but chiefly of disreputable characters, whose bad conduct has brought them into disgrace with their own caste. I firmly believe that you might, at present, as well try and persuade the Archbishop of Canterbury to worship Seeva and Vishnu, as a respectable Hindoo to become a Christian. But you surprise me! Surely it was not Mrs. Mackintosh who made this request?"

"It was indeed," replied Merryweather.

"Then she has seen fit to add hypocrisy to her other virtues. But I suppose Mr. Munroe gave you a full and circumstantial account of all her proceedings when she was in this country?"

"On the contrary," replied Merryweather, "he was always so uncommunicative upon all subjects, and invariably assumed so wearied and injured a look whenever I spoke to him, that had it not been for your letters, I fear I should have remained lamentably unconscious of her worth."

"Yes," replied Mr. Ponsonby, his eyes twinkling with redoubled brilliancy, "She is an artful, intriguing, dishonest—but bah! It is no use getting into a heat, particularly in this climate; though I will say this, that if she obtained the property which rightly belongs to you by fair means, I will throw myself under the wheels of the first Juggernath car I see."

The native servant now reappeared, and informed Merryweather and Somerville that the baths were in readiness. They therefore quitted their host for the present and proceeded to the performance of their toilet. Oh, the delight, of a bath in India! No footpans here with the water an inch or two deep. A large receptacle is daily filled by an industrious " Bheastie" for the enormous pay of four rupees a month! Then there is no need as in England of oil cloth and matting to prevent the water trickling through the floor and spoiling the drawing room ceiling. The bathroom is always on a level with the ground, and carefully covered with chunam— a cement which takes the polish of marble,—while a small parapet around prevents any little rebellious streams from running off into directions where they ought not to go.   In this reservoir revel till you are out of breath! and then if you are not refreshed, there must be something radically wrong in your constitution.

Merryweather had enjoyed to the utmost this novel kind of bathing, and had partially attired himself, when he summoned the native who was waiting outside, and having bid him arrange his things for dressing, inquired his name. The native at first evinced great unwillingness to let it be known that he understood English, but finding that Merryweather was entirely ignorant of Hindustani, he at length told him in answer that his name was "Barjee Gopall."

"And I hear," said Merryweather, "that you were once my father's,——that is to say, Colonel Merryweather's servant ?"

"Ah, Sahib!" replied Barjee Gopall affirmatively, as he became suddenly animated, "I was Colonel Merryweather's servant.   Is master, Colonel's son ?"

Barjee Gopall no sooner understood that this was the case, than he threw himself at Merryweather's feet, and placing both hands in front of his face, exclaimed, "Very many salaams to sahib. I have held sahib in my arms when he was little, little *bachha*, no higher than so much" (holding his hand a little way from the ground). "I very glad indeed to see master again."

"Well, Barjee Gopall," said Merryweather, "my memory is not so good as yours, I fear."

"Cannot master remember that I take him, when little boy, on the back of elephant. Colonel Merryweather have two—three elephant, and plenty camel and horse. He was one *burra sahib*. But master too, is plenty rich I think?"

Barjee Gopall's manner in asking this question manifested some inquisitiveness, though it was uttered with much assurance, as if no doubt was to be entertained on the subject; and Merry-

weather could not avoid noticing the
look of mingled surprise and conster-
nation, whether real or feigned, which
stole over the countenance of the native,
when he replied, "Indeed I am not.
Very little of my father's property
came to me." But as he was allowed
to complete his toilet without any
further manifestation of sympathy on
the part of Mr. Gopall, this conversation
soon faded from his mind. The
incident, however, was again recalled,
after the lapse of some days, by the
perseverance with which Barjee Gopall
seized every available opportunity to
descant upon the splendour of his
father's establishment and mode of life,
his opulence, the number of his retinue,
and the profound respect and homage
that everywhere awaited him—remarks
which generally ended with the oriental
lament of *wah! wah!* that the *burra
colonel sahib's* son should be less rich
than his deceased parent. Barjee

Gopall, in fact, seemed on these occasions determined not to admit the correctness of Merryweather's explanation, and rejected the statement of his limited means as a mark of disrespect to the memory of his old master. Our hero was much amused at what he considered the native's garrulity, and would often encourage him to enter into conversation on the subject, when once happening to remark that Colonel Merryweather had very unaccountably left no papers of any description amongst his other effects, he observed Barjee Gopall staring at him with a look of horror, and apparently rooted to the spot. Suddenly, as if under the influence of some uncon trollable feeling, he hurriedly blurted forth—"Oh Sahib ! Barjee Gopall wicked thief, who take away box from Colonel Sahib's tent. Inside I see plenty papers ! But Sahib very angry, I think, and he will have Barjee Gopall sent beyond the great sea. Ah !" he continued, in a perfect agony at this idea, "*kali pani men beja jaunga!*"

Merryweather who had listened with intense interest to the few words that had fallen from Bargee Gopall, now endeavoured, by many assurances that no harm should befal him, to obtain a little more information. He succeeded at length in pacifying him, and then asked what had induced him to steal things that could never be of any manner of use to him, and whether the papers were still in existence.

To the first of these interrogatories the native replied by allowing that the contents of the box were of no use to him, but he stated in a confused manner, and evidently not without feeling that he put forward a Mussulman's excuse, that he had been bribed to abstract it, declaring, however, much to Merryweather's satisfaction, that he could tell where it was.

Merryweather now hastened to impart to Mr. Ponsonby the information thus acquired; but no sooner did the latter summon Bargee Gopall to his presence and commence questioning him, than his fears predominating, he retracted every word he had said. Threats availed as little as promises of reward, and at last nothing more could be extorted from him than that he was "only a poor humble man *(gareeb admi)* and how therefore was he to know anything of Europe papers?"

He continued to defend himself on this ground with great pertinacity, and all the powers of logic that Mr. Ponsonby could muster, and all the influence he could exercise were found inadequate to drive him from his stronghold.

A search was next made amongst the outhouses appropriated to the use of the servants, but nothing was found amongst Bargee Gopall's effects that could lead to a discovery of what they sought, and Mr. Ponsonby gave up all hope for the present of obtaining the missing docu-

ments.   "It is useless," ·he said to his
nephew on the following day, "to attempt
to gain possession of these papers now,
but I know how to manage these natives.
In a little time, when Bargee Gopall's
fears have subsided, I make no doubt
that I shall be able to make him produce
them.   Were we to use coercion, we
should only urge him to destroy them
in order to screen himself, so I would
advise you to have a little patience, and
not to run the risk by precipitate
measures of losing for ever the property
which may yet be recoverable."

Mr. Ponsonby had long been a resident
in Bombay, and was well acquainted with
the principal civilians and officers, both
of the Queen's and Company's service.
Many opportunities consequently pre-
sented themselves of initiating his nephew
and Somerville into Indian society, and
under his auspices they received nume-
rous invitations, amongst which was one
to a ball about to be given by a member

of the supreme council the day previous
to their intended departure from Bombay
to Poona, whither, pursuant to the orders
of the Adjutant General, they were to
repair with as little delay as possible.

There is a difference between a ball in
England and a ball in India. In England
it is in general a reunion of youth and
health, — a recreation eagerly and
naturally sought by exuberant and
buoyant spirits, where bright hopes of
the future are only surpassed by the
actual enjoyment of the passing hour.
In India, the emaciated victims of tropical
heat, who assemble to indulge in exer-
tions unsuited to the climate, and by
unwonted efforts to increase the daily
discomfort they experience in an atmos-
phere where the thermometer seldom
sinks much below 90°, bear the same
resemblance to their English prototypes,
as it may be supposed their own *larvæ* will
bear to themselves, when they shall have
been ferried over the dark Stygian lake.

On the evening of the appointed day, however, with all the excitement, at least, which novelty could lend to the scene, Merryweather and Somerville, accompanied by Mr. Ponsonby, presented themselves at the house of Mr. Bahawdur. It was a spacious and well-furnished mansion, standing in its own grounds or "compound," to use an oriental phrase, and crowds of Kitmutgars, Khansamans, and every other variety of menial, dark mustachioed and turbaned, glided about with noiseless steps, and were not out of character perhaps with the ideas suggested by the intense heat that prevailed.

A gay scene however presented itself to them as they entered the ball room. The greater part of the gentlemen were officers, and the uniforms of their several corps created at once a striking effect, and presented a strong contrast with the more modest and simple attire of that most efficient body of public men,——the civil servants of the East India Company.

The ladies were in a decided minority, and of these very few were unmarried. The dancing, consequently, for the most part, devolved upon them which, to say the least, became a very arduous amusement, as their suffering appearance abundantly testified. Merryweather also marvelled much at the pleasure a few " subs " who were present, could possibly derive from whirling round the room till their faces became as scarlet as their coats, when it was evident they were treated as mere Automatons by the fair partners to whom they devoted themselves, and when convenient, were discarded with the utmost nonchalance. Business, stern unrelenting business, seemed to be the order of the day, or rather of the night, with these ladies, and they were apparently incapable of alleviating the toil which it imposed by the slightest relaxation of feature or manner. Merryweather had had ample opportunity to indulge in these reflections, and had begun to wish the time for departure was a little nearer at hand, when his uncle informed him that Miss Flirtree, a young and unmarried lady wished to try her fascinations upon him.

" She surely never made you her *confidante* on the subject, uncle?" asked Merryweather.

" Not exactly." said Mr. Ponsonby, " but she has asked me so many questions about the interesting young officer who accompanied me here, and whom I in troduce to no one, that without any great exercise of penetration, this may he considered equivalent to a wish to be introduced to you."

" By all means then let us gratify a wish so flattering to myself. I scarcely thought that there was any person in the room who from disinterested motives would wish to take the trouble of becom- ing acquainted with another."

"Do not be too sure of the disinterested- ness of the motive in the present instance."

" Why what motive can she have ?" said Merryweather, " she knows nothing of me."

" I'll venture to say," rejoined Mr. Ponsonby, " that she knows a great deal more about you, than you imagine, and that she has not only found out when you arrived, and almost everything that you said and did on the passage out, but has also heard that you are generally supposed to be possessed of some private fortune."

" If that is the case I am sure I feel very much flattered by the interest she takes in me."

" Or that she would wish to take in your three per cents."

" Oh, there's no fear of that," rejoined Merryweather, laughing.

" Well, forewarned is forearmed, remember !" So saying he led Merryweather up to Miss Flirtree, and introduced him to that lady. It would perhaps be scarcely fair to say that she was plain, and though she certainly could not be called good looking, yet her pretensions did not sink below mediocrity, while a few judicious artifices effectually concealed from the inexperienced eye, the number of years that had elapsed since her "teens."

"Will you" said Merryweather, after having engaged this lady for the next dance, "allow me to hold your bouquet for you?—what a very beautiful one it is."

"I think it must be, for do you know I have had that said to me so many times this evening. Now do" continued Miss Flirtree, with what was intended to be a captivating glance, " take compassion on me and proceed to some other subject."

" Nay then" said Merryweather, " I must certainly in self defence throw the burden upon you, for I am a complete stranger here, and scarcely acquainted with a single person present. You doubtless know a great many?"

"Yes," said Miss Flirtree, carelessly, "I know almost every body. But when I am so fortunate as to meet one who has just arrived from dear—dear England, I can scarcely find courage to talk of those whom I almost look upon as belonging to this country."

"Then you know" said Merryweather, with affected surprise, "that I have only just arrived from England?"

"Oh dear yes! It is not difficult to perceive that. People who have just come from England, bear such evident marks of home about them, that they are easily distinguished from those who have been in India for any time."

"But it does not appear," said Merryweather, fairly shamed into a little gallantry, "that every-body loses their good looks by a residence here."

"But I," said Miss Flirtree instantly appropriating the compliment, "have not been out here very long. Now I will be very confidential, and tell you that the person seated opposite us, is my poor dear uncle." (Merryweather glanced in the direction, and saw a very large white waistcoat, surmounted by a remarkably acrid looking countenance,) "who has been such a great sufferer, that I have come out to be his nurse, for his gallant spirit will not allow him to return home for the sake of his health, while his services are required here."

"How exceedingly kind of you," said Merryweather, unable to repress a smile.

"But I am in great hopes," continued Miss Flirtree, "that he will yet listen to what I so frequently urge, and return home to recruit his strength for further exertions. I am sure in the sweet green fields of happy England, his health would be quickly restored to him."

"Doubtless," said Merryweather, abstractedly, "the very fact of returning would be sufficient I should think, to invigorate the most enfeebled frame."

" I am delighted to hear you say that, Mr. Merryweather, because it confirms my own opinion. I should also suppose from your manner that you have no intention of remaining in India very long?"

" Very long ?" said Merryweather forcing his thoughts back from a subject which their conversation had suggested to him,—" Oh no. Very far from it. Though," he continued, in a lively manner, and glancing at Miss Flirtree, to see what effect his words produced, " if I had advantages like my friend Mr. Somerville, who accompanied me here this evening, and possessed the ample means which he enjoys, I am not sure if my plans would not be different."

" Mr. Somerville did you say ?" said Miss Flirtree, suddenly changing her manner. " Dear me, how very long this dance is. Really you must let me sit down. I am so very tired. There is a chair by my uncle. My bouquet ?— thank you."

Merryweather bowed and moved away, and in a very short time perceived that Miss Flirtree was dancing with Somerville. He was watching with some interest her proceedings when his uncle came up to him and said,—"

"Well Frank, have you been led into captivity?"

"Why no, uncle. The fact is that I have I believe misled her as to the possessor of the three per cents. She is now under the impression that Somerville is the fortunate man, and as you may perceive has already commenced her operations upon him.

"So she has, by Jove!" said Mr. Ponsonby, with great glee. "She will soon find out however how the case really ˚stands, and will bear you very little good will in consequence."

"That will scarcely matter much, uncle," said Merryweather. "Sufficient to the evening is the mischief thereof. But who is that majestic looking woman, so gorgeously attired, whom you were conversing with just now ?"

" The wife of the Commodore, and her character in every way tallies with her appearance. The present Governor on his first arrival here committed the monstrous solecism of taking down the wife of one of the members of council to his own table in preference to her. This was a slight not to be overlooked. She instantly left his house, and involved her husband, the member of council, the governor and the court of directors in a twelve months correspondence, the result of which was, that the governor in order to get out of the scrape, and to shelter himself from the hot fire she opened upon him, was obliged to apologise for his error."

" Does so much jealousy exist then in the society here ?"

" To an unknown extent ; though the people of India are for the most part kind to one another, I think, when their intercourse is not of a nature to call forth this feeling. But woe to him who steps out of his place in the rank!"

"It will be well to bear that in mind then," said Merryweather, laughing. "But who is that unmistakable votary of Mars, talking to your friend, the commodore's wife?"

"His name is Captain Tossover, and he belongs, I have heard, to a Welsh family, though I can scarcely believe that he is not a lineal descendant of that far-famed duellist whom Sheridan has immortalized,—Sir Lucius O'Trigger. You see he wears his arm in a sling, the consequences of his last encounter, the circumstances of which were not a little singular. An officer of another corps happened one evening to differ from him in opinion at mess, — 'that is quite sufficient, sir,' said Captain Tossover, 'we need not prolong the discussion.' The next morning they went out, and fired at one another three times without effect, when the seconds at last managed to arrange the matter. They thereupon walked away together in the most friendly manner, but had not proceeded far, when Captain Tossover, turning to his recent antagonist, said, ' Then, of course, you agree with me *now* in what I said last night ?'

' Not at all,' returned the other.

' Oh ! then we will just return to the ground if you please,' was the immediate reply, which they accordingly did, and the result was the broken arm which Captain Tossover now wears in a sling.'

" Talking of belligerents, however, there is Major Start, celebrated for his pugilistic encounters. He goes by the name of ' The Rasper.' "

" What ! that infirm looking old fellow who seems as if he had lived upon a curry diet all his life ?"

" The same. He fought, by his own account, I know not how many pitch battles, when he was last in England,

with draymen, cabmen, *et id genus omne,*
who invariably got 'wound up' at last
by such a c--r—uel rasper, a favourite
phrase, to which he owes his *soubriquet.*
I believe though that I should do him
injustice, were I not to add, that a
tendency to extol his own pugilistic
feats is his chief failing. I have known
him act with judgment and impartiality
under extremely trying circumstances.
Look there! If Miss Flirtree has
not managed to get your brother
Griffin to take her into supper! She
certainly casts her net very skilfully,
but will be rather disappointed in the
present instance if she succeed in landing
her game. By the way, yonder there
is one of her cast off suitors who is
also the hero of tail."

"Tell it by all means," said Merryweather.

"Be it known then, that he was
very anxious to make his vows at the
Hymeneal altar, though it did not

appear that his desire for the connubial state was prompted by a partiality for any particular person. Under these circumstances, he frequently applied for leave of absence from his regiment on the plea of being about to marry, but for some cause or other, his efforts were unattended with success, and he as frequently returned in the same state of single blessedness. On one of these occasions he happened to meet Miss Flirtree, and paid her most devoted attention. But that astute young lady kept him hooked on only as a *pis-aller*, holding out hopes that if he obtained a lucrative staff appointment he had applied for, she might take the subject into consideration, but never irretrievably committing herself, and like a prudent general never failing to reserve the means of retreat. In the meantime another governor arose in the land who knew not Joseph, and he consequently lost at one and the same time, all chance of the appointment and of the

hand of Miss Flirtree.   This *contretems*,
however threatened very disagreeable
results, for at the time he became
acquainted with this double disaster, he
had just obtained leave of absence, under
the stringent condition that he should
be placed under arrest if he again
returned to his regiment unmarried!
I cannot say whether his commanding
officer really intended to enforce this
part of the compact, but he appears to
have apprehended such a step, for in
the greatest distress he explained his
situation to a lady whom he had never
spoken to before, and begged her to
take compassion upon him.   She did so,
and within a week they were married,
and as the story book says, have lived
very happily ever since."

"He happened to fall upon his feet
then," said Merryweather.

"Yes.   A circumstance that could
scarcely have been anticipated.   But
let us now follow the example which

every one has set us, and repair to the supper room."

This was a spacious apartment where the refreshments that were to reward the disinterested gyrations of the younger gentlemen in the ball room, were arranged with no slight attention to effect, or to the actual wants of their heated frames. The luscious mangoe, the delicate leechee, and the fragrant but insipid rose apple, and other tropical productions, gave a truly oriental character to the repast, while English preserved fruits, and more substantial viands, intermixed with champagne of excellent vintage and unexceptionably *frappé*, were also there in profusion. Merryweather had devoted himself with considerable satisfaction to some iced mangoes, and was highly applauding, in his own mind, the advantage that an Indian supper room possesses, in being supplied with a sufficient number of attendants, to obviate the necessity for the conversion of spirited and public minded dandies into amateur waiters, when Somerville came up and said,—

" Really Merryweather, the people here are very difficult to comprehend. I was introduced to a young lady— there—that one who is going back to the ball room with the man in a staff uniform ; and she seemed, by some extraordinary means, to know as much about me as I do myself ; oddly enough too, she asked a great many questions about you, as my friend."

" And was the explanation satisfactory ?" said Merryweather.

" Well, I fancy not," replied Somerville, " though that is the most unintelligible part of the whole affair, for I had no sooner become slightly confidential, and told her, as I thought in my best manner, that it was enough to make the fortune of a poor sub to be welcomed in India by such bright eyes, or something to that effect, when she instantly asked her present companion for an ice, then for his arm back to the ball room, to find her uncle, and so left me to console myself with a glass of champagne."

Our hero and Somerville soon after took their departue; and as they were waiting in the hall for their bearers Miss Flirtree and her uncle passed them, the former of whom cast upon both, a mingled look of resentment and mistrust as she left the house.

CHAPTER VIII.

Black Driver (with great vigour.)   "Ally Loo!
Hi.   Jiddy, Jiddy.   Pill.   Ally Loo!"
Horses almost do it.
Black Driver (with his eyes starting out of
his head.)   "Lee, den.   Lee, dere.   Hi.   Jiddy,
Jiddy.   Pill.   Ally Loo, Lee-e-e-e-e!"

Dickens' American Notes.

AT an early hour next morning Merry-
weather and Somerville having taken leave
of Mr. Ponsonby left the island of Bom-

bay in obedience to the orders of the Adjutant-General, and embarked in a Patoma, or native boat, for Panwell, on the main land of India, and the first stage on the journey to Poona. These boats are about the size of a small English fishing smack, and have a cabin or poop, which, although not quite high enough to admit of an upright posture, is in other respects comfortable, and being furnished with port-holes, a current of air is thus kept up which renders the whole pleasantly cool. Underneath these port-holes are seats with cushions, long enough to admit of the traveller lying down if he feel so inclined, a valuable privilege, as he is not unfrequently detained half way between Bombay and his destination by the turning of the tide.

For some miles a fair wind attended their progress, and a few green and luxuriant looking islands, that lay in their course, were rapidly passed. The water sparkled and foamed beneath the sharp prow of their boat, and Bombay with its forest of masts, soon became indistinct in the distance. In front the view improved every minute, and even promised to justify the extravagant ideas that each had formed of Indian scenery. But soon a small headland was turned, and then a far different prospect opened before them. Muddy swamps were now seen to extend for miles, and rank grass and stunted herbage, the growth of the fever-breeding soil, bore evidence of the baneful influence of the pestilential vapours that hung around. Perhaps the scene in all its combinations was a fair emblem of the high visions formed by an aspiring youth at the commencement of his Indian career, and of the fallacies so soon to be revealed to him—the life he is doomed to lead, as little verifying his anticipations as the nauseous wilderness around could have been expected to follow the pleasing view our hero and Somerville had enjoyed at starting.

The wind now died away, and compelled them to anchor till the turn of the tide should again facilitate their progress up the creek which they had entered. Slowly the thick glutinous liquid, which it would be libellous to call water, contracted on either side of them, gradually exposing to view the slimy bed on which it had so lately reposed. The stream, as if conscious of its loathsome properties, and ashamed of the appearance it presented, glided down in sullen stillness. Not a ripple disturbed its surface, nor could any obstruction provoke its torpid movements. Stealthily would it flow round whatever might oppose its course, and without marking its disapprobation by so much as a murmur or a bubble, pass on in silence. How different, thought Merryweather, from the fresh, gurgling, leaping, restless stream that ran through Ulvacombe, every drop of which seemed animate with life, and through whose transparent waters could be discovered the pebble, the rock, or the firm soil over which it held its course.

To be compelled to wait in a place where every object suggests some disagreeable association is not an enviable event, and wearily under such circumstances do the hours pass by. Merryweather and Somerville endeavoured to alleviate the monotony of their position by talking over all that had happened to them since their arrival in India, and for some time they were successful; but their conversation, as if oppressed by the influences which surrounded them, gradually drooped, till they relapsed into silence and waited with forced resignation till the tide should begin to flow. This they at last perceived had commenced, and being impatient to proceed, they left the cabin to ascertain why the anchor was not being taken up. The cause was sufficiently apparent. Seated round an immense iron pot were all the boatmen, their eyes fixed with intense interest upon its contents.

Merryweather was at first under the impression that they were performing some religious rite, but this idea was soon dispelled by seeing them one after another dip their fingers into this culinary utensil, and after extracting a handful of rice, perform the same operation in another vessel filled with a yellow substance, and then convey the savoury mess to their mouths.

"Why they were eating like that when I looked out an hour ago," said Somerville.—" Here! you boatmen! when are you going on?"

"Go on soon," replied the man who had the guidance of the rest, and who had acted as steersman, but whose only apparent claim to superiority consisted in his wearing a larger cloth round his loins, and in perhaps possessing a blacker skin. "De Boatmen eat!"

"There is no occasion for you to tell us they do that, darky," said Merryweather, "the fact is sufficiently obvious.

L 5

But the time has now come to proceed on our way, and as we particularly wish to leave this delightful spot, perhaps you will be so obliging as to get up the anchor."

Mr. Ram Chandah, the person whom Merryweather had addressed, understood enough English to know that he was just then required to do what was exactly contrary to his own wishes, and therefore appealed very vehemently to Merryweather on the necessity of the men fortifying themselves for their exertions, by laying in a good stock of provisions, and finally succeeded in obtaining a quarter of an hour's grace. At the expiration of this time however, no intention was visible on the part of Mr. Ram Chandah and his crew to get ready for departure. On the contrary, repletion, and a subsequent devotion to a "hubble bubble" pipe, which was handed about from one to the other, had produced a state of apathy, from which they seemed to have no intention of rousing themselves. Under these circumstances, Merryweather and Somerville, having previously conferred together, seized Mr. Ram Chandah by the ankles and wrists, and notwithstanding his cries, which much resembled those of a pig about to be slaughtered, forcibly conveyed him from the alluring spot. Thus suspended between the two " sahibs," his person after a few preliminary vibrations, and a *one, two, three,* was successfully launched on to the poop, where he alighted with considerable force on that portion of it, which however well adapted by nature for the reception of thumps and bumps, is not, on that account, less susceptible of the injuries they entail. After measures had been taken to prevent him returning to his astonished associates, it was delicately intimated, that if his hands and feet were tied, perhaps the water just under the stern, was deep enough to drown him, on the possibility of which he manifested considerable uneasiness, and cast a wistful look in the direction pointed out as favourable for his immersion. He was however a man of pride, and conceiving the hint thrown out about the course that would be adopted, should he prove refractory, as merely done to terrify him, he resolved upon making an effort to assert his dignity. " Sahib," he said, " belong to Ridgement, Boatman make complaint to Ridgement officer, Sahib get dismissed."

" Oh, you are beginning to threaten," said Merryweather. " Come, say your prayers, you have but a short time to live. Tie his hands, Somerville. That's right. Now overboard with him, unless——

Merryweather was here interrupted by the most violent vociferations on the part of Mr. Ram Chandah, over whose spirit there came a wonderful change. His hostile words were now changed into the most piteous supplications for mercy.

varied with hurried words to the boatmen to get up the anchor and proceed with all speed, which they instantly set about, and in a marvellous short space of time, were pulling away with their paddles as hard as they could. Mr. Ram Chandah was now released from his bonds, but given to understand that he would be held responsible for the behaviour of the others; and being entirely subdued, followed the instructions he received with the most implicit obedience. His black satellites, whom he immediately harangued in a most lively and excited manner if they showed the slightest indication of a wish to relax their exertions, were informed, (though not to the knowledge of our hero and Somerville, who, of course, did not understand the language,) that there were two devils on board, dressed up like sahibs, and that, if they did not make haste and get to Panwell, the boat would divide and swallow them all up, a statement they fully believed. The consequence was, that for the remainder of the way to Panwell, the boat was propelled at a rate, which it had probably never exceeded since the days of its construction.

On arrival there, whether it was that the belief of Mr. Ram Chandah and his crew, in the supernatural powers of Merryweather and Somerville had become shaken, or that they were under the impression that their devilish propensities could not be exercised on dry land, must remain doubtful: but be this as it may, they were not backward in urging their claims to some larger remuneration than usual, on account of their late unwonted exertions, and Merryweather so far satisfied them on this score, that even Mr. Ram Chandah, himself, seemed to consider that he had been sufficiently compensated for the indignity offered to his person.

On leaving the landing place, their attention was attracted to a vehicle,

apparently the hybrid of a bathing
machine and a tax cart, which some en-
terprising person had in vain endeavoured
to metamorphose into a phæton. To
this conveyance, on close examination,
it was just possible to trace a caricature
resemblance, and they were wondering to
what use it could possibly be applied,
when a native under whose charge it
seemed to be placed, informed them that
if they were the Sahibs who had engaged
a phæton to Poona, here it was, ready
for their accomodation, and that the
horses would be brought out immediately.
The bare idea of travelling seventy miles in
a trap of this description, appeared to them
so preposterous, that their first impulse
was to laugh at the statement just made
as a joke, but the solemn aspect of the
man, not unmixed with a look of pride,
as he contemplated the property of his
master, soon convinced them of the
fallacy of their supposition, and they
gradually drew the painful conclusion,

that the house to which Mr. Erskine's
name is generally attached was the only
one at hand, and being thus compelled
to yield to circumstances, they resolved
to treat the matter philosophically, and
not to increase intolerable discomforts
by unavailing regrets. Hearing, however,
of the existence of a Government Bunga-
low in the immediate vicinity, they
required neither. Having therefore in
their equipage to be got ready
and brought round to the place
which we will now attempt to describe.
A large thatched roof which protected
four mud walls from the weather, was
pointed out to them as the place deno-
minated, the "Government Bungalow,"
in which they were informed was a
"mess man," who provided travellers
with every thing they could possibly
require, and who, to justify the commen-
dations passed on him, ought to have
rivalled a *restaurateur's* of the Boulevards
or the Palais Royal. The appearance of

the building outside was certainly unin-
viting enough, nor did they feel their
desire to enter it at all increased by the
obstructions that opposed their doing so.
These consisted of a drain, meandering
in front of the principal entrance, and in
which several pigs were reclining, whose
approbation of the spot was occasionally
testified by a lazy grunt, unmistakably
expressive of their satisfaction. Pariah
dogs of the most emaciated, mangy, and
loathsome description, that ever disgraced
the canine species, were snarling over
a heap of dry bones, horns, and refuse
of every kind on one side, while on the
other, the picture was diversified by
broken-kneed ponies, apparently in the
last stage of consumption, and sickly
looking ducks and fowls, the latter having
a particularly long, lanky, parched look,
which gave them the appearance of walk-
ing upon stilts. After a vigorous assault
upon the various tribes in possession of
the soil, who at first showed some inten-

tion to defend their sanctum against
intrusion, Merryweather and Somerville
managed to effect an entrance into the
bungalow itself.   They found the area
enclosed by the four mud walls, divided into
three small rooms, in each of which was
a table, four chairs, and a sofa or bedstead
with a cane bottom.   Each room besides
boasted of a piece of canvass overhead,
meant to imitate a ceiling ; a mud, or
what appeared to be a mud floor, and
some pictures hung on the white-washed
walls.   One of these was a coloured
representation of a sentimental scene
between a gentleman and lady,
underneath which were inscribed the
affecting words, " Don't say nay."
The lady, who was about to leave the
room was turned towards the door, but
her head which, by some wonderful
means, was twisted completely round—
had its downcast eyes fixed upon the gen-
tleman at her feet, who had hold of one
of her hands, and was apparently making

the touching appeal we have quoted. This gentleman's toilet had been performed with such care that not even a hair of his beautifully curled whiskers was out of place. His coat fitted him with a precision that was never before witnessed except on the dummies in a ready-made clothes shop, while his trousers were strapped down over the most unexceptionable boots, so tightly, that one gazed in momentary expectation of their relieving themselves by wrenching off the buttons, and rending the paper on which they were painted.

Another was the portrait of a middle-aged gentleman, with a rubicund nose, who apparently was enjoying his own reflections over a bottle of wine of a bright cherry colour, and a bunch of grapes that in size would have shamed the produce of any vine in Brobdignagia. His lips were pursed up in a way which plainly implied that his thoughts were his own, and would not on slight grounds

be communicated to the curious or im-
pertinent. But to the remaining works of
art which adorned this saloon no descrip-
tion of ours could possibly do justice, and
for this reason alone we pass them over.

After some time had been employed
by our Hero and Somerville in the vain
endeavour to attract attention by loud
vociferations, they thought it expedient
to try if they could succeed by other
means. For this purpose they entered a
verandah formed by the projection of the
thatch beyond the walls, and supported
by frail looking stakes nearly eaten
through with the dry rot. They then
saw, what at first seemed to be a bundle
of the striped cotton stuff, used sometimes
as a carpet in the East, till a slight move-
ment by the object on which their eyes
rested convinced them that it was alive.
Upon this bundle being pushed about, it
slowly began to unroll itself, and the
inanimate portion having by this process
been removed, the interior was found to

consist of a human being of the male sex, though the close resemblance he bore to a monkey caused Merryweather to hesitate before he addressed him. His dress was European, so far at least as a dirty shirt and a pair of trousers, apparently made out of blue check dusters, entitles it to that designation, while his features and general appearance indicated a Portuguese origin.

"Master want tiffin or dinner?" said the object mechanically, and speaking before Merryweather or Somerville had had time to address a word to him, getting up and rubbing his eyes; an enquiry suggested by the fact that his mind so constantly dwelt upon subjects connected with eating, that his waking thoughts immediately led him to the conclusion that his professional services were required in some shape or other.

"We should like anything that we can get," replied Merryweather. "Dinner would be preferable if you can get it in any reasonable time."

An assurance that they should have it immediately was given much in the same vague manner as the inquiry had been made. Their new found *maitre d'hotel* then very leisurely proceeded to the front of the house, and with a dexterity that could only have been the result of long practise, had soon whipped up a bilious looking duck in one hand, and a long legged fowl in the other, with which he quietly sauntered to a hut adjoining the bungalow, that served the purpose of a kitchen, a sleeping apartment for a man with his wife and family, and occasionally a dressing room. From the door of this little sanctum, which was devoid of a chimney, there soon issued a quantity of smoke and feathers, showing that the process of killing and plucking had been going on inside, and that a fire had been kindled to prepare for the

table the animals whose span of life had
been so unexpectedly shortened.

In the course of an hour, during
which time Merryweather and Somer-
ville had taken a stroll, which had
produced in each of them a strong desire
never to see Panwell again, symptoms
of their repast being nearly ready were
manifested by a table cloth, with unequi-
vocal signs of former service, knives and
forks, a saltceller and cruet stand, being
laid in one of the rooms of the bungalow,
and at last came the dinner itself. Nor
would there have been any just cause
of complaint if the quality had been in
any proportion to the quantity. About
a dozen dishes were placed upon the
table by their attendant, who had
evidently shaken off his apathy, and in
addition to cooking their dinner had
found time to improve his personal
appearance by the addition of a pair
of shoes, a white jacket, and an old
black silk cravat, arranged *a la* Byron.

His hair, too, which before presented a tangled mass of wool which it seemed no comb could possibly penetrate, had by the copious application of cocoanut oil, been reduced to order, and arranged in two shining curls, plastered against each side of his face.

Merryweather and Somerville now took their seats at the table on which the dishes had been arranged with mathematical precision, and on the covers being removed by the Portuguese servant, the delicacies on which they were to break their fast were one by one disclosed to view. There was the duck, looking a great deal more bilious without its feathers, and the fowl a great deal drier and more parched. There again was some bacon, which had of course been contributed by the Society of Swine whose knowledge of worldly bliss was confined to wallowing in the drain outside. There were some vegetables also, and " side dishes," but to the latter it would have been extremely hazardous to assign any definite character or name, though upon looking upon them more attentively, it occurred to Merryweather and Somerville with singular force that they belonged to a species of quadrupeds not generally made use of for food, but which even then were pouring forth their melodious croakings within a stone's throw of the Bungalow.

The fowl being the least objectionable of all the good things set before them satisfied their appetite. The other viands, including those of doubtful appearance and character, were sent away untouched, probably not for the first time, and with equal probability destined to be again subjected to the culinary art, and to reappear for the next traveller in the shape of a curry, or a stew. By the time their meal had been disposed of, the vehicle which was to convey them to Poona came to the door, and as the evening had closed in, and they were informed that

they would arrive in Poona before the
reappearance of the sun, they caused the
cumbrous looking hood to be pushed
back, a feat which could only be accom-
plished by great exertion, and the destruc-
tion of a large portion which broke off in
the struggle.

They set out at last, however,
and rattled through the dirty-looking
village to the evident admiration of the
inhabitants. Standing behind the carriage
was a man, making ridiculous efforts to
imitate an English post horn, and always
taking care to favour each knot of his
acquaintance larger than usual with a
sample of his skill.   If a cart in the road
caught his eye, though a quarter of a
mile distant, it was the immediate cause
of a succession of the most unearthly
sounding blasts till the obstruction was
passed, while in the interval between
these musical performances, besides the
usual noise which accompanies a carriage
in motion, a confused and ominous sound

of jingling, chafing and rumbling was heard in every part of the conveyance, which forcibly suggested to the inexperienced mind that its immediate dissolution was at hand. By dint, however, of flogging, the jaded animals, whose united exertions were but just equal to their task, accomplished the first stage, a distance of about five miles, within the hour. Here an unexpected difficulty arose. Bad as were the horses which had brought them thus far, they nevertheless were the best in the postmaster's stud, and were always placed in the phaeton at first starting, in order to insure the departure of the traveller. Now, however, that Merryweather and Somerville had arrived at the second stage, and to go back would present the same difficulty as to proceed, they were forced to remain passive witnesses of the new scene which passed before them. Two bony looking animals much against their inclination, were brought out of a

M 2

ruined looking shed that served them for a stable, to replace those that had just been released. With their ears well back, and an evident desire to kick everything that came within reach of their hind legs. The appearance they presented was not one to impress the beholder favourably as to their future behaviour, even if the hazardous attempt to harness them to the phaeton should be attended with success. This task, however, by a judicious combination of force and skill, was at last accomplished. The reins were handed to the driver. The " guard" took up his position behind, and began blowing his horn. Everything was in readiness, but for some reason the phaeton remained immovable. A vigorous application of the whip on the backs of the horses was next heard, the result of which was the counter-application of their heels on the phaeton, which vibrated throughout with the shock. Merryweather and Somerville now sprung up on the front seat. There were the horses, with their ears still as far back as they could get them, their fore legs firmly planted on the ground, and their whole attitude evincing a most decided repugnance to proceed. Two men advanced to their heads and endeavoured to pull them forward by the bridle, making use at the same time of a few encouraging words. But they had listened too often to these blandishments for any such mild expedient to be effective, and their whole demeanour showed that could they, like Balaam's ass of old, have suddenly become gifted with the power of utterance, "gammon," would have sprung spontaneously to their lips. Kindness, therefore, being evidently lost upon them, they were assailed with a shower of thumps, kicks, and pokes, by the men at their heads, while the driver kept his whip unceasingly employed. All three at the same time maintained a running fire of abuse, principally addressed

to the female relations of the objects
of their wrath,—a species of eloquence in
which it may, *par parenthæse*, be observed
the natives of India are wont to indulge
in, whether their indignation be provoked
by their own species, or by dumb
animals.

On the present occasion the most
philosophical contempt was evinced by
the two quadrupeds for the epithets made
use of in connection with their families,
as well as for the illtreatment which was
being so freely administered to them by
their persecutors, and a pause having in
consequence taken place, till the men at
their heads, who had numerous resources
for every emergency, should determine
upon what course they were `next to
pursue ; the horses took advantage of
the respite to back towards the stables,
and were on the point of depositing our
Hero and Somerville in a ditch, when
this retrograde motion was arrested by a
fore leg of each being held off the ground

by means of ropes, which, with great dexterity, the men slipped on in time to prevent the catastrophe. The next phase of the contest showed the men who had so skilfully thrown the lasso round the fore legs of their opponents, applying with the assistance of several others their whole strength to the ropes, to the evident discomfiture of the horses, who, in order to prevent the dislocation of their shoulders, trotted on a little way up the road, but again became stationary upon finding that the cause of annoyance had been suspended. Again the ropes were applied, and again they advanced till they felt themselves free, and then came to a stop as before. They were evidently horses of deep calculation, and considered their present troubles preferable to dragging the phaeton to the next stage. Things now reached a crisis. Human ingenuity, however, prevailed, though by a device so cruel that had Merryweather and Somerville been aware of what was intended, they would have interposed in time to prevent the experiment. A small bundle of straw was placed under each of the horses. This was set fire to, and as the flame ascended, singing the hair and scorching their bodies, they cantered forwards, and stopped no more, till they arrived at the next stage. Similar difficulties were frequently encountered during the remainder of the journey, but strange to say, it was without any accident that they found themselves the next morning at Poona.

CHAPTER IX.

Sanguine et igne micant oculi : riget ardua cervix ;
Et setæ, densis similes hastilibus, horrent.
Fervida cum ranco latos stridore per armos
Spuma fluit : dentes œquantur dentibus Indis.
Fulmen ab ore venit : frondes afflatibus ardent.
                                    Ovids Met :

FOR six months after Merryweather and
Somerville had arrived at Poona, they
were constantly employed in learning

M 5

the practical part of their profession, a
necessary business, but not on that
account the more interesting.   To handle
about a musket in every conceivable
way—to practise the sword exercise till
the possibility of being struck anywhere
by any gladiator, however fierce, is re-
duced to an absurdity—to successively
turn, wheel, retire and advance in the
presence of an imaginary enemy of
infinitely superior numbers, whose forces
are finally routed without the loss of a
man on the victorious side, are acquire-
ments doubtless of the greatest importance
to the young soldier ; but whether, after
being thus engaged for six months in a
climate like that of India, the youthful
aspirant to military fame thinks the
colour of his jacket as gaudy as the first
day he put it on, may be considered
problematical.

One morning after Merryweather had
been examined in these various branches
of the art of war, and pronounced eligible

for service, he received a letter from his uncle, stating that Bargee Gopall had at last afforded a clue to the missing box of papers. He now confessed that he had received instructions from some person whose name he would not at present disclose to destroy them, but that he had determined to conceal the box and its contents, till some future period and had in fact buried it at the time under-ground. The letter then went on to say that the native had offered to proceed to the spot with Merryweather and surrender the long hidden treasure. Mr. Ponsonby added that he had immediately closed with this proposition, and strongly recommended his nephew to apply for the necessary leave of absence, to enable him to prosecute the search, stating moreover that he had stimulated the zeal of Bargee Gopall by promising him a considerable reward should the result of his proceedings be successful.

Merryweather had not long perused
this epistle, and was about to write a
formal application for leave of absence
on ' urgent private affairs ' when Somer-
ville rode up to the door. They were
not now perhaps on such intimate terms
as formerly, for though they had not
had   any   misunderstanding,   yet   the
coolness which exists between the two
services of which they were members, had
imperceptibly communicated itself to them
individually.   But,   envy,   which   Mr.
Locke describes as " that uneasiness of
mind caused by the consideration of a
good we desire, obtained by one we think
should not have it before us," would per-
haps best convey an idea of the feeling
that exists between the two branches of
the military profession in India, for one
service looks with a jaundiced eye upon
the preference shown to the Company's
officers in the distribution of staff appoint-
ments and local honours, while the latter
are stung at the precedence given to the

Queen's troops, and at the more favourable reception in society, undoubtedly experienced by the officers in Her Majesty's service. Still this state of affairs had not materially affected the friendship of Merryweather and Somerville, and it was with great pleasure the former perceived who his visitor was.

"How are you?" he said, "pray come in. *Ho Ghorawallor! sahib ka ghora pakarao.* You see I have managed to pick up sufficient Hindustani to tell them to hold your horse. What has been your success with the language? You are obliged to pass an examination, are you not?"

"Yes, a colloquial one, and I have already passed it," said Somerville.

"Well you have not been long about it. But come and sit out in the verandah. It is cooler here than anywhere else. And now, how do you like your Regiment?"

"I confess that I am disappointed."

" My predictions are then fulfilled ?"

" I am not prepared to admit as much as that," said Somerville, " I was merely speaking of my Regiment. From all accounts, it appears to be the very worst in the service, and my disappointment consists in finding that as there is no similarity of ideas, tastes, or feelings between myself and the officers whom I have yet seen, no friendship can exist between us, as these are amongst its most essential components."

" There is no doubt," said Merryweather, tilting his chair back, " that you have acted upon misconceived notions, and that the expectations you formed were altogether misplaced."

" You are prejudiced," said Somerville.

" No, I think not," replied Merryweather, " I am quite ready to change my opinion if you will show me sufficient cause for doing so ; but you yourself say that you are disappointed."

"You will not deny, I suppose, that there are indifferent regiments in the Queen's service. A part does not condemn the whole."

"No! But your only means of judging of the whole is from your experience of the part; and if a part is admitted to be bad, that certainly is not a premiss from which you would infer the perfection of the remainder."

"But listen a moment, and then say if you think that my regiment is a fair sample. You know, of course, that our regiments contain only half the number of officers that there are in yours. Notwithstanding this, six of them are away on staff employ, most probably all of them officers who have distinguished themselves, and whose presence, on that very account, is the more required in the regiment, where their influence would create a better feeling and more gentlemanly tone. Then there are officers away on sick certificate, on furlough, and

on leave.   The commanding officer even
is amongst the latter, and for the last
two months the regiment has been under
the command of the adjutant, who has
had only three subalterns under him
doing duty !"

"If that is the way they conduct
matters in your service, I am sure I am
not astonished at the state into which it
has fallen.   I only wonder that it is so
good.   What ensues in your regiment
from this state of affairs ?"

The result is what might be anti-
cipated.   There is no emulation.   Every
one acts exactly as he thinks fit, and
such a thing as *esprit-de-corps* is un-
known, for although the exploits of the
regiment, ever since its formation, are
constantly the theme of conversation,
yet the officers themselves take no
measures to preserve its credit ; but on
the contrary, by constant disagreements,
by forming parties, or by combining
against a particular individual, who, for

some cause, real or imaginary, has excited their resentment, they bring it into general disrepute. Practices, too, are indulged in, under the idea that they are extremely fast and knowing, of a very questionable character."

"What may they be?"

"One of them is what is termed 'sticking a griffin,' which is no other than quietly swindling a young officer who comes to join his regiment of anything he possesses that happens to excite the cupidity of his new associates."

"And upon what plan do they proceed?"

"Generally, by way of exchange, passing off worthless native articles, which they persuade their dupe are indispensable to him, for some portion of the serviceable English outfit, which a new comer invariably brings with him."

"And how did you fare in this mart for despoiling the unwary?"

"I escaped pretty well, though not without some unsuccessful attempts at extortion. For instance, a horse was offered to me for sale for five hundred rupees, but happening to receive some doubtful information about him, I declined buying him just then, and said I would think about it. Two months later, and without any further negotiation or agreement, the horse was sent round to me one morning, with a note containing a request that I would send a check for the price that had been agreed upon between us, and also expressing a hope that as the fore legs of the horse had now been rendered stronger than ever by the operation of firing and blistering, I should not object to pay the farrier's bill. Now assuming that a somewhat lax morality prevails in horse dealing, this I think was rather a strong proceeding."

"Unquestionably," said Merryweather, with a smile, "and yet you are determined, notwithstanding all this, to think well of the service; why, it is not only acting contrary to your judgment, but in defiance of your own convictions."

"Granted, if I thought the whole service resembled this particular regiment, but there is another here of a totally different character, and into which I hope soon to exchange."

"I have heard of the Regiment you mention," said Merryweather, "and from all accounts there is in it a superior class of men. But I have no hesitation in affirming that it must necessarily be an exceptional case, for whether it is that the Court of Directors are of opinion that their military establishment, which they maintain at so vast an expense, is constructed upon such infallible principles as not to require efficient officers, or that they find it necessary to yield to the influence of the holders of East India Stock in return for their independent support; yet it is beyond a doubt that they admit into their service many whose

previous education and pursuits have **not**
exactly qualified them for a profession.
Now I do not for an instant mean to say
that this, *a priori*, is a reason for their
not being admitted.   On the contrary
my opinions lie quite the other way.
Had such a person the attributes of a
gentleman, and were he moreover an
agreeable fellow, I for one should feel
just as disposed to make him my friend
as if he could trace his descent in a direct
line from one of the Barons who came
over with William the Conqueror.   But
these persons when they reach India
bring with them all the preconceived
notions, habits and feelings of their class,
and so overwhelm the service, that if any
particular Regiment has escaped the
effect of their presence, I maintain that it
it must be an exception to the general rule."

"Then you take it for granted that
those whom you have described are in
sufficient numbers to infuse a bad tone
into the whole service?"

" Undoubtedly—because as you have just observed, a large number of the best men in every Regiment are always away on staff employ. The remainder I conceive, must have peculiar disadvantages to struggle against. They find those of their own set in a minority. Many of them moreover have arrived in this country when quite boys ; without any fixed ideas or principles on any subject, and withdrawn at an early age from all the social influences of home—finding themselves irretrievably involved with persons whose tastes are opposed to their own, they grow callous—old recollections fade away, and they gradually sink into the habits of thought and action which belong to those around them. This is the process by which a service, that might be rendered one of the finest in the world, becomes irremediably contaminated. I am also inclined to think that the efficiency of the native Regiments depends even more entirely than that of the European, upon the moral influence and military character of their officers, for as far as my experience has gone the people of India are excessively quick at appreciating character."

" I will grant you that," replied Somerville, " for it was only the other day that I happened when on guard to overhear some of the men discussing the merits of their respective officers. They described some as being ' *bahut achha sahibs*,' by which they meant generally that they liked them. Others were pronounced ' *kabil*,' that is to say, clever. Another was a ' *bewukuf*,' literally, a person devoid of sense, or, as we should express it, an idiot. Another was a ' *shaitan*'—*anglice*, devil, and so on. As I was not supposed to understand the language at that time, I took no notice of what they were saying, but I could not help thinking that some of these strictures, however improper for them to indulge in, were nevertheless remarkably correct. By the way, I have not yet mentioned the principal thing I came about. The regiment which I told you I hoped to exchange into have made me a member of their hunt, and we meet to-morrow for the first time. Will you come?"

"With great pleasure," said Merryweather.

"Well then, you had better make up your mind to start this evening, as the place where the boar are 'marked down,' is about twelve miles from hence. I have sent out a small tent to sleep in, and the hunt have sent out a large one for all other purposes. You will therefore have no trouble on that score, but you had better send out the horse you intend riding immediately. Yellerly is the name of the place."

"'I will do so," said Merryweather, "and what say you if we ride out there together this evening?"

"Agreed. I will call for you at five. *Au revoir*."

Merryweather had now to determine which of his horses to send out to Yellerly. There were three in his stable. One a common hack, which would do to ride to cover upon, but of the other two he was for sometime undecided which should carry him on the morrow's chase. "Legacy," a powerful half-bred horse, would shirk nothing, but then his speed would probably not be equal to the horses against whom he would have to contend. "Phantom" was the name of the other horse, and was a thorough-bred Arab, the gift of his uncle. But to hunt 'Phantom,' Merryweather felt would be impossible.

'Phantom' would follow him about like a dog, come into his bungalow, and even eat bread out of his plate while he was at breakfast. 'Phantom' would neigh with delight if he heard Merry-weather's voice, and if the bars of his box were withdrawn, would instantly gallop up to his side. No. " Phantom" must remain. Having therefore so resolved, he despatched "Legacy" with all speed to the scene of action.

According to his appointment, Somerville called for our Hero at five, and both then started for Yellerly, whither they had already been preceded by the greater portion of those who intended to join the hunt. The sun was fast nearing the horizon, and about an hour after they had started entirely sunk from view. Twilight, that delightful but evanescent time in India, set in. But every minute the darkening folds of night acquired a more sombre hue. The rays of light receded by swift and perceptible degrees, and the fierce ruler of the tropical day had scarcely relieved them from his presence, when it was dark. Twelve hours respite ! Twelve hours had to elapse ere his apparent progress through the trackless heavens would recommence but then again he would glare over the site of his former power, scorching the parched earth with his perpendicular rays, extracting from stream and river every cooling quality, dispersing or drying up with jealous anger the friendly cloud which might shelter the wayfarer from his potent beams, and finally sink to rest, only to rise again on each succeeding morrow the same unrelenting persecutor.

The evening was beautifully calm and every sound that disturbed the stillness of the heated atmosphere, was heard with wonderful distinctness. From every swampy piece of ground the confused screaming of a multitude of frogs now assailed their ears. Now the shrill and plaintive cry of the jackall followed by the barking of some village dog were wafted past them, and occasionally as they cantered on a heard of startled deer would dart across their path and with a few bounds place themselves beyond reach of danger from the intruders. At last some lights shining out from amidst a clump of trees at a short distance in front revealed the place of rendezvous, and spurring on they were soon in the midst of the tents pitched by their brother sportsmen.

The call of "Ghorawallor" immediately brought some natives to take charge of their horses, and dismounting, they made the best of their way in the direction from whence they now heard sounds of mirth and festivity. The encampment, for such it was, consisted of five or six tents of various sizes, in the centre of which was one much larger than the rest. On a nearer approach Merryweather saw through the open "fly" of this tent a number of officers, seated round a table, on which was placed wine, glasses, fruit, and cigars. A more favourable position could not have been chosen, and the whole scene which now presented itself

was strikingly picturesque. The trees
were sufficiently high and far apart to
admit of tents being pitched under
them, whilst their spreading tops inter-
posed an effectual barrier to the sun.
Horses were picketted in various
directions with head and heel ropes,
and now greeted those of their kind
which had just arrived with loud neighs.
At the foot of the trees fires had been
kindled, and as they crackled and
blazed, a bright red glare was thrown
around, which showed the swarthy figure
of many a native, preparing his simple
meal. Nor were the agreeable asso-
ciations produced by this first view
diminished, when in company with
Somerville, Merryweather entered the
tent set apart for gastronomic purposes.
Contrary to his expectations, he was
introduced to men with whom he could
make himself instantly at home. They
were the officers of the —— regiment,
and their renown in the field had not

more entitled them to be considered the first regiment in the service, than the harmony and good feeling which prevailed in their social intercourse had established their claim as " *bons camarades*."

Their new guests were received with the frank hospitality which distinguishes every true lover of the chase, whether under the burning sun of India, or when the echo of hound and horn blends every feeling into harmony in the green fields of merry England. The next day's sport, with all its exciting anticipations, immediately became the theme of conversation. Songs were sung and toasts went round, and when the advanced state of the evening warned Merryweather to seek the repose necessary to recruit his strength for the exertions of the morrow, he felt that the evening had been one of the pleasantest which he had passed since quitting home.

The next morning the whole party started for the scene of action,—a jungle at a short distance from the encampment where an enormous boar was reported to have taken up his abode. This jungle was exceedingly thick in many places, and covered entirely one side of a long precipitous hill. Immediately on the arrival of the huntsmen, a hundred natives who had previously received their instructions, advanced in a long extended line, which reached from the base to the summit of the hill, and with loud shouts endeavoured to drive the game from his fastness. The boar, however, had taken refuge at the opposite extremity of the jungle, and some hours therefore elapsed before the beaters arrived at the spot where he lay concealed. In the meantime, expectation, which had been at its height amongst the assembled cavalcade below, now began to wane, and the most sanguine were on the point of desponding, when a loud and continued shouting from the beaters, echoed by the cheering cry of 'there he bursts' from the sportsmen, proclaimed that the boar had broken cover.

The natives, alarmed at the gigantic size of the animal whose lair they had invaded, receded on every side, and free access was thus given to the upper part of the hill. A body of men who had been stationed on the summit as a reserve, rushed to the spot which the boar was approaching, and with shouts and yells, and by setting on their their dogs, succeeded in turning him back. But he quickly sees his enemies beneath him, and makes another desperate effort to cross the hill. At a long swinging trot he dashes through the tangled brake and soon leaves his pursuers far behind. Again he nears the summit. This time there is no one to oppose his progress. He passes the debateable ground and disappears on the opposite side.

The huntsmen, in the meantime, who had expected that the boar would be driven to the plain below, had now no other resource than to follow him. Putting spurs to their horses, therefore, they force their way through briar and thicket, and urge the gallant steeds up the precipitous face of the hill. Now a rider and his horse suddenly disappears in some deep nullah formed by the mountain torrent, whose treacherous abyss lay hid beneath a thicket of shrubs. Now on some almost perpendicular ascent the willing horse is seen to strain every muscle in his exertions to bear his rider forward, but unable to proceed, pause, and with every limb quivering with excitement, appear as if his next movement must be a headlong plunge into the yawning chasm beneath.

Merryweather was amongst the foremost of the party and having taken the most direct course found himself in a position of imminent peril. Woe

to him if his saddle girths break,—
inevitable destruction must be the result.
Woe to him if the ground crumble
beneath his horse's hoofs—no means
were there to avert a dreadful doom.
To turn was impossible. "One more
effort, 'Legacy,' and we reach the
summit." The noble animal responded
to the encouraging tones of his master
and struggled desperately to proceed.
The stones and earth displaced in the
attempt fell leaping and bounding hun-
dreds of feet below, but he succeeded
and stood panting and exhausted on the
top of the hill. A few minutes breathing
were all that could be allowed for
presently his competitors for the spear,
three in number, made their appearance.
The rest of the field were far away, and
had but little chance of joining in the sport.

An anxious enquiry was now made
of a native as to the direction the boar
took on disappearing from the view of the
party who had clambered up the ghaut.

N 5

"*Dekho, sahib !*" (Look, sahib,) replied the man in a tone of the greatest excitement, pointing with his finger to the middle of a deep valley, and at the same time bestowing epithets on the boar, which even in Hindustani we hesitate to record.

There was some reason however for the extreme enmity he displayed, for a deep wound in his back to which he did not fail to draw attention was evidently the recent rip of a boar's tusk, and he proceeded to inform them that it was done by the identical animal now endeavouring to escape. There was no time to be lost for the boar under cover of the bushes was rapidly seeking the plains below, and Somerville, who was of the party happening to catch sight of him led the way, closely followed by his companions. Deep in their horses flanks they bury the inciting spur and with impetuous speed rush down the mountain side. Nor rock, nor bush, nor precipitous descent, can check their headlong career. Now they gallop in quick succession along some narrow path which skirts the edge of a deep ravine. Now again where the ground permits they strive for the foremost place, leaping over obstructions, disappearing in the beds of intervening nullahs, or emerging on the opposite side almost at the same moment.

They soon reach the bottom of the hill, and now the boar's fate is sealed. In the very centre of the plain, striving his utmost to gain the shelter of a neighbouring jungle, the huge animal is seen plodding over the heated ground. His speed, which over the wooded hills had defied competition, is now reduced to a pace not much faster than that of a man, and his panting sides show with what difficulty even this is maintained. His immediate pursuers have now an equal chance of the spear. The horses partake of their riders' ardour, and each gallantly endeavours to outstrip his opponent. At racing speed the plain is crossed, and long before the boar can reach the haven within his view, the loud tramp of horses in swift career warn him of his approaching fate. Vain now he knows is the attempt to escape, and with dauntless resolution he turns to face his foes. Close at hand are some stunted trees and bushes, and betaking himself to this cover, he sullenly remains at bay. On rush the hunters, but a long deep wound, extending from the saddle girths to the saddle front, greets the horse of the first assailant. Severely, however, did he that crossed suffer in his attack, ere Merriweather buried his spear deep in the back of the animal's neck, and tried to withdraw the reeking wound, ...

his life as dearly as possibie, he made a final rush at his enemies, but the hero of a hundred such fights received the furious charge, awaiting the attack with a composure that ensured success. At the moment that the sharp tusk of the boar was about to scoop its way into the unprotected flesh of his horse, the practised hand of its rider forced the spear's resistless point through and through him till buried in the ground beneath, the monster's writhing form was kept pinioned to the earth. Gradually his fierce struggles became fainter and fainter. Fastly flowed the life stream from his wounds, and when the deadly weapon was withdrawn, a tremor passed through the huge form of their late formidable antagonist, and he rolled over a lifeless carcase on the plain.

The boar's quivering limbs had scarcely assumed the appearance of death, when the greater portion of those who had started for the hunt were seen galloping across the plain, and although they came too late to join in the sport, all dismounted and viewed with wonder the gigantic proportions of their victim. Perhaps, too, a feeling of remorse passed through the breasts of some that so gallant an animal should have suffered death merely for the sake of affording them a temporary amusement. But it was not long before some natives arrived on the spot with two thick bamboo poles resting upon their shoulders, to which the animal was quickly lashed by the legs, and with the disappearance of their conquered foe, this generous sympathy we fear also vanished.

The day now being far advanced, there was no longer any inducement to beat the jungles a second time. The whole party, therefore, recrossing the hills, returned to the encampment which they had left in the morning.

CHAPTER X.

In vain the circling chieftains round them closed,
For Otho's frenzy would not be opposed;
And from his lip those words of insult fell,
His sword is good who can maintain them well.

Lara.

PLEASURABLE are the sensations which take possession of us, when the excitement created by strong personal exertion, not unaccompanied by danger has passed away, and if the reaction be enhanced by the inspiring juice of the grape, and the soothing influence of a fragrant cigar, it is grateful under such circumstances to dwell on the feats we have performed and the perils we have escaped.   But if these seductive moments must be indulged in with caution and prudence in the temperate north, with tenfold greater distrust should we yield to their influence in tropical India.   Fatigued with their exertions, and parched with thirst, their brain already made dizzy by an unwonted exposure to the mid-day sun, Diana's votaries here return from the chase, and but too frequently by copious and refreshing, but treacherous draughts, to tarnish the laurels they have won in her service.

Merryweather and Somerville, from inexperience of the rapid effect produced by even the mildest Bacchanalian indulgence at such a time, quaffed deeper than the rest of the enticing fluid, which with the transparent ice floating on the top, was so invitingly placed before them. The consequences were soon visible. Loud and angry words arose, and they carried on their dispute with an asperity and waywardness which set the well meant intervention of the remainder of the party at defiance.

"You will, I suppose," said Merryweather, after the discussion had been continued for some time, "allow that the boar could never have lived after the wound he received in the neck from my spear, although I admit that Mr. Elliot did give the finishing stroke?"

"I believe," said Somerville, who in addition to being excited with wine, was with the rest considerably nettled that the only Queen's officer present should have been successful in so large a field, "I believe that in a few days he would have been none the worse for it. You have by accident won the spear, I grant, but not a particle of honour with it."

"Well," said Merryweather, with the view of stopping a discussion, which he now felt threatened a quarrel if further prolonged, "it matters little to whom the honour is due. We have had a capital day's sport, and between us have killed it appears as large a boar as has ever been seen in these jungles."

"That's true," said Somerville, "but that does not alter what I said—that you did not inflict a death wound, and that your striking the boar at all was a pure accident. Now to prove this I'll lay you a wager that if you go out singly with any person present,—myself even included—and a boar should be killed, you will have no share in his death."

"Really," said Merryweather, getting angry, "I am at some loss to discover your motive for so unnecessary a taunt. I have not attempted to laud my own acts. It is yourself who attach so much

importance to them, and I begin to
think that the uncalled for remarks you
have indulged in, are either prompted by
inordinate vanity, or by a wretched
jealousy of an event which is hardly of
sufficient importance to warrant such a
feeling."

"Apologize!" replied Somerville, start-
ing up with every evidence of ungovern-
able passion displayed in his countenance.
"Apologize for what you have just
said!"

"Certainly not," replied Merryweather,
"you drew my retort upon yourself."

"I ask you once more," said Somer-
ville, seizing a decanter, "if you will
apologize?"

"You have heard my answer," said
Merryweather.

"Take the consequences then," said
Somerville, now losing all command over
himself, and hurling the decanter across
the table at Merryweather. The missile
only touched his shoulder, and glancing

off was shivered into a thousan pieces
on the ground.

Merryweather rose and said, with as
much coolness as he could assume,
though the twitching of his upper lip,
and the constraint he evidently put upon
his voice to prevent it trembling,
sufficiently indicated that he was greatly
excited, "There is, of course, only one
way in which this can be atoned for."
He then bowed stiffly to the company,
left the tent and ordered his horse to be
saddled in order to ride back to Poona.

As he was impatiently waiting for
its appearance, one of the officers he
had just quitted came up to him, and
after expressing his regret at the occur-
rence which had just taken place, begged
Merryweather to allow him him to try
and effect a reconciliation.

"You can have but one motive,"
said Merryweather, "in offering to be
a mediator, and that a most laudable
one, but you must remember that every
circumstance connected with this affair

will soon be known throughout the camp, and that any undue haste on my part in settling it, will not only compromise me in the opinion of my brother officers, but cast a reflection on the regiment to which I belong. I shall consult with one of them as to the best course to pursue, and if it be not an amicable one, you may rest assured it will arise from no vindictive feeling on my part, for now that the momentary resentment caused by the act you witnessed has subsided, I would myself, willingly propose to Mr. Somerville, who has been my greatest friend for years, a mutual forgiveness for what has taken place. I think, however, you will allow that I have unfortunately ceased to be a free agent."

The officer who had addressed Merryweather was obliged to admit the justice of this remark, and pressed his services no further. He, however, held out his hand to our hero, as he was about to ride off, and after cordially expressing a hope that this unfortunate affair might be satisfactorily arranged, wished him a pleasant ride back to Poona.

It was with far different feelings from those which had attended him on the previous evening that Merryweather now rode over the ground between Yellerly and Poona. A sense of depression weighed upon his spirits, which he in vain endeavoured to shake off. To fight a duel, he felt was inevitable, and had it been with a stranger, after the insult he had received, perhaps he would have felt no great compunction about the matter. But to engage in what might prove to be a deadly strife with one for whom he had entertained the most friendly feeling for years, occasioned him unmitigated pain.

His thoughts therefore were harassing in the extreme, and impatient of their goading influence, he urged his steed forward at a rapid pace, in the vain hope of escaping by this means from his sensations. But he soon felt that had he even bestrode the winged horse Pegasus, his feelings would have mocked the reputed fleetness of that animal, and as he became aware how idle it was to attempt to escape from the dilemma in which he was placed by such an expedient, he checked the speed of his horse, and allowing him to relapse into a walk, determined to face the enemy he could not evade.

"After all," he said to himself, "there is no occasion to be so much distressed about it. The past cannot be recalled, and if I am obliged to fight a duel with Somerville I need not fire at him, so that really there is nothing to regret except the repugnance which every one must naturally feel to engage in such an encounter." This idea had no sooner struck him than he resolved to act upon it, and instantly his mind felt as if lightened of a load. When therefore he

again urged on his horse, it seemed as
though some kindly spell had displaced
the gloomy fiend which had haunted
him; or that his steed, endowed with
magic speed had this time distanced his
unseen tormentor.

It was late before he arrived at Poona,
but notwithstanding this he resolved to
visit Lieutenant Pinkem, the officer of his
own regiment to whom he had determined
to apply for *friendly* assistance should
it be necessary to have recourse to hostile
measures.

Lieutenant Pinkem had just returned
home from mess, and bore certain
unequivocal signs of having "dined"
very well. "Hurrah!" he shouted, as
soon as Merryweather made his appear-
ance. "Come in, and we'll have a night
of it—you shall not go home till gun-
fire. There's no parade to-morrow
morning. But in the first place," he
continued, assuming a ludicrously grave
countenance, "let us hear of your

delinquencies and give a satisfactory explanation of your absence from mess to-night. Ah, reprobate! Stand off. The *natch!* I've hit it."

"Your conclusions are rather hastily drawn, if I understand you aright," replied Merryweather. "The fact is, that I have been out hunting all day, and have only just returned. But what I have come about is to ask your advice *à propos* to a scrape I have got into."

"And you shall have it with the greatest pleasure, my dear fellow," replied Lieutenant Pinkem, "but first of all we must send for some champagne from the mess, for of all dry things to talk about, what you call a scrape is the driest. Boy!" he shouted at the top of his voice.

"*Sahib!*" replied a man of about fifty years of age, instantly making his appearance.

"Go to the mess and get two bottles of champagne, and look sharp about it."

"Yes sir," replied the native, in almost the only English words he could utter, disappearing as fast as his legs could carry him.

"Thank Heaven!" continued Lieutenant Pinkem, "I am not acquainted with one word of the language, and what is more, I hope I never shall. I should fancy I was becoming a heathen, and that my face was turning black, if I jabbered Hindustani all day long."

"But you may chance," said Merryweather, "some day to feel the inconvenience of not being able to make yourself understood, besides you get things so much more readily done by being able to explain to the natives what you want, in their own language."

"Quite wrong, Merryweather,—quite wrong, I do assure you,—I know these fellows well, and I'll tell you how I manage them. Although the man you saw just now cannot speak one word of English, yet I make him understand it a great deal better than he does his own language. For instance, I tell him to get some champagne from the mess. He understands the words 'champagne' and 'mess' well enough, and he knows that my boot-jack has an uncontrollable propensity to fly across the room in the direction of his person if he delays a second. Well, that is all plain English, and since it produces what I want in a far shorter time than the same result could be obtained by the longest explanation in Hindustani, I naturally infer that he comprehends me much better than if I spoke to him in his own language."

"Not a very logical conclusion," said Merryweather, "though certainly your proceedings have the effect of making him extremely expeditious, for here he returns."

"That's right, boy," said Lieutenant Pinkem, in a patronizing tone, to the native, who at this moment reappeared quite out of breath, "I shall increase your wages if you go on in this way.

Put some tumblers on the table. Open the champagne—and go. Now Merryweather help yourself, and let us hear what your scrape is about."

Merryweather here recapitulated what had taken place at Yellerly, to the whole of which Lieutenant Pinkem listened with a mock seriousness peculiar to the state into which he was verging.

" The only thing I can blame you for," he said, when the account was finished, " is for being so lenient. You may depend upon it, Merryweather," he continued, swaying himself backwards and forwards in his chair, and tapping the finger of one hand in the palm of the other, to give more significance to his words, " that if you treat these 'N I's' so indulgently, they will be sure (hic.) to take advantage of it. But how can I assist you ? you should have returned the compliment at the time, and with an effective aim. It's too late to do that now."

I came with the intention of asking you to call upon Mr. Somerville for an apology if you think the case will admit of one, or for satisfaction. It is impossible to pass over such conduct unnoticed."

"Very proper, — very proper indeed of you to think of that. Yes ; I'm your man. And of course, to prevent all mistakes, I will go provided with the means calculated to uphold the credit of the regiment."

"I give you *carte blanche* to act for me, as you may deem advisable," said Merryweather, misunderstanding his companion, "and if you find it necessary that I should go out, I shall not hesitate to place myself in your hands."

"Go out!" exclaimed Lieutenant Pinkem, who seemed so much taken aback at this view of the question, that he fairly staggered with surprise. "Go out!! Fight a duel with an 'N. I!' Why it will soon scarcely be worth a man's while to enter her Majesty's service. But if you have really made up your mind to so Quixotic a proceeding, I must see that such an arrangement is made as not to give them any undue advantage over you. Now you know, " continued Lieutenant Pinkem, with a comical increase of gravity, " that a duel ought to be fought upon equal terms. But in the ordinary way of proceeding, an ' N I' would have a decided advantage ; because, even if he is killed, he gains far more distinction by meeting his death at the hands of one of her Majesty's officers, than any exploit of his own would entitle him to, though he lived as long as that old fellow Methusalah ; whereas it would be just the reverse with you. Therefore, in order to make all fair, you must have two shots to his one. Although, if this sort of thing is to go on, I plainly see we shall have to shoot a quantity of them, before they come to their senses.

"Your opinions on this subject," said Merryweather, laughing in spite of himself, "are I suppose those of Ajax, who you know modestly proclaims,—

'Losing he wins, because his name will be
Ennobled by defeat who durst contend with me.'

But since I am not disposed to consider myself, individually, so surpassing a character, the arrangements you contemplate will not be necessary; and seriously, I assure you that whatever may be the result of your negotiations, I shall not fire at Mr. Somerville."

The volubility with which Lieutenant Pinkem had found himself able to express his views on the case that had been laid before him, had produced a secret satisfaction that was indicated by a bland smile suffusing itself over his features, but it was suddenly arrested by the latter part of Merryweather's observation, and with a vacant stare he exclaimed, "not fire at him?"

Merryweather repeated his determination, at which Lieutenant Pinkem, who could snuff a candle at twelve paces, and who knew that Merryweather was nearly as good a shot as himself, was apparently so overwhelmed, that, possibly with a view of calming his excited feelings, he without further delay quaffed off two tumblers of champagne, and having in his own opinion considerably cleared his intellects by this process, replied, "Why, it is absolute suicide ; positively throwing yourself away ;"——and as if to illustrate so reckless an action, he threw himself forward with a serio-comic air, in strict keeping with his other proceedings during the evening, but unable to preserve his equilibrium, sunk upon the couch which furnished this part of the bungalow, and after a few unsuccessful efforts to continue the conversation, in a short time fell fast asleep.

Merryweather now rose and after casting a look upon Lieutenant Pinkem that would scarcely have flattered that gentleman had he witnessed it, left the house, and having arrived at his own bungalow, shortly forgot the adventures of the day in a repose, which after the fatigue he had encountered, not even his excited feelings could disturb.

CHAPTER XI.

He left his home with a swelling sail,
Of fame and fortune dreaming,——
With a spirit as free as the vernal gale,
Or the pennon above him streaming.
He hath reach'd his goal ;——by a distant wave,
'Neath a sultry sun they've laid him ;
And stranger forms bent o'er his grave,
When the last sad rites were paid him.
                              Alaric Watts.

LIEUTENANT Pinkem whom we intro-
duced to our readers in the last chapter
under rather unfavourable circumstances,

had many redeeming qualities. He
entered the army at a very early age, and
soon after that event, carried the colours
of his regiment in one of the severest
actions in which it was ever engaged.
After a short repose he was again ordered
upon service, and distinguished him-
self as an active, enterprising, and
intelligent officer. In the "piping time of
peace," his restless disposition seemed to
chafe from lack of employment. He be-
came a careless, roving, idle character; and
his notions of right and wrong, acquired
in the battle field and in the camp, it must
be confessed, were somewhat ill defined;
but he was generous withal, and ever
ready to do a kind turn for a friend,
though his generosity was not always
very nicely graduated to the extent of his
means. He was much liked in the
regiment, and his bungalow, which was
frequently made a place of rendezvous,
on the morning after the scene we have
described, contained a general assemblage

of his brother officers. Lieutenant Pinkem, consequetly, with as much accuracy as his memory would permit, proceeded to recapitulate the communication he had received on the previous evening. A council was thereupon held, and every one having quickly come to the conclusion that it was necessary for Merryweather to " go out " with the " N I," it was agreed *nem. con.* that Pinkem ought without further delay to take the challenge.

Lieutenant Pinkem upon hearing this opinion lost no time in performing his toilet, and having mounted his horse, was soon at the other end of the cantonments, where Somerville resided. He found him at home, and having explained the nature of his visit, briefly stated that the circumstances were of too aggravated a nature to admit of reconciliation. He therefore begged that he might be referred at once to some friend who would be willing to act as his second.

Somerville mentioned the name of one of his brother officers, to whose bungalow Pinkem instantly repaired, and it was then arranged that the duel should be fought that evening.

Pinkem next went to Merryweather, informed him of the " arrangement" that had been made, and that the place agreed upon for the meeting was on some waste ground about a mile from camp, and little frequented either by Europeans or natives. He now again urged upon Merryweather the necessity of firing at the " N I" and though his proposition of the previous night seemed to strike him as rather extravagant, yet he did not fail to lament what he termed the inequality of the contest, now rendered doubly so by Merryweather's infatuated decision.

When all the " arrangements " are made in a matter of this sort, there is little inclination on the part of the principal to enter into conversation, and although Lieutenant Pinkem, with his usual vivacity, at first chattered away with great ardour, yet perceiving that Merryweather evinced no desire to reply to him, he gradually relapsed into silence. Indeed, men who have so serious a reality before them cannot estrange their thoughts from the painful subject which engrosses their attention, and though by an effort of the mind they may, for a brief space, counterfeit indifference, the deceit is too harassing to admit of any long continuance. It was nearly in silence, therefore, that the day passed away. Merryweather having completed the letters he deemed it necessary to write, took up a book and endeavoured to beguile the time by its perusal, but the unturned page and his motionless eye showed that its contents did not engage his mind. Lieutenant Pinkem on the other hand relieved the monotony of the intermediate hours in a way peculiar to himself. He smoked a cigar in the stables, and gave gratuitous advice to the *Ghorawallors* in English, who plainly indicated by the expression of their countenances they had no doubt that what " *Sahib* " said well merited their respectful attention, though they did not happen to understand one word that he uttered. Lieutenant Pinkem then had recourse to some soda water, and in the middle of the day took a short nap, which had the effect of making him very hungry, if the " tiffin " he eat upon awaking was any criterion. He afterwards tried a few favourite airs upon the German flute, and indulged in occasional draughts of pale ale and cigars till five in the afternoon, at which time it had been arranged they were to start for the appointed meeting.

Merryweather and Pinkem then ordered their horses, and having consigned to the care of a *Ghorawallor*, who had directions to follow them, a parcel, wrapped up in a manner which would prevent any suspicion of the real nature of its contents, they mounted, and rode leisurely through the cantonments. As they proceeded Merryweather could not help glancing at the various objects that met his eye, and wishing, what perhaps few men have not under such circumstances failed to wish, that the present hour had passed away, and that he was now looking at the same objects on his *return* from the approaching conflict.

On reaching the ground they saw Somerville and his friend advancing from an opposite direction. Dismounting therefore from their horses, they gave them in charge to the native by whom they were accompanied, and bade him remain with them in a hollow, where the nature of the ground would conceal their operations, and Pinkem, taking the parcel under his arm, they proceeded to the spot before agreed upon.

As they advanced together arm in arm, Pinkem took occasion to dilate upon the superior nature of the weapons he carried, assuring Merryweather at the same time that they were in excellent order, and that, as he had no intention of wounding his adversary, they might be relied upon to take a button from the " N I's" coat, or to shave a lock of hair from his head, or even to send a bullet through his foraging cap, as a proof at once of his forebearance and his skill ; but observing that Merryweather was not paying much attention to his remarks he attributed his silence to despondency, and thought it advisable to rally him.

" There is not much after all," he said, "in standing up to be shot at. You have no idea how accustomed one gets to it in time. Now just assume a careless sort of manner, and if you don't feel inclined to smoke a cigar, atallevents help yourself from my snuff-box when we get close enough to be observed. When we are within hearing too, begin talking on indifferent subjects——where you intend passing the evening for instance, or any other matter equally unconnected with what you have come about."

"You need not trouble yourself about my behaviour," replied Merryweather, coldly. "I am not aware that I have given you reason to suppose that there is any necessity in my case to have recourse to those blustering expedients which are not unfrequently adopted to conceal a really faint heart."

"Not at all, my dear fellow, not at all. But it has a good appearance—that's all."

"There again I differ from you," replied Merryweather. "I think such proceedings have a very bad appearance. All fantastic tricks are quite out of place on such an occasion, and in my opinion have falsehood stamped upon them, for no man can feel indifferent at a time when he knows that the next minute may be his last. But though I have no intention of swaggering about the ground

in the manner that is sometimes prac-
tised, I believe I am a great deal more
light hearted at this moment than many
would be who so conducted themselves,
from the simple fact, that though it is
impossible to say what may happen to
myself, I run no risk of having the blood
of another on my hands, for, as I said
before, I mean to fire in the air, and
consequently the excellence of your
pistols will avail me little."

Pinkem had too much shrewdness
and good feeling not to feel the justice
of Merryweather's remarks, and from
a desire to do his duty towards his
friend, had been led to suggest expe-
dients which in his own case he would
at once have rejected. Passing over,
therefore, what was unanswerable, he
confined himself to Merryweather's last
observation, and said,—

"That is a point on which you have
an undoubted right to exercise your
own discretion, though, were it my

case, I certainly should not allow him
to go unpunished. But suppose you
stop here. This is as good a position
as you can have, I think; and the
' N I' can stand near that mound.
You will be under no disadvantage
with such an arrangement ?"

"None at all, that I am aware of,"
said Merryweather; "this will do very
well; and now, the sooner the ground
is measured out and the signal given
the better."

Pinkem then left Merryweather's side,
and after speaking for a few minutes
with the adversary's second, returned
and informed him that everything was
settled,—that the distance was to be
twelve paces,—the signal, one—two—
three, upon which they were to fire,
and that whatever was the result, the
contest was then to terminate.

Merryweather merely assenting,
Pinkem walked away a few paces, but
lingered for a moment. He then

returned to him, and with more earnestness of manner and feeling than he had previously evinced, said, "I have never thought of asking you before, and perhaps the present is not a time to suggest such a possibility, nor is it at all likely; but if an accident should happen, is there anything you would wish done?"

"I have fully contemplated such a possibility," replied Merryweather, "and there are letters addressed to all my friends in my desk. If what you suggest should happen, pray see them forwarded."

"I promise you that, though God knows, Merryweather," said Pinkem, "I hope my services will never be required for such a purpose. But there is no use in thinking of such matters now," he continued, his old associations resuming their influence over him. "It will be all over in a minute, and then we will drink your health at mess to night."

The ground was now measured by the two seconds, and then Merryweather and Somerville between whom since their childhood the most undivided friendship had existed until this unhappy quarrel occurred—who at that moment would willingly have cast down the deadly weapons with which they were armed, and have become reconciliated— these men were obliged to threaten each other's lives, not because they wished it, but to comply with the usages of society, and to satisfy the scruples of those who were utterly indifferent as to the result of the contest.

The seconds now retired a few paces, and Pinkem having then asked the combatants whether they were ready, to which he received an affirmative reply, gave the signal one—two—three ! Scarcely had the last word left the mouth of Pinkem when Merryweather's pistol exploded. He had intended, as he had before said, to fire in the air, but upon raising his pistol, the hair trigger, with which he was ignorant it was provided, was accidentally brushed against the skirt of his coat. The ball sped upon its deadly errand, and Somerville, pierced through the breast, fell backwards to the earth.

" Heavenly mercy !" exclaimed Merryweather, completely bewildered, " what have I done ?" He first gazed vacantly upon the pistol he still grasped, then at the form which his own hand had laid prostrate. Suddenly he threw the weapon from him, darted across the intervening space, and throwing himself by the side of his dying friend, propped up his head, tore open his clothes and endeavoured to stop the stream of life that was fast flowing from his wound.

The manifest fruitlessness of his attempts almost bereft him of reason. With the wildness of a maniac he begged the man whose stay in this world, was at the furthest limited to a few minutes, to say that he was not hurt, bewailing in the same breath that he could not purchase Somerville's life with his own.

" I am beyond any help that you can give me," said Somerville, in a faint tone. " Tell them at home"——he paused at the associations that this word conjured up, but continued, " yes——at home——that I thought of them in my last moments, and that my dying conviction is, that you were as innocent of any intention to cause my death, as I was to cause yours."

His voice had sunk lower and lower, till the last words were scarcely louder than a whisper, but still they were heard by the whole party, who had now come up, and were kneeling on the ground by his side.

He remained motionless for a minute, and then his lips again moved, but no sound proceeded from them, and he could only gently press Merryweather's hand. For an instant a smile hovered on the countenance on which death was rapidly stamping his indelible marks, and then the jaw sunk, the eye glazed, and Merryweather's arms held but the corpse of his once generous, noble-hearted friend.

Merryweather could scarcely believe the evidence of his own senses. The whole scene appeared like some frightful dream, and he still continued, when life was extinct, to gaze upon the inanimate countenance of Somerville. Pinkem endeavoured to rouse him from the stupor into which he had fallen, and raising him from the ground, conjured him to mount his horse and proceed to Bombay, and if possible to embark for England, assuring him that in his absence he would vindicate his character, and explain the facts as they occurred.

As he spoke, a mounted patrole was seen galloping towards them, for it had reached the ears of the Commander-in-Chief that a duel was to be fought. Had the troopers arrived ten minutes sooner the duel would never have taken place. Upon such trivial things does the destiny of man depend! and strange to say, the wounded feelings of the most susceptible man of honour would have been quite as much appeased by the readiness the parties evinced to give " satisfaction," as if the most desperate conflict had taken place.

The patrole now rapidly approached, but Merryweather remained immoveable. Assisted by Pinkem on his horse, his hands seized the reins, but he made no effort to escape. More than once while he held Somerville in his arms he had eyed the loaded pistol that had fallen by his friend's side, when the fatal shot arrested the hand that was about to discharge its contents in the air, and it is probable, that had he remained longer on the ground, his insupportable agony would have sought relief in the last desperate act a man can have recourse to; but with his wild gaze fixed on vacancy, he now seemed unconscious of what was passing around him.

Scarcely had he been thus mounted when the guard reached the ground. The officer in command, after a glance at the group, instantly ordered his men to seize Merryweather. They galloped forward to obey, but only one got sufficiently near to reach him. It was fortunate that this attempt to capture him was made, for roused to action by the rude grasp of the soldier, his thoughts were for the moment diverted from the dreadful scene in which he had taken so prominent a part, and setting spurs to his horse, the man who had leant forward to obey his officer's commands was dragged from his saddle and fell to the ground.

Instinctively he again dashed his spurs into the flanks of "Phantom," who, indignant at such unwonted treatment,

bounded high in the air, and sprang
forward at a rate that soon doubled the
intervening space between him and his
pursuers.   Merryweather then checked
the ardour of his horse, but took care to
preserve the distance that he had already
obtained.   For miles thus they rode, the
pursuers alternately gaining and losing
ground as Merryweather pulled or slack-
ened the reign of his willing steed.   The
pace however at which they were proceed-
ing could not be kept up for any length
of time by the pursuers.   Their horses
began to show evident symptoms of
distress, and, reeking with foam, they
lost ground at every stride.   The men,
therefore, seeing the fruitlessness of their
efforts, reined in, and gave up the chase.
" Phantom," on the other hand, had
not yet turned a hair, and the proud way
in which he bore himself shewed that
what had beaten the horses of the
pursuers was but just sufficient thoroughly
to rouse the spirit of the steed of the

desert. When the bit occasionally checked his progress, he would champ and chafe under its control, while, with dilated eye, expanded nostril, erect carriage of the head, and a spirited action that fully displayed his fine proportions; he was a picture that canvass could not have successfully pourtrayed, though Verné himself had been the artist.

But a more formidable impediment than his pursuers now threatened to arrest the progress of Merryweather. It was near the middle of June, the time for the setting in of the monsoon. For days previously heavy looking clouds tossed to and fro by the contending blasts, had, with their menacing folds, at times usurped every part of the heavens. As they were driven forward or repulsed by the powerful antagonists which were struggling for supremacy, they were at times lost sight of beneath the horizon, but only till the conquered foe, gathering fresh strength, again spread them over the space from which they had lately been driven. These well known signs, the muttering of distant thunder, the heavy drops of rain that occasionally fell, and at night the lightning's vivid flash, all betokened the speedy advent of the Elephanta, the storm that invariably ushers in the periodical wind, which for four months in the year deluges the heated soil with rain.

Symptoms of its immediate approach now manifested themselves. The wind, descending from the upper regions, began to blow in fitful gusts along the surface of the earth, forcing in its progress masses of dust before it, so dense as completely to shroud from view even the nearest objects. This annoyance was at last removed by torrents of hail and rain, but with such force were they urged by the furious storm, that Merryweather was compelled to turn his horse in the opposite direction to that from which they were driven.

In the mean time night set in, and then darkness rapidly spread around. It was in truth " a darkness that might be felt." Nothing but the most intense blackness prevailed on all sides. Not a particle of light in any direction presented itself on which to fix the eye. Not a star glimmered, but still the wind rising higher and higher continued its impetuous course. Still the clouds shot forth their deluging streams. Suddenly the whole scene was illumined by one of those brilliant flashes of lightning that are only seen in the tropics. The electric fluid passed close by Merryweather, and striking a tree at a short distance from the road side, rent its bulky form in twain. The crashing report that followed had not died away, before the lightning again darted forth on some destructive errand, and reverberating peals of thunder swiftly succeeded each other. But trifling to Merryweather was the warring of the elements as compared to the tempest that raged within his own breast. It seemed to him as if the vengeance of heaven tracked the flying footsteps of the murderer. The dying countenance of Somerville, with its resigned expression, was ever present before him, and the last noble words he had uttered sounded in endless repetition in his ears. Remorse with cruel and invincible power now seized his mind, and despair nearly hurled it from its tottering seat. From this maddening conflict of feeling, he again sought refuge in action, and turning his horse's head, once more faced the storm. He rode onwards at the peril of his life, for he had wandered from the road, and was now ascending one of the ranges of ghauts that traverse this part of India. A false step would in many places be certain death. But what recked he of danger? What object had he in preserving himself from a death that would at once relieve him from the torture of self condemnation? As this occurred to him, the enemy of mankind, ever near to encourage us in evil, blew the spark thus kindled till Merryweather eagerly hoped for the relief which had at first only indistinctly suggested itself to his mind. On, on, he then spurred, and at every stride impiously wished that his horse's hoofs might spring into void space, and hurl him into eternity. Providence, however, decreed otherwise, and he pursued his dangerous course unhurt, though at times he passed so close to the mountain torrent that leapt with resistless force into the depths below, that showers of spray were blown over him by the wind, and though the next day the prints of his horse's feet were traced on the edge of the deepest precipices.

He had nearly traversed the ghauts when the storm began sensibly to abate, and though the rain still continued to descend in undiminished quantity, it was driven with less force. The moon, too, which had risen, now dispelled the intense darkness which had hitherto prevailed, and shortly afterwards making her appearance through some broken clouds, shed a pale light over the dripping prospect, and enabled ' Phantom' with the instinctive quickness for which his race is so celebrated, to regain the high road.

As Merryweather became aware of this, and of the comparative safety in which he now travelled ; as he became sensible that he had been protected not only against inevitable dangers, but against those which he had madly and impiously sought, better and calmer thoughts took possession of his mind. It may have been that the obstacles he had surmounted, and his miraculous escape from the perils that had beset his path, led him to hope that the feelings which now raged in his breast might be controlled and subdued. It may have been that the consciousness of owing his escape from destruction to the almost visible interposition of Providence, suggested to him the duty of bearing his present sufferings with more humility and patience. But to whatever cause it might be traced, reaction began to take place in his mind, hope again asserted her empire, and his thoughts slowly reverted to those channels which were the best safeguard against the desperate act he had so nearly committed He pictured to himself the beautiful countenance of his cousin, wondered whether she would believe him capable of having purposely caused the death of Somerville, and then again as his avowed intentions recurred to him, and his conscience acquitted him of all design against his friend's life, he thought her blue eyes looked reproachfully though kindly upon him.

But the terrible excitement under which he had laboured, and the hours he had passed in his saddle began to tell upon him. He became faint with exhaustion and fatigue. His brow throbbed with incipient fever, and his whole frame shook as with the palsy. Dreading in this extremity that he would be unable to reach Bombay, he again pressed his horse forward, now jaded with the distance he had come, and stiff with wet and cold. But " Phantom " soon mended his pace, and as his blood warmed and circulated more freely through his veins, his breeding again shewed itself, and gallantly he resumed his devotion to the service of his master.

The ghauts were soon left behind, but every mile that Merryweather now advanced found him less and less capable of sustaining further fatigue, and at last unable to hold himself upright, he twisted his hands in his horse's mane and leant forward for support on his neck till he reached a village where there was a government bungalow.

Riding up to the door he succeeded, after some trouble, in awaking a man who was sleeping within, and making him understand that he wanted some brandy. After an incessant talking of several minutes duration with some people inside, all of whom lighted lanterns and torches, and moved about in every direction but the right one, a bottle of brandy was brought to him. First mixing some of it with water, he poured it down his horse's throat, and then endeavoured to recruit his own failing strength.

Though the fiery liquid increased the malady that was every minute making such rapid strides, yet it gave him temporary relief, and, remounting his horse, also refreshed by the stimulating draught it had swallowed, he prepared to resume his journey. He was now quickly reminded that he had omitted to pay for his entertainment by a native taking hold of his horse's rein, and rather peremptorily demanding the required sum. Merryweather was still in so nervous and excited a state, that he instantly supposed this was some attempt to capture him, and he immediately put spurs to his horse. But the man, sure of the assistance of his companions, kept hold of the rein, and succeeded in backing the horse till Merryweather was thrust against the low thatch of the bungalow. On any other occasion it is possible that he would have had recourse to measures not quite agreeable to his assailant's feelings, but as he now understood, from the oft repeated word of " pice " the cause of his proceedings, he instantly expressed his willingness to accede to the demand. It is not however the practice of residents in India to carry money about with them. Each individual is well known, and the demands for ordinary expenditure are provided for in another way. Merryweather therefore was devoid of the necessary "pice," but taking his watch from his pocket, offered that, and was thereupon allowed to proceed without further molestation.

The native eyed the handsome gold watch of which he had so unexpectedly become possessed for some minutes, pondering at the same time over the probable circumstances under which it had come into his possession. He then carried it to a box in which all his worldly wealth was deposited, placed it therein with the greatest care and secresy, extracted from the same receptacle two rupees, and having closed and locked his stronghold, sauntered back to his comrades, handed the money to the "Messman," and talked incessantly till morning, over the remainder of the brandy that had been so extravagantly paid for, of the great prowess he had displayed in obliging the "sahib" to pay the two rupees they had seen him produce.

Merryweather, ignorant, and heedless if he had not been so, of the fate of the watch he had thus been obliged to surrender, continued his journey. He now made every effort to reach Panwell before the strength given him by the cordial he had taken should go off, and leave him, as he was aware would be the case, in a greater state of prostration than before. Ten long miles were still before him, but at last the distance was accomplished,—the long dirty village of Panwell was reached, and both horse and rider, in a deplorable condition, stopped at the door of the bungalow, of which a description has been given in a previous chapter.

Merryweather managed to dismount, and to relieve his horse of the saddle and bridle, and as soon as he could obtain assistance ordered him to be properly attended to. It was useless.

Just as the man advanced to obey the order, a dull sound as of a heavy weight falling was heard, a few groans followed, and all was again still. "Phantom," had expired.

John, the monkey faced servant, proved himself a valuable acquaintance on this occasion, for after finding that all his arguments to persuade Merryweather to remain in the bungalow were fruitless, he assisted him down to the place of embarkation for Bombay, and procured him a canoe just large enough to hold two men, and which from its size could be propelled at a great rate. John, after seating him in this and propping him up in the best way he could, bade him good-bye, and thrust the light craft from the landing steps.

At every stroke of the paddles the canoe shot swiftly ahead. The swamps that had before struck Merryweather as so loathsome were rapidly passed,

and after two or three hours of unre-
laxed exertion on the part of the rower,
the lights of Bombay became distinctly
visible. As they neared the shore, the
diminutive boat, skimming over the
water on her rapid course, shot through
the congregated shipping, which in the
deceptive light afforded partly by the
moon and partly by the breaking day,
looked like huge monsters at rest.

But Merryweather, was far too ill
to notice what passed around him.
He knew not even where he was, or
what time had elapsed since he left
Panwell, having been insensible the
greater part of the time; and now
that the boat stopped at the wharf, and
he was informed that he had arrived
at Bombay he found himself unable to
rise from his recumbent position, and
after being assisted into a palanquin,
could with difficulty tell the bearers to
take him to his uncle's house, whither he
arrived as that gentleman was about to

mount his horse and proceed on his morning's ride.

Pity soon took the place of surprise with Mr. Ponsonby, when he perceived the condition of his nephew. His faded eye, hollow cheek, and ghastly countenance already marked but too distinctly the ravages of the disease that had fastened upon him. He instantly therefore had him conveyed within and placed on a bed—a bed that for many weary weeks was to be the scene of his sufferings.

CHAPTER XII

With that methought a legion of foul fiends,
Environ'd me and howled in mine ears,
Such hideous cries, that with the very noise,
I, trembling, wak'd, and for a season after
Could not believe but that I was in hell!
Such terrible impression made my dream.
                              Shakspeare.

GREAT was the excitement that prevailed
amongst the military circles at Poona,
when the disastrous result ot the duel

became known.   A court of enquiry met the next day, but the evidence of the seconds, and particularly of Pinkem, was decisive, and the court pronounced an unanimous opinion, establishing the accidental nature of the unhappy event which had just taken place.   The Commander-in-Chief also expressed himself satisfied with the verdict, upon the proceedings being forwarded to him.

Merryweather, therefore, had nothing to fear from this source as he had at first gloomily apprehended, but the knowledge that he was not obnoxious to official blame in no degree mitigated the feelings of remorse which in his lucid intervals pressed upon his mind.

In his uncle's house he remained unmolested, a surgeon having certified that he could not be removed without fatal consequences.   A further inquiry was therefore instituted, occasioned by his absence from regimental duty, and a general order was afterwards issued, entirely exculpating him on this ground also. The affair consequently blew over, and had ceased even to be a subject of conversation, long before Merryweather had risen from his bed of pain.

For four weeks the fever maintained its undivided power over his prostrate frame, defying the skill of his physician, and reducing his strength to so low an ebb, that death appeared not unlikely to ensue from mere exhaustion. During this period Merryweather's sufferings were unremitting, for even when sleep at long intervals visited him, it brought no respite with it.

At one time during his restless slumbers his heated imagination placed him amidst a vast multidude, by whom, with ignominious gibes, he was being led to the scaffold. His limbs were bound so tight that the cords in some places pierced to the bones. The halter which was to end his existence was placed around his neck. The cap was drawn

over his face. The bolt which supported
him was withdrawn. He fell heavily—
and at the same moment awoke from
his imaginary sufferings, only to expe-
rience the reality of pain, which the
merciless fever inflicted upon him.

He then fancied himself in the streets
of a large town, where the wildest
confusion and riot reigned. The air
appeared to teem with offensive sounds,
and at every step horrible sights met
his unwilling eye. Oaths and coarse
jokes, and hoarse discordant laughter
struck his ear on the one side,—shrieks
of murder and piteous cries for help
on the other. A fountain that was
playing near him was throwing up *blood*
instead of water. Blood too was flowing
in profusion along the streets. Blood
was written in large crimson letters
on the houses. Suddenly, as he remained
in speechless horror regarding this
scene, a man came up and accused
him of murder, then another and

another, till at last he was surrounded
by a raving mob with yelling and angry
voices, pouring forth accusations against
him.   " Kill him !" cried one, and in-
stantly a hundred voices cried "Kill him!"
He saw an opening in the crowd and
darted through it. The whole multitude
were instantly in pursuit. The foremost
gained on him. Their footsteps sounded
nearer and nearer. He was felled to the
ground, buffeted and stabbed, and seemed
to breath his last amidst the triumphant
shouts of his persecutors.

Again he awoke, and shuddered as
he reviewed the whole scene, the
minutest particulars of which were so
vividly impressed upon his mind, that
for many minutes he doubted if they
had only existed in his imagination.
For hours after this he lay awake, not
daring again to trust himself to the
caprice of a disordered imagination,
unrestrained by reason ; but at last
sleep again asserted her dominion.

His truant fancy now carried him to a vast desert, where at every step he sank into the loose sand, and the air, radiant with the reflected heat of a vertical sun, played against his face like the exhalation of some immense furnace. He had toiled onwards for half the day, but as far as the eye could reach, interminable mounds of sand were the only objects it encountered. Wearily he still struggled on to a hill in front, higher than any he had yet ascended, and the hope of seeing some termination to the frightful scene of desolation which surrounded him encouraged him to persevere. With renewed energy therefore he climbed up its burning side. But the disappointment he experienced when the same dreary sight met his gaze, was too much to bear. His fortitude forsook him, and sinking down he fervently prayed that death might speedily bring him relief. At that moment a light shadow flitted across the

Q

place where he sat, and a voice familiar
to his ear said—"Take courage. Trust
in the Providence that protected you
during the midnight storm on the
ghauts."

" Constance !"

" Nay, speak not. Ask me nought ;
but believe that your sufferings shall
soon be over."

So saying, she took his hand. The
earth seemed no longer to attract him.
He had merely to wish to move and he
moved without an effort, without even
touching with his feet the burning
surface through which he had toiled
with so much difficulty. Rapidly they
now fled through space. At length from
an acclivity he perceived green meadows
and meandering streams, and beautiful
groves of trees covered with luxuriant
foliage. The streams seemed to bathe
their feet in their onward flight. A cool
and refreshing breeze, bearing on its
wings the perfume of violets, and the

songs of many birds was then wafted by. A few moments more elapsed, and the hand that had clasped his own presented to his parched lips a cup, wreathed with flowers, and brimming over with the purest water.

"Constance!" exclaimed Merryweather, "that I had the power of adequately expressing my gratitude!"

"Promise," was the reply, "that the love you once said you bore me shall ever remain undiminished."

"Can love of mine ever repay such acts as these?" Merryweather was about to say, but at this instant he awoke, and found that during a sleep of several hours duration the crisis of his disorder had passed, and the fever had nearly left him. "I do promise, though," he continued, still thinking of what he was about to say in his dream, "always to love her, and if ever hereafter even a momentary unkind thought of her should arise in my breast, the remembrance of this dream shall that instant crush it."

Although Merryweather was now pronounced free from danger, many days yet elapsed before he could arise from his bed, and when he was at last able to do so, he found that he was but the shadow of his former self.   His mind had also suffered.   If he attempted to peruse a book, the meaning of the words eluded his grasp, and a settled melancholy seemed to fall upon his spirits.   All his ideas and wishes now centred in one object—to leave India, a place connected with such unhappy associations, and his uncle who viewed these symptoms with the greatest alarm, recommended him to travel for a few months on the continent of Europe, and at once to make the necessary application for leave of absence.   So urgent did this step appear, that Mr. Ponsonby would not even wait for the return of Bargee Gopall, who had voluntarily started alone for the spot where he represented the box of papers to be concealed ; but having made his own arrangements, left, with his nephew, by the next mail for Suez. Previous to doing so, however, he entrusted the whole secret to a friend, who willingly consented to use every effort to obtain possession of the valuable documents.

Mr. Ponsonby was glad to perceive that the sea air effected a slight change for the better in Merryweather. He was unremitting in his exertions to rally him, and seized every opportunity to divert his thoughts from the subject to which they were chained. Nor were these kind efforts totally unsuccessful, and once he even produced a smile on his countenance by pointing out to him amongst the passengers the *ci-devant* Miss Flirtree, who had at last become a bride. She had been married a month, and had already insisted upon being sent home by her amiable spouse to recruit her health in

the " green fields of dear—dear Eng-
land."

Having crossed the desert and descended
the Nile, Mr. Ponsonby determined to
embark at Alexandria for Malta, and
commence his plan of travelling on the
continent of Europe by proceeding at
once to Naples. This he found no
difficulty in accomplishing, and after
spending a sufficient time at the latter
place, to render them as familiar with its
glorious scenery as our readers doubtless
are, either from actual experience, or
from descriptions or paintings, which
leave nothing for experience to supply,
they passed a month at Rome and
Florence, and, crossing the Appenines,
proceeded to Venice. Merryweather
was naturally keenly alive to the attrac-
tions which these places afforded, and
it had been one of his favourite plans to
make such a tour as he was now engaged
in. But neither Rome, nor the Pitti
Palace, nor the Florentine Gallery, nor

Venice, as rich in the noble works of its artists as in its historical traditions, could dispel the confirmed melancholy that had settled upon him. Mr. Ponsonby perceiving this, and that his young spirit had received a wound which time alone could heal, proceeded by slow stages through the Tyrol to Munich, and from thence to Frankfort and down the Rhine to England, whither they arrived in the early part of spring, nearly a year having elapsed since their departure from India.

END OF VOL. I.

London : Printed by T. C. Newby, 30, Welbeck Street, Cavendish Square.

CPSIA information can be obtained
at www.ICGtesting.com
Printed in the USA
BVHW082207110819
555624BV00019B/2676/P